fault lines

in the

CONSTITUTION

The Graphic Novel

fault lines

in the

CONSTITUTION

The Graphic Novel

The Framers, Their Fights,
and the Flaws That Affect Us Today

written by C Y N T H I A   L E V I N S O N
A N D   S A N F O R D   L E V I N S O N
art by A L L Y   S H W E D
color by G E R A R D O   A L B A   R O J A S
lettering by A N G E L A   B O Y L E

First Second
NEW YORK

contents

PART IV

"HURRAH! I'M 18. I CAN FINALLY VOTE FOR THE PRESIDENT!" "NOT SO FAST."

125

PART V

CAN THE PRESIDENT REALLY DO THAT?!

142

PART VI

WHO'S RUNNING AMERICA?

171

PART VII

EMERGENCY! EMERGENCY!

210

PART VIII

KEEPING PACE WITH THE TIMES

245

Issues and information addressed in
Fault Lines in the Constitution inevitably
evolve. The authors blog updates at
faultlinesintheconstitution.com.
Join the conversation!

about this book

Most Americans take pride in the constitution that established our system of self-government.

But the men, called Framers, who crafted it at the **Constitutional Convention of 1787** weren't at all certain about the decisions they were making.

They debated heatedly, each predicting the frightful results of the others' ideas.

Then they negotiated, hoping that their compromises would head off disaster and provide stable ways to govern their new country. And they built in ways to amend it.

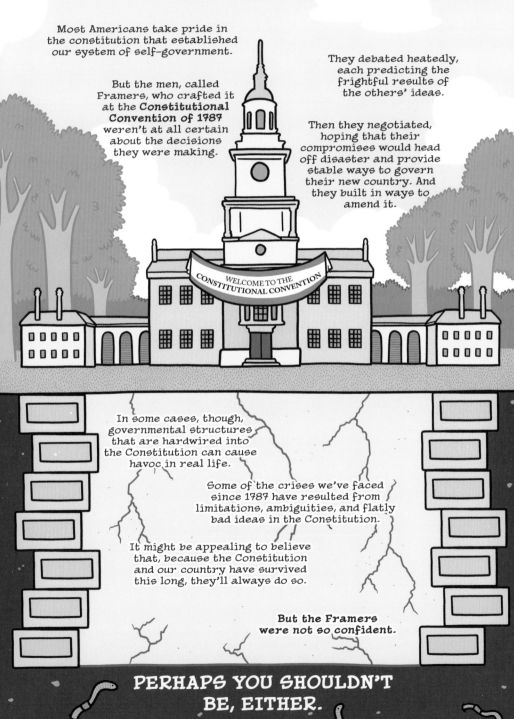

WELCOME TO THE
CONSTITUTIONAL CONVENTION

In some cases, though, governmental structures that are hardwired into the Constitution can cause havoc in real life.

Some of the crises we've faced since 1787 have resulted from limitations, ambiguities, and flatly bad ideas in the Constitution.

It might be appealing to believe that, because the Constitution and our country have survived this long, they'll always do so.

But the Framers were not so confident.

PERHAPS YOU SHOULDN'T BE, EITHER.

WHAT IS A CONSTITUTION?

WHY HAVE ONE?

A constitution is an agreement that describes how an organization is governed: who makes the laws, how those decision makers are chosen, how long they serve, and what powers they have.

Constitutions can be broad outlines or detailed rules about how to make laws.

They can emerge through discussion or by force.

Almost all countries, except Britain, New Zealand, and Israel, have written constitutions.

So do all fifty states, Puerto Rico, most American Indian Nations, and many organizations, including civic groups, clubs, and schools.

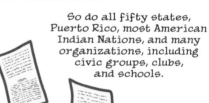

Regardless of how it is developed and what it contains, a constitution is intended to help a group of people accept leadership and reduce friction.

That's the idea, at any rate.

FROM INDEPENDENCE TO A CONSTITUTIONAL CONVENTION

In the **Declaration of Independence**, issued on July 4, 1776, "the thirteen united States of America" pronounced themselves:

Free and Independent States with full Power to levy War, conclude Peace, contract Alliances, establish Commerce, and to do all other Acts and Things which Independent States may of right do.

But their independence was about the only thing these states could agree on.

The states were Free and Independent not only from Britain but also from each other. The "united" part of United States was vague and not very accurate.

Thirteen disjointed mini republics were strung along the Atlantic seaboard. Each state had its own political system, money, and constitution.

VIRGINIA, SIR, IS MY COUNTRY.

MASSACHUSETTS IS OUR COUNTRY.

Thomas Jefferson

(neither attended the convention)

John Adams

Without a king to order them around, the states had to figure out how to get along with each other and how to reach decisions everyone would abide by, even when some states objected to them.

IT IS THE FIRST INSTANCE, FROM THE CREATION OF THE WORLD . . . THAT FREE INHABITANTS HAVE BEEN SEEN DELIBERATING ON A FORM OF GOVERNMENT.

James Madison

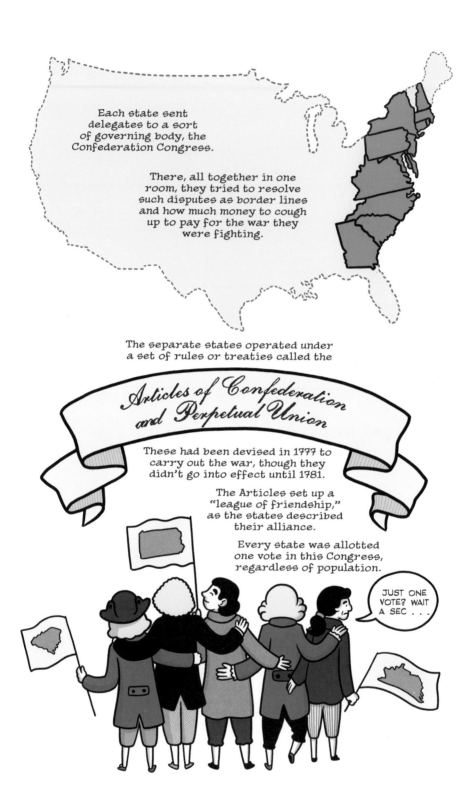

Each state sent delegates to a sort of governing body, the Confederation Congress.

There, all together in one room, they tried to resolve such disputes as border lines and how much money to cough up to pay for the war they were fighting.

The separate states operated under a set of rules or treaties called the

Articles of Confederation and Perpetual Union

These had been devised in 1777 to carry out the war, though they didn't go into effect until 1781.

The Articles set up a "league of friendship," as the states described their alliance.

Every state was allotted one vote in this Congress, regardless of population.

JUST ONE VOTE? WAIT A SEC . . .

But the delegates often didn't show up, and when they did, they spent much of their time bickering, after which they went home empty-handed and frustrated.

There was a limit to **what** could be accomplished.

The Articles allowed few powers beyond making **treaties** with other countries and printing **money**, which turned out to be nearly worthless.

ARTCLES OF
CONFE ERATION
A ND
PERPETUAL UNION

Probably worst of all, the national government was not allowed to tax the citizenry. It could only issue requests, called requisitions, from the states, which were often ignored.

Consequently, the treasury didn't even have enough money to pay the soldiers who had won the Revolutionary War.

In June 1783, four hundred of those soldiers stormed Congress's headquarters in Philadelphia and locked the delegates inside.

WE WANT OUR BACK PAY!

WE GOTTA STAY A STEP AHEAD OF THOSE SOLDIERS!

When the officials were finally released, they ran for their lives, conducting business in a series of temporary quarters in Maryland, New Jersey, and New York.

In 1786, Congress tried to requisition **$3.8 million** (worth about $100 million today) to pay off war debts, including soldiers' back pay.

The states forked over a measly **$663**.

IMBECILITY!

Alexander Hamilton

Meanwhile, states imposed their own taxes on residents. These taxes were so high that many farmers lost their land and were thrown into paupers' prisons.

In Massachusetts, a band of two thousand men rebelled. Led by **Daniel Shays**, a former captain of the Continental Army, they executed vigilante raids on munitions depots, surrounded courthouses, and mobbed sheriffs.

The Articles of Confederation called for an appointed president, who served for one year.

So America's first president was not George Washington but **John Hanson**.

Washington could be considered our ninth!

However, none of the first eight presidents had any real power.

Both the national government
and the states were in turmoil.

George Washington despaired.

I PREDICT THE
WORST CONSEQUENCES
FROM A HALF-STARVED,
LIMPING GOVERNMENT,
ALWAYS MOVING
UPON CRUTCHES AND
TOTTERING AT
EVERY STEP.

His friend General Henry
Lee begged Washington
to use his influence to
quell the uprising.

INFLUENCE IS
NOT GOVERNMENT.
LET US HAVE ONE
BY WHICH OUR LIVES,
LIBERTIES, AND
PROPERTIES WILL
BE SECURED.

Monumental change was needed, and
quickly, if the "united States" were to
survive as a genuine union. Otherwise,
the young nation would dissolve into
several separate, sparring countries.

To prevent such chaos, Congress
called for a convention of delegates
from the states to convene in
Philadelphia on May 13, 1787.

DISTINGUISHED CHARACTERS

At first, hardly anyone showed up. Many dreaded abandoning their families, farms, and businesses to make the tiresome trek by stagecoach or horseback. But by May 25, enough people had gathered in the Assembly Room at the State House to begin deliberations.

Most were prominent men of means (yes, all fifty-five delegates who attended at various times were men), lawyers, doctors, or merchants. Many were young.

Twenty-six-year-old **Jonathan Dayton** of New Jersey, who had fought in the Revolutionary War when he was only sixteen, was the youngest.

James Madison, later described as the "father" of the Constitution, was thirty-four. **Alexander Hamilton** was also in his early thirties.

The oldest delegate was eighty-one-year-old author, statesman, inventor, and diplomat **Benjamin Franklin**, who arrived in a sedan chair carried by prisoners.

8

James Madison sat in the front row and took detailed notes on the debates, though these were not published until 1840, four years after his death. Scholars now know that, over the years, he edited his notes for political purposes, so they are not completely accurate.

Several other Framers occasionally made notes, too. We have a pretty good idea of the general arguments presented in Philadelphia, but we don't always know who made them or exactly what the delegates said.

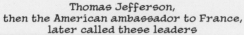

Thomas Jefferson,
then the American ambassador to France,
later called these leaders

an assembly of demi-gods

Congress had instructed
the delegates to revise the
Articles of Confederation, but
they knew that much more than
mere revision was needed.

Working six days a
week for just under
four months, in a
stifling room behind
barred doors and
latched windows, they
concocted an entirely
new and daring kind
of government,
faults and all.

We the People...

the framers

George Washington

James Madison

Gouverneur Morris

William Samuel Johnson

David Brearley

Pierce Butler

Nicholas Gilman

John Francis Mercer

Elbridge Gerry

William Few

Richard Dobbs Spaight

Gunning Bedford, Jr.

Alexander Hamilton

William Leigh Pierce

Luther Martin

George Clymer

Rufus King

William Churchill Houston

Jared Ingersoll

Charles Pinckney

Hugh Williamson

Richard Bassett

Roger Sherman

James Wilson

George Read

William Blount

James McHenry

Edmund Randolph

Abraham Baldwin

William Livingston

Robert Yates

Jacob Broom

John Langdon

Oliver Ellsworth

George Mason

Daniel Carroll

William Houstoun

John Dickinson

Alexander Martin

Caleb Strong

Thomas Mifflin

John Blair

James McClurg

William Paterson

Benjamin Franklin

Jonathan Dayton

Robert Morris

George Wythe

Daniel of
St. Thomas Jenifer

William Richardson
Davie

John Lansing, Jr.

Nathaniel Gorham

John Rutledge

Charles Cotesworth
Pinckney

Thomas Fitzsimons

preamble

We the People of the United States, in Order to form a more perfect Union, establish Justice, insure domestic Tranquility, provide for the common defense, promote the general Welfare, and secure the Blessings of Liberty to ourselves and our Posterity, do ordain and establish this Constitution for the United States of America.

This statement opens the United States Constitution. It's called the **Preamble** because it "walks before" the rest of the document.

Even though it's the first paragraph, composing it was one of the last tasks the Framers took up before signing their Constitution and going home.

ACTUALLY ONE FRAMER IN PARTICULAR DID THE JOB: GOUVERNEUR MORRIS.

I DIDN'T CREATE IT FROM SCRATCH.

I BORROWED IDEAS FROM THE CONSTITUTIONS OF SEVERAL STATES, INCLUDING MY HOME STATE OF PENNSYLVANIA!

OTHER FRAMERS HAD DRAFTED A PREVIOUS VERSION A MONTH EARLIER, IN AUGUST 1787. BUT MORRIS WANTED TO MAKE SOME EDITS.

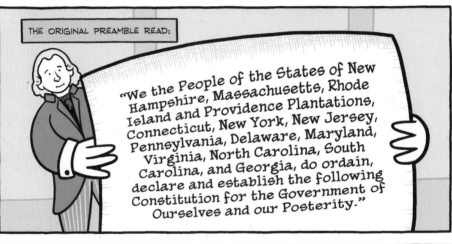

THE ORIGINAL PREAMBLE READ:

"We the People of the States of New Hampshire, Massachusetts, Rhode Island and Providence Plantations, Connecticut, New York, New Jersey, Pennsylvania, Delaware, Maryland, Virginia, North Carolina, South Carolina, and Georgia, do ordain, declare and establish the following Constitution for the Government of Ourselves and our Posterity."

MORRIS KEPT *"WE THE PEOPLE."* BUT HE DIDN'T THINK THE ORIGINAL DRAFT REFLECTED THE OVERARCHING GOVERNMENT THAT THE FRAMERS HAD CREATED.

SWIPE!

MORRIS WANTED TO DO MORE TO BRING THE COUNTRY'S WIDELY DISPERSED CITIZENRY TOGETHER UNDER THE CANOPY OF THE NEW CONSTITUTION.

LET US DELETE THE NAMES OF INDIVIDUAL STATES AND INSERT THE TITLE OF THE COUNTRY, WITH A CAPITAL *U* AND *S*!

WHEN THE CONSTITUTION WAS PUBLICLY DISTRIBUTED AT STATE RATIFYING CONVENTIONS, THIS LAST-MINUTE SWITCH CAUSED A FUROR.

NORTH CAROLINA IS NOT READY TO TRANSFER POWER TO SOME LARGE ENTITY THAT DOESN'T EVEN EXIST YET!

I WISH TO KNOW WHERE THEY FOUND THE POWER OF CONSOLIDATING THE STATES.

WHY ARE THEY SO DISTRESSED?

IT'S A MATTER OF REMAINING LOYAL TO THEIR *SEPARATE STATES* OR THINKING OF THEMSELVES AS *AMERICANS*.

AND THEY WANT TO KNOW WHO WILL HOLD MORE POWER: INDIVIDUAL STATE GOVERNMENTS OR THE FEDERAL GOVERNMENT?

I'M TOTALLY OKAY WITH THE PHRASE "WE THE PEOPLE," THOUGH!

IT'S A GIVEN THAT WE ARE GOING TO RULE OURSELVES!

NO LONGER WILL WE BE RULED BY A MONARCH WHO REFUSES TO LET US DECIDE THINGS ON OUR OWN!

BUT WAIT, THIS DOESN'T QUITE CLARIFY WHO "WE THE PEOPLE" ARE.

FREE, ADULT, WHITE MEN WHO OWN PROPERTY OR PAY TAXES?

IN 1787, NEITHER WOMEN, NOR NATIVE AMERICANS, NOR ENSLAVED PERSONS COULD ATTEND THE CONVENTION OR RUN FOR ELECTION TO ANY OF THE NEW OFFICES.

UH, LET'S WORRY ABOUT THIS LATER . . .

NEVERTHELESS, NO OTHER COUNTRY AT THE TIME WAS BASED ON SELF-GOVERNMENT.

THIS WAS REVOLUTIONARY.

ESTABLISHING A NEW SOCIETY. AT LEAST THAT'S SOMETHING WE CAN AGREE ON!

SELLING THE CONSTITUTION

Once the Constitution was drafted, it was distributed to the states for discussion and approval. This process was called **ratification**.

The Framers decided that **nine of the thirteen states** would have to ratify the Constitution before it could go into effect. Voters in each state would choose **delegates** who would attend ratification conventions to determine the Constitution's fate.

LIKE ME.

Morris may have worried that the delegates might not agree to exchange the flawed but familiar Articles of Confederation for the unheard-of new arrangements.

WHO COULD TURN DOWN "THE BLESSINGS OF LIBERTY"?

He probably penned the Preamble to make the Constitution more appealing.

THE REST OF THE PREAMBLE DESCRIBES WHAT THE FRAMERS HOPED THEIR NEW SOCIETY WOULD LOOK LIKE—THE AIMS THE CONSTITUTION WAS WRITTEN "IN ORDER TO" ACCOMPLISH.

WE HAVE TO NOTIFY THE PEOPLE UPFRONT THAT THEY'RE MERGING INTO A SINGLE "MORE PERFECT UNION."

IT'S GOING TO TAKE SOME EFFORT!

PEOPLE WILL HAVE TO START OBEYING LAWS AND PAYING STATE AND NATIONAL TAXES.

THEY'RE GOING TO HAVE TO ACCEPT AN ADDITIONAL LAYER OF LEADERS AND DECISION MAKERS!

THEY WILL HAVE TO STRETCH THEIR LOYALTY FROM ONE STATE ALONE TO THE COUNTRY AS A WHOLE!

OTHERWISE, AS THOMAS JEFFERSON SAID, WE MAY ALWAYS BE AN UNIMPORTANT DIVIDED PEOPLE.

NO, WE'RE SUPER IMPORTANT.

WHAT'S NEXT ON THE AGENDA?

WE'LL ESTABLISH JUSTICE BY CREATING A SYSTEM OF FEDERAL COURTS.

IT WILL PROTECT CITIZENS' RIGHTS BETTER THAN THE EXISTING STATE COURTS!

UNDER THE ARTICLES OF CONFEDERATION, THE COUNTRY'S HIGHEST COURTS WERE AT THE STATE LEVEL.

HE'S FROM DELAWARE? I'M FROM DELAWARE!

I RULE IN FAVOR OF THIS GUY!

FEDERAL JUDGES, ON THE OTHER HAND, WOULD BE PICKED BY THE PRESIDENT, CONFIRMED BY THE SENATE, AND PAID BY THE NATIONAL GOVERNMENT, NOT THE STATES.

YOU'LL REMAIN ON THE COURT FOR LIFE, AS LONG AS YOU BEHAVE YOURSELVES!

AND TRY TO BE IMPARTIAL, OKAY?

BUT WHAT ABOUT TOUGH ISSUES, LIKE PROPERTY . . . AND **SLAVERY?**

THE FRAMERS CARED ABOUT A NUMBER OF RIGHTS, AND PROTECTING PROPERTY WAS AN ESPECIALLY IMPORTANT ONE. BUT IN MOST OF THE THIRTEEN STATES, ENSLAVED PERSONS WERE CONSIDERED PROPERTY.

SO IF I ESCAPE FROM A SLAVE STATE, I HAVE TO BE RETURNED TO MY OWNER?!

THAT'S THE JUST THING TO DO.

WHAT?! THAT'S THE WORST FORM OF INJUSTICE!

THE FRAMERS DISAGREED FERVENTLY ABOUT SLAVERY.

SEE, THIS IS SOMETHING THE FEDERAL COURTS CAN HELP US FIGURE OUT!

MAYBE IT'LL HELP US "INSURE DOMESTIC TRANQUILITY," TOO?

America in the 1780s could
be a tumultuous place to live.

Daniel Shays and his
rebellious farmers
caused mayhem in
western Massachusetts.

New York and New
Hampshire tussled
over their boundaries.

Vermonters tried to secede
from New York and New
Hampshire, creating their
own minuscule republic.

Slave owners feared
that their chattel
(human beings owned as
property) would band
together and revolt.

The Framers yearned for a national government
that would ensure peace in the homeland.

BUT INTERNAL STRIFE WASN'T THE
ONLY SOURCE OF HOSTILITIES DURING
THE LATE 1770S AND 1780S . . .

Great
Britain!

Indigenous
nations!

Spain!

UNDER THE ARTICLES OF CONFEDERATION,
CONGRESS DID NOT HAVE THE AUTHORITY
TO RAISE A NATIONAL ARMY TO PROTECT
THE INHABITANTS OF ANY STATES.

SO WAIT,
YOU CAN'T
HELP US?

NO, NOT
PHYSICALLY OR
FINANCIALLY.
BUT . . . WE'RE
ROOTING
FOR YOU!

THE FRAMERS KNEW THEY MUST
"PROVIDE FOR THE COMMON
DEFENSE" BEYOND LOCAL MILITIAS.

IN GENERAL, THE FRAMERS AGREED THAT THE NEW GOVERNMENT SHOULD HAVE THE MEANS TO DO WHAT IS NECESSARY FOR THE GOOD OF ITS CITIZENS.

WHAT EXACTLY DO WE MEAN BY "THE GENERAL WELFARE"?

WELL, WE DEFINITELY NEED TO SHIFT THE MINDSET OF PEOPLE FROM THEIR *STATE* TO THE *NATION.*

WHEN GOODS ARE SOLD ACROSS STATE LINES, PEOPLE SAY THEY'RE BEING *"IMPORTED,"* AS IF THEY'RE BEING BROUGHT IN FROM ANOTHER COUNTRY!

AND STATES CHARGE *TARIFFS* ON THESE "FOREIGN" PRODUCTS!

WE SHOULD PROBABLY ELIMINATE THOSE.

VIRGINIA GAZETTE

Just imported from Philadelphia: Dr. Martin's Celebrated Medicine

WHAT ABOUT MONEY FOR ROADS AND BRIDGES? ABOUT 80% OF AMERICANS LIVE IN RURAL AREAS!

FARMERS AND MERCHANTS WANTED THEIR GOODS TO REACH MARKETS RELIABLY AND QUICKLY.

GREAT WAGON ROUTE?!

MORE LIKE GREAT IMPASSABLE TRAIL OF MUD, DUST, AND BROKEN-DOWN WAGONS . . . ROUTE.

GREAT WAGON ROUTE

I GUESS OUR *YOUNG COUNTRY ON THE MOVE* NEEDS INFRASTRUCTURE TO PROMOTE ITS GENERAL WELFARE, HUH?

Through the amendment process, the Constitution has changed over time. So has our perception of the terms and concepts in the Preamble. We have a right to evaluate the Constitution in the 21st century.

How well has the Constitution succeeded since 1787?

What meanings do you assign to the Framers' original terms and concepts?

★ PART I: ★
how bills become
(OR, MORE LIKELY, DON'T BECOME)
law

The Framers' Constitution set up
a three-part government:

**A lawmaking
legislature**

Congress, which is
divided into the
Senate and the House
of Representatives

**An executive
branch**

headed by the
President

**A judicial
branch**

headed by the
Supreme Court

This arrangement, called **separation of powers**,
makes some sense; each player has some power over
the others but none can necessarily dominate.

But the structure can also cause turmoil that
traces back to the Constitution. Several factors
too often cause our basic system to grind to a
stop and lead to widespread unhappiness with
the federal government.

1

it takes two to tango

bicameralism

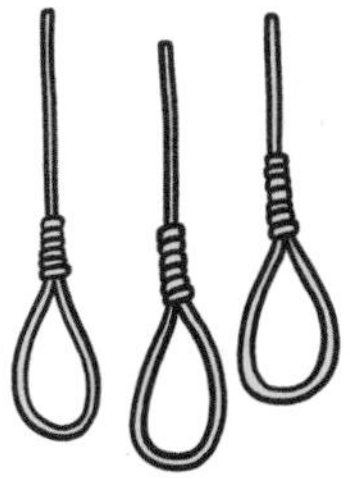

From 1877 to 1950, 4,384 black people were murdered by **hanging**.

99% of the perpetrators went free because state-level courts failed to prosecute them.

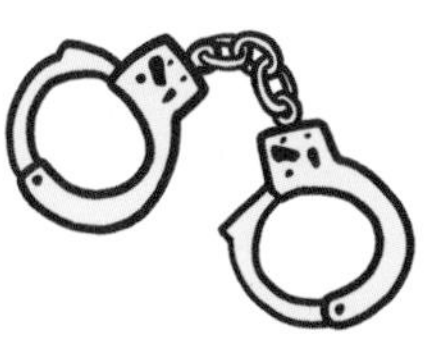

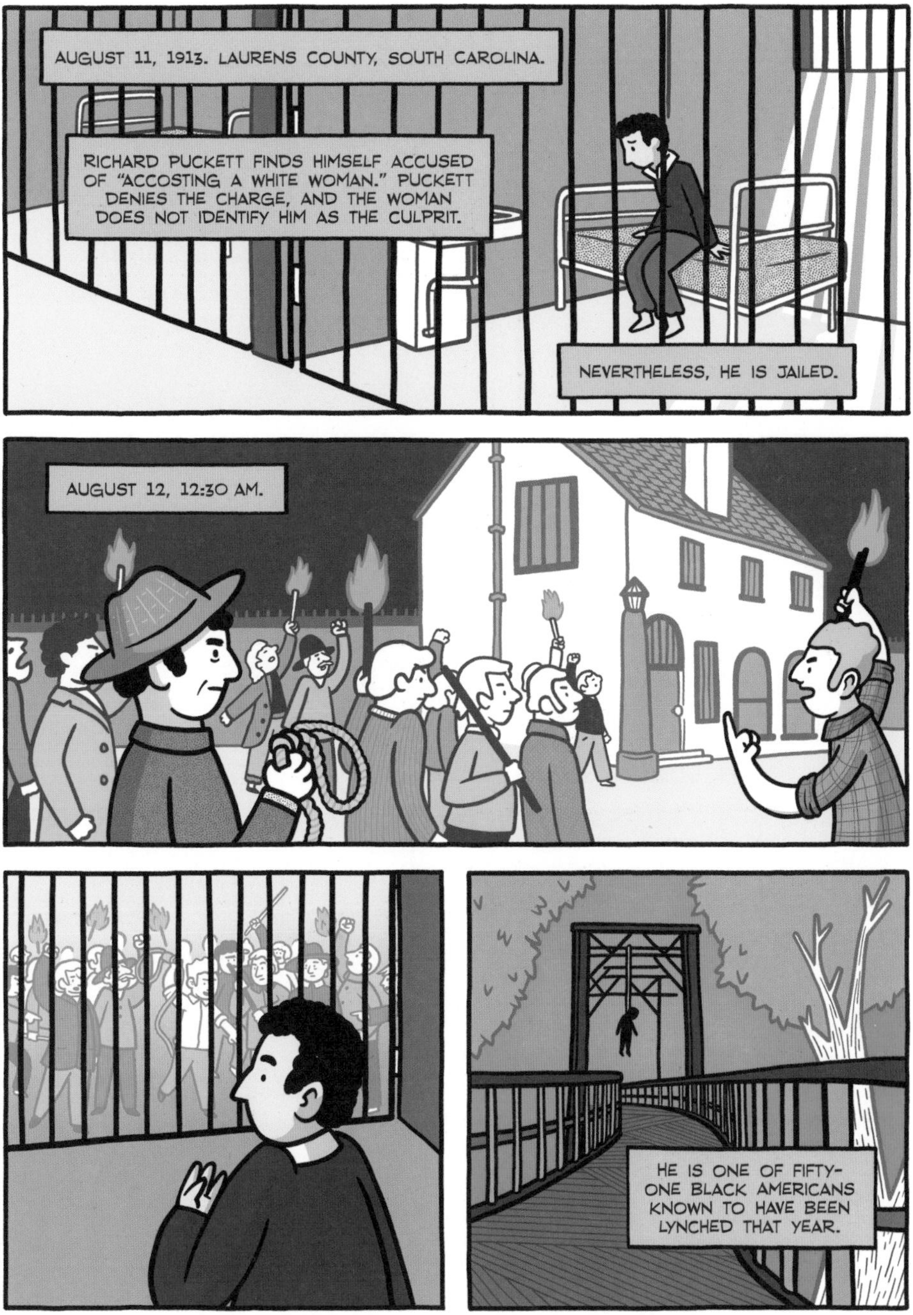

AUGUST 11, 1913. LAURENS COUNTY, SOUTH CAROLINA.
RICHARD PUCKETT FINDS HIMSELF ACCUSED OF "ACCOSTING A WHITE WOMAN." PUCKETT DENIES THE CHARGE, AND THE WOMAN DOES NOT IDENTIFY HIM AS THE CULPRIT.
NEVERTHELESS, HE IS JAILED.
AUGUST 12, 12:30 AM.
HE IS ONE OF FIFTY-ONE BLACK AMERICANS KNOWN TO HAVE BEEN LYNCHED THAT YEAR.

IN 1918, REPUBLICAN REPRESENTATIVE LEONIDAS C. DYER INTRODUCED ANTI-LYNCHING LEGISLATION INTO CONGRESS.

I AM *OUTRAGED* AT THE VIOLENCE BY WHITE GANGS AGAINST MY BLACK CONSTITUENTS IN ST. LOUIS, MISSOURI!

HIS BILL INTENDED TO HAVE PEOPLE ACCUSED OF LYNCHING TRIED IN FEDERAL COURT. SOUTHERNERS IN THE HOUSE DEFEATED THE BILL SEVERAL TIMES, BUT IN 1922, IT FINALLY PASSED.

DYER'S LEGISLATION THEN MOVED TO THE SENATE FOR CONSIDERATION. SOUTHERN MEMBERS OF THAT CHAMBER, ALL OF THEM DEMOCRATS, DENOUNCED THE BILL.

TO PREVENT THE BILL FROM EVER COMING UP FOR A VOTE, A GROUP OF SENATORS *FILIBUSTERED*—THAT IS, THEY TALKED ON AND ON UNTIL IT WAS CLEAR THEY'D NEVER STOP. DYER'S MEASURE FAILED.

IT'S AN ATTACK ON THE RIGHTS OF STATES TO DEAL WITH LYNCHERS HOWEVER THEY SEE FIT!

LYNCHING IS A WAY TO PROTECT WHITE WOMEN FROM BLACK MEN!

IT KEEPS THE RACES SEPARATE!

MORE ABOUT THE FILIBUSTER IN *CHAPTER 4*!

OTHER REPRESENTATIVES INTRODUCED SIMILAR BILLS IN THE 1930S AND 1940S.

THE HOUSE PASSED THREE OF THESE BILLS. THE SENATE FILIBUSTERED TWO OF THEM, AND THE THIRD WAS "PASSED OVER" THREE TIMES THROUGH LEGISLATIVE TRICKERY.

IT DIDN'T MATTER THAT A 1937 OPINION POLL FOUND THAT *72%* OF AMERICANS, INCLUDING 57% OF SOUTHERNERS, SUPPORTED ANTI-LYNCHING LAWS.

OVER THE YEARS, SEVEN U.S. PRESIDENTS URGED CONGRESS TO PASS AN ANTI-LYNCHING LAW.

PASS THIS BILL!

SORRY, PRESIDENT HARDING.

NO BILL EVER CAME UP FOR A VOTE IN THE SENATE, HOWEVER, BECAUSE MEMBERS EITHER FILIBUSTERED OR THREATENED TO DO SO.

Meanwhile, back in 1787 . . .

THE **ARTICLES OF CONFEDERATION** HAD ESTABLISHED ONE LEGISLATIVE HOUSE CONSISTING OF REPRESENTATIVES FROM EACH STATE TO THE CONFEDERATION CONGRESS.

BUT WE'RE ALREADY FAMILIAR WITH BRITAIN'S **BICAMERAL** PARLIAMENT, THE HOUSE OF LORDS AND THE HOUSE OF COMMONS . . .

AND MOST OF THE AMERICAN COLONIES ADOPTED **BICAMERAL** GOVERNMENTS WHEN THEY BECAME STATES AFTER THE REVOLUTIONARY WAR . . .

SO, THE CONSTITUTIONAL FRAMERS ESTABLISHED A **BICAMERAL** LEGISLATURE: THE **SENATE** AND THE **HOUSE OF REPRESENTATIVES.**

All legislative Powers herein granted shall be vested in a Congress of the United States, which shall consist of a Senate and a House of Representatives.

(Article I, Section 1)

Every bill which shall have passed the House of Representatives and the Senate, shall, before it becomes a law, be presented to the President of the United States.

(Article I, Section 7)

BUT WAIT! THE HOUSE OF COMMONS IS ELECTED—

—EVEN THOUGH ONLY 10% OF BRITISH CITIZENS ARE ENTITLED TO VOTE.

AND THE HOUSE OF LORDS IS ALL ARISTOCRATS WHO INHERITED THEIR SPOT!

SO, WHAT'S THE BIG PROBLEM?

A MAJORITY OF THE MEMBERS OF **BOTH** HOUSES OF CONGRESS MUST APPROVE **THE EXACT SAME VERSION** OF A BILL FOR IT TO BECOME LAW.

THIS MEANS THAT EITHER BODY CAN BLOCK BILLS PASSED BY THE OTHER, EVEN IF A MAJORITY OF MEMBERS OF ONE HOUSE SUPPORTS A PIECE OF LEGISLATION.

WE CAN VOTE AGAINST A BILL THAT THE OTHER HOUSE HAS PASSED.

WE CAN ADOPT RULES THAT DELAY OR PREVENT PASSAGE OF BILLS.

WE CAN FAIL TO BRING A BILL UP FOR A VOTE.

WE CAN PASS A BILL THAT IS VERY SIMILAR BUT NOT IDENTICAL TO A BILL ADOPTED IN THE FIRST HOUSE.

THE TWO VERSIONS HAVE TO BE IDENTICAL; THEY CAN'T DIFFER BY EVEN A SINGLE COMMA!

IN 2010, FOR EXAMPLE, THE PUBLIC CLAMORED FOR AN OVERHAUL OF U.S. IMMIGRATION POLICIES.

WITH THE SUPPORT OF BOTH REPUBLICANS AND DEMOCRATS,

WE, THE SENATE, HAVE PASSED A BILL THAT WILL PROVIDE WAYS FOR ALMOST ALL OF THE MORE THAN ELEVEN MILLION UNDOCUMENTED ALIENS TO EVENTUALLY BECOME CITIZENS!

BUT THE REPUBLICAN LEADER IN THE HOUSE OPPOSED THE BILL.

I REFUSE TO BRING THIS UP FOR A VOTE.

WHETHER AMERICANS THOUGHT IT WAS A GOOD BILL OR NOT, THEIR REPRESENTATIVES NEVER HAD THE CHANCE TO DEBATE OR VOTE ON IT.

POLITICAL PARTIES CAN MAKE GRIDLOCK ESPECIALLY LIKELY IN A BICAMERAL SYSTEM.

THERE ARE ONLY TWO EXCEPTIONS TO THE RULE THAT BOTH HOUSES MUST AGREE BEFORE ACTION CAN BE TAKEN:

ONLY THE SENATE IS INVOLVED IN CONFIRMING PRESIDENTIAL APPOINTMENTS. A MAJORITY VOTE IS NECESSARY.

ONLY THE SENATE RATIFIES TREATIES WITH OTHER COUNTRIES. TWO-THIRDS OF THE MEMBERS MUST AGREE.

THE FRAMERS HAD HOPED TO STAVE OFF THE FORMATION OF *FACTIONS.*

MEMBERS OF FACTIONS CARE ONLY ABOUT WHAT'S GOOD FOR THEMSELVES, NOT WHAT'S GOOD FOR THE COUNTRY!

NEVERTHELESS, PARTIES TRIUMPHED. BY 1796, THERE WERE TWO.

DEMOCRATIC-REPUBLICANS

FEDERALISTS

BUT IF YOU CONTROL ONE HOUSE AND YOU CONTROL THE OTHER, BUSINESS CAN GRIND TO A HALT IF YOU CAN'T COMPROMISE ON LEGISLATION!

HEY, THAT CAN HAPPEN EVEN WHEN THE SAME PARTY HOLDS THE MAJORITY OF SEATS IN BOTH HOUSES.

IF MEMBERS CAN'T COME TO AN AGREEMENT, THAT'S THAT. THE PRICE WE PAY FOR CHECKS AND BALANCES IS LOGJAM!

During the 114th Congress (2015–2016), **10,659 bills** were introduced. Only **189** (fewer than 2%) became laws, and many of them involved such insignificant matters as naming post offices after local notables.

This might explain why **more than 85%** of Americans say they disapprove of Congress . . .

. . . the same number who dislike **cockroaches** and **traffic jams.**

HEY, YOU STINK.

BUT, THERE ARE OTHER WAYS!

TAKE NEBRASKA, THE COUNTRY'S ONLY UNICAMERAL STATE LEGISLATURE SINCE 1937.

WE JUST ELECT OUR LEGISLATORS FROM DISTRICTS OF APPROXIMATELY EQUAL POPULATION.

NO SENSE IN HAVING THE SAME THING DONE TWICE!

WE COULD PROBABLY OPERATE JUST AS WELL WITH ONE AS WITH TWO SEPARATE HOUSES.

WE ARE A SMALL STATE, THOUGH.

WHAT ABOUT THE BRITISH PARLIAMENT?

IN 1911, THE POWER OF THE HOUSE OF LORDS OVER THE HOUSE OF COMMONS WAS SIGNIFICANTLY LIMITED.

PARLIAMENT PASSED A LAW TAKING AWAY THE LORDS' ABSOLUTE VETO OVER LEGISLATION.

IT CAN DELAY LEGISLATION, BUT NOT PERMANENTLY SQUASH IT.

FRANCE AND GERMANY BOTH ALLOW, UNDER SOME CIRCUMSTANCES, THEIR LOWER HOUSES TO ENACT LEGISLATION WITHOUT THE APPROVAL OF THE UPPER HOUSE.

IN NORWAY, IF THE TWO HOUSES DISAGREE, THEY MUST MEET TOGETHER.

IF TWO-THIRDS OF THE GROUP VOTE IN FAVOR OF A LAW, THEY CAN PASS IT.

PERHAPS THE U.S. COULD ADOPT SUCH SYSTEMS.

MAYBE THEN WE COULD ENACT AN ANTI-LYNCHING LAW.

THERE IS STILL NO FEDERAL LAW AGAINST LYNCHING.

BUT ON JUNE 13, 2005, THE SENATE PASSED RESOLUTION 39.

THIS RESOLUTION APOLOGIZES TO THE VICTIMS OF LYNCHING AND THE DESCENDANTS OF THOSE VICTIMS FOR THE FAILURE OF THE SENATE TO ENACT ANTI-LYNCHING LEGISLATION.

AMONG THE GUESTS IN THE CHAMBER THAT EVENING WAS WINONA PUCKETT, RICHARD'S NIECE.

THIRTEEN YEARS LATER, IN 2018, THE SENATE UNANIMOUSLY PASSED ANTI-LYNCHING LEGISLATION INTRODUCED BY THREE SENATORS—TWO DEMOCRATS AND A REPUBLICAN. THE HOUSE FAILED TO TAKE ACTION. THE SENATE PASSED THE SAME BILL IN 2019 AND SENT IT TO THE HOUSE.

2

big states, little say

the senate

SEPTEMBER 20, 2001.

LADIES AND GENTLEMEN OF THE CONGRESS, I THANK YOU FOR WHAT YOU HAVE ALREADY DONE AND WHAT WE WILL DO TOGETHER . . .

TO IMPROVE AIR SAFETY . . .

TO GIVE LAW ENFORCEMENT TOOLS TO TRACK DOWN TERROR . . .

TO STRENGTHEN OUR INTELLIGENCE CAPABILITIES . . .

PRESIDENT GEORGE W. BUSH'S POST-9/11 ADDRESS LED TO THE CREATION OF THE

USA PATRIOT ACT

Uniting and Strengthening America by Providing Appropriate Tools Required to Intercept and Obstruct Terrorism

THE LEGISLATION WAS PASSED BY CONGRESS ON OCTOBER 26, 2001.

THIS WILL ALLOCATE $13.1 BILLION FOR STATES TO PREVENT LOCAL ACTS OF TERRORISM.

CHAIRMAN OF THE SENATE JUDICIARY COMMITTEE PATRICK J. LEAHY SAW TO IT THAT THE PATRIOT ACT MANDATED EVERY STATE, REGARDLESS OF SIZE OR NEED, WOULD RECEIVE A MINIMUM OF 0.75% OF THE FUNDS.

WHETHER IT'S A STATE OF HALF A MILLION OR 4 MILLION PEOPLE, YOU'VE GOT TO DO CERTAIN BASIC THINGS.

Welcome to VERMONT

LEAHY IS A DEMOCRATIC SENATOR FROM VERMONT, A RATHER SMALL STATE.

Welcome to VERMONT
2001 POPULATION 612,223
0.0045% OF THE TOTAL U.S. POPULATION

HE WANTED TO MAKE SURE HIS HOME WOULD NOT BE SHORTCHANGED.

STATES USED MUCH OF THE MONEY THEY WERE GIVEN . . .

2009

TO HIRE MORE EMERGENCY WORKERS

AND

TO PAY FOR EQUIPMENT AND TRAINING.

STATES ALSO SENT THE DEPARTMENT OF HOMELAND SECURITY (DHS) LISTS OF SITES THEY CONSIDERED POTENTIAL TARGETS FOR TERRORISTS, LIKE

The Hoover Dam!

THESE LISTS HELPED DHS DETERMINE ADDITIONAL FUNDING TO PROTECT THOSE SITES.

SOME OF THE SMALLEST STATES, HOWEVER, SUBMITTED THE LONGEST LISTS OF POSSIBLE TARGETS . . . WHICH UPPED THEIR FEDERAL FUNDING.

WHY ARE WE CITED AS A MAGNET FOR TERRORISTS?

MAYBE BECAUSE POPCORN EXPLODES?

WELCOME TO BERNE INDIANA

AMISH COUNTRY POPCORN

THE FUNDING FORMULA MEANT THAT THE LEAST MONEY PER RESIDENT WENT TO THE TEN LARGE STATES DHS CONSIDERED THE MOST LIKELY TARGETS.

AND THE TEN STATES AT THE BOTTOM OF THE RISK LIST—ALL SMALL—RECEIVED THE HIGHEST AMOUNTS PER RESIDENT.

ISN'T THE MATH A BIT UPSIDE DOWN?

BUT WE HAVE BIG BUILDINGS YOU CAN PUT A LOT OF PEOPLE IN!

PATRIOT ACT

DOUG FRIEZ
CHIEF HOMELAND SECURITY OFFICIAL
NORTH DAKOTA

CNN

3:45 PM

WITH THE LOPSIDED FORMULA, SMALL STATES HAD ENOUGH MONEY LEFT OVER TO BUY SOME DUBIOUS ITEMS . . .

WYOMING
BOUGHT A ROBOT NAMED MISS DAISY THAT COULD DISMANTLE BOMBS AND DISPOSE OF TOXIC CHEMICALS

COLORADO
INVESTED IN FITNESS PROGRAMS

NEW JERSEY
BOUGHT AIR-CONDITIONED GARBAGE TRUCKS

AND
WASHINGTON D.C.
COMMISSIONED A HOMELAND SECURITY RAP SONG

HERE ARE THE NUMBERS: The USA PATRIOT Act formula gave

$61 per person to WYOMING

but

CALIFORNIA only received $14 per person

(the lowest amount of any state)

BUSH ENCOURAGED CONGRESS TO REVISE THE FORMULA, BUT LEAHY AND HIS COLLEAGUES FROM RURAL STATES HAD A LOT OF LEVERAGE IN THE SENATE.

WE CAN HOLD HOSTAGE A BILL WE DON'T LIKE!

WORLD WAR III BREAKS OUT AT MEETINGS IF WE EVEN TALK ABOUT CHANGING THE FORMULA!

In 1790, about 59,100 people lived in Delaware; of these approximately 8,900 were enslaved.

By comparison, about 434,400 people lived in Pennsylvania (3,700 or so enslaved). That's seven times the size of Delaware.

And about 747,600 people (including 292,000 slaves) lived in Virginia—twelve times the size of Delaware.

NO ONE AT THE CONVENTION KNEW IF OR HOW SLAVES WOULD BE COUNTED.

ON JUNE 11, TWO DELEGATES FROM CONNECTICUT, ROGER SHERMAN AND OLIVER ELLSWORTH, PROPOSED A COMPROMISE.

HOW ABOUT *PROPORTIONAL REPRESENTATION* IN THE LOWER HOUSE . . .

AND *EQUAL REPRESENTATION* IN THE UPPER?

. . .

I'M GOING HOME TO NEW YORK!

YEA!

NAY!

PROPORTIONAL!

EQUAL!

NAY!

NAY!

YEA!

I PRAY FOR THE ASSISTANCE OF HEAVEN!

IT'S FINE WITH ME IF THE SMALL STATES WANT TO PULL OUT OF THE UNION!

I FULLY EXPECT THE CONVENTION TO DISSOLVE!

ON JULY 2, HUGH WILLIAMSON OF NORTH CAROLINA TRIED TO BRING EVERYONE TO THEIR SENSES.

IF WE DO NOT CONCEDE ON BOTH SIDES, OUR BUSINESS WILL SOON BE AT AN END.

HE'S RIGHT!

LET'S LET A SMALLER GROUP DEAL WITH THIS SO WE CAN CELEBRATE INDEPENDENCE DAY!

AND SO, AN ELEVEN-PERSON SUBCOMMITTEE WAS TASKED WITH DEVELOPING A COMPROMISE ON REPRESENTATION.

TWO WEEKS LATER.

HERE ARE THE SUBCOMMITTEE'S RECOMMENDATIONS:

THE LOWER BRANCH OF THE LEGISLATURE, THE HOUSE OF REPRESENTATIVES, SHOULD BE SELECTED PROPORTIONALLY, ACCORDING TO THE SIZE OF THE STATE POPULATIONS.

THE UPPER BRANCH, THE SENATE, SHOULD CONTAIN THE SAME NUMBER OF REPRESENTATIVES FROM EACH STATE.

ALL IN FAVOR OF THIS GREAT COMPROMISE?

YEA! YEA! YEA!

YEA!

ALL OPPOSED?

NAY . . .

NAY.

IT IS SETTLED!

"THE HOUSE OF REPRESENTATIVES SHALL BE COMPOSED OF MEMBERS CHOSEN EVERY SECOND YEAR BY THE PEOPLE OF THE SEVERAL STATES." (ARTICLE I, SECTION 2)

BUT HOW MANY SENATORS WILL EACH STATE HAVE?

THREE IS TOO EXPENSIVE.

ONE SEEMS RISKY; WHAT IF HE GETS SICK?

ON JULY 23, IT WAS (FINALLY) DECIDED.

"THE SENATE OF THE UNITED STATES SHALL BE COMPOSED OF TWO SENATORS FROM EACH STATE, CHOSEN BY THE LEGISLATURE THEREOF, FOR SIX YEARS;

"AND EACH SENATOR SHALL HAVE ONE VOTE." (ARTICLE I, SECTION 3)

HUH!

THIS IS MORE OF A DEFEAT THAN A COMPROMISE.

BUT I GUESS THIS IS BETTER THAN SPLINTERING INTO SEMI-INDEPENDENT STATES?

MAYBE?

Were James Madison's doubts valid?

In 2018, less than half the U.S. population (those in small states) was represented by **eighty-two senators**. More than half (including big states with larger cities and more diverse populations) was represented by only **eighteen senators**.

And the situation is likely to worsen: forecasts indicate that in 2040, 70% of Americans will congregate in fifteen states, represented by thirty senators. Unless another state joins the Union, the remaining 30% of people will get the other seventy senators.

LARGE STATES

SMALL STATES

SENATORS FROM SMALL STATES CAN SECURE MORE FEDERAL MONEY PER CONSTITUENT THAN THOSE FROM LARGER STATES.

IN 2014, CALIFORNIA RECEIVED $1,549 PER RESIDENT, WHILE VERMONT RECEIVED $3,091!

AND RESEARCHERS POINT OUT THAT EQUAL REPRESENTATION HAS EVEN AFFECTED SNACKS AND SCHOOL LUNCHES, AS WELL AS THE RISING NUMBER OF OBESE AMERICANS.

THE FIVE FARM-BASED STATES OF THE UPPER MIDWEST—IOWA, KANSAS, MINNESOTA, AND THE TWO DAKOTAS—HOLD 10% OF THE SENATE, BUT ONLY 4% OF THE U.S. POPULATION.

SINCE THE 1930S, RURAL SENATORS HAVE PERSUADED CONGRESS TO PASS A FARM BILL THAT ENCOURAGES FARMERS TO GROW CERTAIN CROPS BY GIVING THEM SUBSIDIES—MONEY TO BUY SEEDS, FOR INSTANCE.

THIS HELPS OUR CONSTITUENTS.

The crop for which farmers have received the most subsidies over the years is **corn**.

So, corn appears in feed for cattle and hogs . . .

making meat more caloric.

And it's used to make high-fructose corn syrup . . .

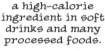

a high-calorie ingredient in soft drinks and many processed foods.

As one study concluded, "Taxpayers are paying for the privilege of making our country sick."

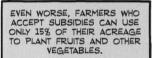

EVEN WORSE, FARMERS WHO ACCEPT SUBSIDIES CAN USE ONLY 15% OF THEIR ACREAGE TO PLANT FRUITS AND OTHER VEGETABLES.

SO, RARER CROPS BECOME MORE EXPENSIVE, AND CALORIE FOR CALORIE, CORN CHIPS COST LESS THAN CARROTS.

BECAUSE OF THE MAKEUP OF THE U.S. SENATE, HEALTHY FOOD IS MORE EXPENSIVE THAN UNHEALTHY FOOD!

CORN

CARROTS

Madison was right: equal representation **does** injure the majority of the people.

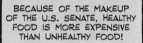

BUT THERE ARE OTHER WAYS!

LITTLE FEDERALISM

Many American states initially modeled themselves after the national government and established bicameral legislatures in which the upper house was like the Senate: equal representation in county or district, regardless of population.

BIG FEDERALISM

THIS PRACTICE WAS CHALLENGED IN 1964, WHEN THE SUPREME COURT HEARD THE CASE OF REYNOLDS V. SIMS.

I, M.O. SIMS, AM SUING THE STATE OF ALABAMA BECAUSE I AM NOT FAIRLY REPRESENTED IN THE STATE SENATE!

THE DISTRICT WHERE SIMS LIVED HAD FOURTEEN TIMES AS MANY PEOPLE AS ANOTHER ONE.

THE COURT AGREED WITH SIMS, DECLARING "LITTLE FEDERALISM" TO BE UNCONSTITUTIONAL: BECAUSE OF *THE EQUAL PROTECTION CLAUSE.*

THIS VIOLATES THE 14TH AMENDMENT, WHICH PROMISES EQUAL PROTECTION OF THE LAWS.

ALL PEOPLE SHOULD BE TREATED FAIRLY, AND LEGISLATIVE DISTRICTS WITHIN EVERY STATE SHOULD BE EQUAL IN POPULATION!

THE DECISION, WHAT THE COURT CALLED "ONE-PERSON/ONE-VOTE," APPLIED TO ALL FIFTY STATES.

THIS MAKES AS MUCH SENSE FOR THE U.S. GOVERNMENT AS IT DOES FOR STATES!

BUT THE GREAT COMPROMISE EMBEDDED EQUAL REPRESENTATION INTO THE CONSTITUTION, AND THE EQUAL PROTECTION CLAUSE REFERRED ONLY TO THE STATES.

MANY COUNTRIES HAVE BICAMERAL LEGISLATURES!

SOME, LIKE SWITZERLAND AND AUSTRALIA, ALSO HAVE UNEVEN REPRESENTATION IN ONE OF THEIR CHAMBERS, JUST LIKE THE U.S.!

BUT THE POPULATION DIFFERENCES BETWEEN SMALL AND LARGE STATES IN THE U.S. IS GREATER THAN ANYWHERE ELSE IN THE WORLD!

On top of that, in many other countries, the chamber that is more representative of the **people** has more power than the one that is not.

AUSTRIA

POLAND

FRANCE

CZECH REPUBLIC

SPAIN

In these countries, for example, the upper house generally cannot kill laws passed by the lower house. (This is different from the U.S., where the House and Senate have equal influence on legislation.)

THE WAYS THAT MEMBERS OF THE UPPER HOUSE ARE SELECTED IN OTHER COUNTRIES ALSO DIFFER FROM OURS.

IN AUSTRALIA, EACH OF THE SIX STATES IS REPRESENTED BY TWELVE SENATORS, WHO ARE ELECTED BY PROPORTIONAL REPRESENTATION.

THIS SYSTEM MAKES IT EASY FOR SMALL PARTIES TO WIN A SEAT! AS A RESULT, THERE IS A GREATER VARIETY OF VIEWPOINTS IN THE UPPER HOUSE THAN THE LOWER ONE.

IN ADDITION, THE AUSTRALIAN NATIONAL TERRITORY, WHERE THE CAPITAL CANBERRA IS LOCATED, AND THE NORTHWEST TERRITORY EACH GET TWO SENATORS.

EVEN IF EQUAL RATHER THAN PROPORTIONAL VOTING POWER BY THE STATES WAS A GOOD IDEA, QUESTIONS REMAIN:

WAS IT WISE FOR US TO SPECIFY TWO SENATORS PER STATE IN THE CONSTITUTION?

SINCE 1959, WHEN HAWAII BECAME THE LAST STATE TO JOIN THE UNION, THERE'S BEEN A TOTAL OF ONE HUNDRED MEMBERS IN THE SENATE.

BUT THE NATIONAL POPULATION HAS ALMOST DOUBLED SINCE THEN!

AND CONGRESS TODAY FACES MANY MORE ISSUES THAN WE EVER DID!

MAYBE IT WOULD BE A GOOD IDEA TO INCREASE THE NUMBER OF SENATORS TO THREE OR FOUR AS THE POPULATION GROWS AND ISSUES GET LARGER?

SPEAKING OF THE WHOLE COUNTRY . . .

IN 2007, THEN-SENATOR BARACK OBAMA SUPPORTED A BILL THAT DECREASED THE MINIMUM GRANT TO EVERY STATE FROM 0.75% OF PATRIOT ACT FUNDS TO 0.25%.

THIS BILL DIED.

TO STEER MONEY TO AREAS MOST AT RISK OF TERRORISM AND VIOLENCE, WHEN HE BECAME PRESIDENT, OBAMA DIRECTED DHS TO AWARD FUNDS FROM VARIOUS PROGRAMS TO STATES ALONG AMERICA'S VULNERABLE BORDERS AND TO URBAN AREAS.

USING A CALCULATION BASED ON THE LIKELIHOOD OF THREATS, THE DEPARTMENT HAS DONE EXACTLY THAT.

NEVERTHELESS, WYOMING STILL GETS MORE MONEY PER PERSON FROM THE PATRIOT ACT THAN CALIFORNIA DOES.

3

delete!

presidential veto

JANUARY 2004. LEBANON, OHIO.

PAULA AND JEFF NOVAK WELCOME THEIR THIRD SON INTO THE FAMILY.

SETH WAS BORN WITH DOWN SYNDROME, AND LIKE MANY INFANTS IN THIS CONDITION, HE NEEDED OPEN-HEART SURGERY, GENETIC AND HORMONE TESTING, EYE AND EAR EXAMS, SPECIAL FOOTWEAR, AND SPEECH THERAPY.

FOR SEVERAL YEARS THE NOVAKS COULD AFFORD THESE SERVICES BECAUSE OF *MEDICAID*, A FEDERAL INSURANCE PROGRAM THAT USES STATE AND FEDERAL FUNDS TO HELP LOW-INCOME PEOPLE WITH MEDICAL EXPENSES.

SO . . . I GOT A RAISE TODAY.

JEFF! THAT'S GREAT NEWS!

WHY DO YOU LOOK SO UPSET?

BECAUSE THAT MEANS WE'RE GOING TO LOSE OUR MEDICAID COVERAGE.

EVERY OTHER INSURANCE PROGRAM THEY LOOKED INTO LABELED SETH UNINSURABLE BECAUSE OF HIS CONDITION.

FORTUNATELY, LESS THAN A YEAR LATER, OHIO GOVERNOR TED STRICKLAND APPROVED A BUDGET THAT ALLOWED FAMILIES LIKE THE NOVAKS TO RECEIVE MEDICAID, EVEN IF THEIR INCOMES ROSE SLIGHTLY.

I FEEL PRIVILEGED THAT SETH CAN ONCE AGAIN SEE THE DOCTORS AND THERAPISTS HE NEEDS!

BUT THEN THE PRESIDENT STEPPED IN.

ON AUGUST 17, 2007, PRESIDENT GEORGE W. BUSH DIRECTED THE STATES TO LIMIT WHO COULD BE COVERED BY MEDICAID.

THE PROGRAM SHOULD SUPPORT ONLY VERY POOR PEOPLE, AND THE FEDERAL GOVERNMENT SHOULD NOT COVER THOSE WHO ARE MERELY LOW-INCOME.

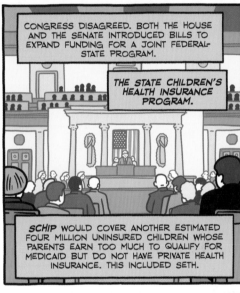

CONGRESS DISAGREED. BOTH THE HOUSE AND THE SENATE INTRODUCED BILLS TO EXPAND FUNDING FOR A JOINT FEDERAL-STATE PROGRAM.

THE STATE CHILDREN'S HEALTH INSURANCE PROGRAM.

SCHIP WOULD COVER ANOTHER ESTIMATED FOUR MILLION UNINSURED CHILDREN WHOSE PARENTS EARN TOO MUCH TO QUALIFY FOR MEDICAID BUT DO NOT HAVE PRIVATE HEALTH INSURANCE. THIS INCLUDED SETH.

WITH SUPPORT FROM BOTH REPUBLICANS AND DEMOCRATS, THE LEGISLATION PASSED OVERWHELMINGLY AND WAS SENT TO THE PRESIDENT FOR HIS SIGNATURE.

BUSH VETOED THE BILL.

CONGRESS WAS OUTRAGED.

SUPPORTING A HEALTH BILL FOR CHILDREN IS THE MORALLY RIGHT THING TO DO!

BUSH HAD MADE AN IRRESPONSIBLE USE OF THE VETO PEN.

ONE OF THE THINGS THE PRESIDENT CAN DO IS SAY, I'M NOT GOING TO SIGN A BILL THAT HAS POLICIES IN IT THAT SHOULD NOT BE A PART OF U.S. POLICY.

Republican Senator Orrin Hatch, Utah

Republican Senator Gordon Smith, Oregon

Dana Perino, White House spokesperson

THE PRESIDENT WOULD NOT NECESSARILY HAVE THE LAST WORD.

THOSE OF US COMMITTED TO SCHIP CAN OVERRIDE BUSH'S VETO . . .

. . . IF AT LEAST TWO-THIRDS OF THE MEMBERS OF EACH HOUSE VOTE TO DO SO.

THE BILL HAD ALREADY PASSED THE SENATE BY THAT MARGIN, BUT GETTING IT THROUGH THE HOUSE, WHERE OPINIONS WERE MORE EVENLY SPLIT, WAS MORE PROBLEMATIC.

WHEN THE BILL CAME UP FOR VOTE AGAIN, IT PASSED WITH 273 MEMBERS IN FAVOR AND 156 OPPOSED.

THIS SHOWED OVERWHELMING SUPPORT—BUT NOT THE NECESSARY TWO-THIRDS MAJORITY.

CONGRESS SENT A REVISED BILL TO BUSH, BUT HE VETOED IT AS WELL. AFTER THAT, CONGRESS GAVE UP.

SETH AND THE APPROXIMATELY FOUR MILLION OTHER LOW-INCOME KIDS REMAINED UNINSURED.

Meanwhile, back in 1787 . . .

AS AMERICANS DESIGNED A GOVERNMENT FOR THEMSELVES, THEY HAD TO DECIDE HOW POWERFUL THEY WANTED THEIR NEW PRESIDENT TO BE.

COME NOW, MEN!

WE'VE BEEN QUARRELING ABOUT THIS FOR MORE THAN THREE MONTHS!

SHOULD HE BE MORE OR LESS POWERFUL THAN THE LEGISLATURE?

WHAT ABOUT THE COURTS?

THE COLONISTS' VERY FIRST COMPLAINT AGAINST KING GEORGE III WAS THAT HE OVERRULED LAWS PASSED BY THE COLONIAL LEGISLATURE.

BUT WE WERE ALSO CRITICAL OF KING GEORGE WHEN HE DIDN'T VETO LAWS PASSED BY THE BRITISH PARLIAMENT THAT WE THOUGHT WERE UNCONSTITUTIONAL.

THE PRESIDENT SHOULD DEFINITELY HAVE VETO POWER.

HE WILL TAKE AN OATH TO PRESERVE, PROTECT, AND DEFEND THE CONSTITUTION.

WON'T THIS INCLUDE REFUSAL TO SIGN LEGISLATION HE THINKS CONTRADICTS THAT CONSTITUTION?

I AGREE, THE PRESIDENT SHOULD HAVE AN ABSOLUTE VETO.

THE HOUSES SHOULD BE ABLE TO OVERTURN THE VETO.

MIGHT THAT NOT TURN HIM INTO A DICTATOR?

BUT HOW MUCH OF A VOTE WOULD THAT NEED?

THREE-QUARTERS?

TWO-THIRDS OF EACH HOUSE?

IF WE DON'T MAKE UP OUR MINDS, WE'RE GOING TO BE STUCK HERE IN PHILADELPHIA UNTIL THE END OF THE YEAR!

IS THREE-QUARTERS OKAY WITH EVERYBODY?!

I GUESS SO

FINE

YES

OKAY

YES

TWO WEEKS LATER, THEY CHANGED THEIR MINDS AND SWITCHED TO TWO-THIRDS, WHICH IS WHAT WE OPERATE UNDER TODAY.

SO . . . WHAT?

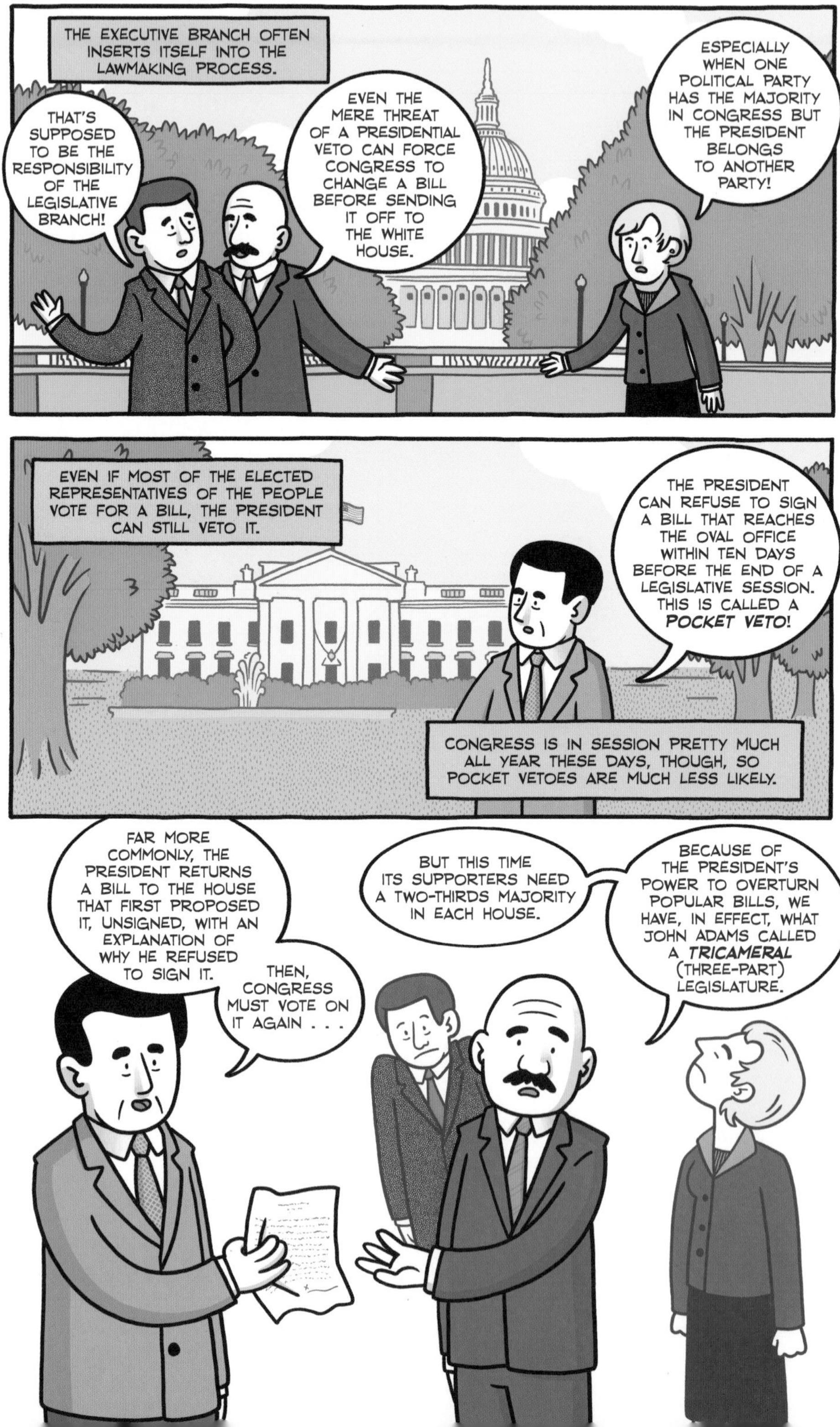
THE EXECUTIVE BRANCH OFTEN INSERTS ITSELF INTO THE LAWMAKING PROCESS.
THAT'S SUPPOSED TO BE THE RESPONSIBILITY OF THE LEGISLATIVE BRANCH!
EVEN THE MERE THREAT OF A PRESIDENTIAL VETO CAN FORCE CONGRESS TO CHANGE A BILL BEFORE SENDING IT OFF TO THE WHITE HOUSE.
ESPECIALLY WHEN ONE POLITICAL PARTY HAS THE MAJORITY IN CONGRESS BUT THE PRESIDENT BELONGS TO ANOTHER PARTY!
EVEN IF MOST OF THE ELECTED REPRESENTATIVES OF THE PEOPLE VOTE FOR A BILL, THE PRESIDENT CAN STILL VETO IT.
THE PRESIDENT CAN REFUSE TO SIGN A BILL THAT REACHES THE OVAL OFFICE WITHIN TEN DAYS BEFORE THE END OF A LEGISLATIVE SESSION. THIS IS CALLED A ***POCKET VETO***!
CONGRESS IS IN SESSION PRETTY MUCH ALL YEAR THESE DAYS, THOUGH, SO POCKET VETOES ARE MUCH LESS LIKELY.
FAR MORE COMMONLY, THE PRESIDENT RETURNS A BILL TO THE HOUSE THAT FIRST PROPOSED IT, UNSIGNED, WITH AN EXPLANATION OF WHY HE REFUSED TO SIGN IT.
THEN, CONGRESS MUST VOTE ON IT AGAIN . . .
BUT THIS TIME ITS SUPPORTERS NEED A TWO-THIRDS MAJORITY IN EACH HOUSE.
BECAUSE OF THE PRESIDENT'S POWER TO OVERTURN POPULAR BILLS, WE HAVE, IN EFFECT, WHAT JOHN ADAMS CALLED A ***TRICAMERAL*** (THREE-PART) LEGISLATURE.

Here are some examples of this veto power:

In 1971, Richard M. Nixon vetoed a bill to establish childcare centers for working parents based on their income.

FAMILIES, NOT GOVERNMENT, SHOULD RAISE CHILDREN!

In 1990, President George H. W. Bush vetoed a civil rights bill that would have strengthened the ban on racial discrimination in hiring and promoting workers.

CONGRESS WITHDREW THE BILL RATHER THAN SEE IT GO DOWN IN DEFEAT.

And in 1997, President Bill Clinton vetoed legislation regarding late-term abortions.

THE HOUSE OVERRODE MY VETO WITH A SUPERMAJORITY, BUT THE SENATE FELL THREE VOTES SHORT.

IN 1996, CONGRESS HAD VOTED TO GIVE CLINTON, AND ALL SUCCEEDING PRESIDENTS, AUTHORITY FOR *"LINE-ITEM" VETOES* UNDER CERTAIN CIRCUMSTANCES.

THIS MEANS THE PRESIDENT CAN DELETE BITS AND PIECES OF A BILL BUT APPROVE THE REST.

BUT IN 1998, THE SUPREME COURT RULED THAT LINE-ITEM VETOES WERE UNCONSTITUTIONAL.

THE CONSTITUTION REQUIRES AN ALL-OR-NOTHING DECISION BY THE PRESIDENT. NO PICKING AND CHOOSING ALLOWED!

Only **111** overcame the supermajority barrier and became law.

That's just **4%**!

Most people agree that some laws should be vetoed.

From 1789 to 2017, forty-four presidents vetoed **2,574 bills**.

But should there be so many hurdles in the way of congressional majorities?

ARE THERE OTHER OPTIONS?

THE EXECUTIVES—THAT IS, GOVERNORS—OF ALL FIFTY STATES CAN VETO LAWS, BUT THE PROCESS VARIES.

MOST STATES FOLLOW THE FEDERAL PRACTICE OF REQUIRING A *SUPERMAJORITY*—TWO-THIRDS OF THEIR STATE LEGISLATORS.

IN NORTH CAROLINA, THE GOVERNOR HAD NO VETO POWER UNTIL 1996. NOW, THREE-FIFTHS OF THE MEMBERS OF THE N.C. HOUSE AND SENATE MUST VOTE TO OVERRIDE THE VETO.

ALABAMA, ARKANSAS, INDIANA, KENTUCKY, TENNESSEE, AND WEST VIRGINIA ALLOW A MAJORITY OF THE LEGISLATURE'S MEMBERS TO OVERRIDE A VETO.

AND MOST GOVERNORS HAVE THE RIGHT TO A LINE-ITEM VETO.

IN OTHER COUNTRIES, DIFFERENT VERSIONS OF THE EXECUTIVE VETO ARE PRACTICED.

IN SWITZERLAND, THE PRESIDENT CANNOT VETO ANY LAWS PASSED BY THE FEDERAL ASSEMBLY, THE COUNTRY'S LEGISLATURE.

IN CYPRUS, THE PRESIDENT CAN VETO ANY PIECE OF LEGISLATION RELATING TO FOREIGN AFFAIRS, DEFENSE, AND SECURITY. SHE OR HE CANNOT BE OVERRULED.

IN SOUTH AFRICA, PRESIDENTS CAN SEND A BILL BACK TO THE NATIONAL ASSEMBLY (THE LOWER HOUSE) BUT ONLY IF THEY BELIEVE IT'S UNCONSTITUTIONAL AND EXPLAIN WHY.

IF THE ASSEMBLY DISAGREES AND READOPTS THE BILL UNCHANGED, IT GOES TO THE SOUTH AFRICAN CONSTITUTIONAL COURT, A SPECIAL COURT CHARGED WITH ASSESSING THE CONSTITUTIONALITY OF LEGISLATION.

IF THAT COURT AGREES WITH THE ASSEMBLY, THEN THE PRESIDENT MUST SIGN IT.

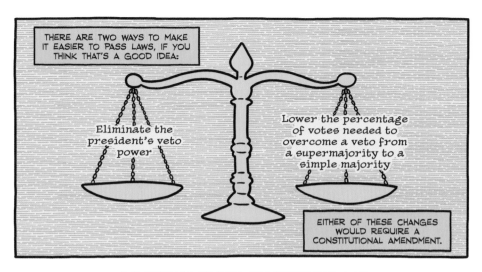

THERE ARE TWO WAYS TO MAKE IT EASIER TO PASS LAWS, IF YOU THINK THAT'S A GOOD IDEA:

Eliminate the president's veto power

Lower the percentage of votes needed to overcome a veto from a supermajority to a simple majority

EITHER OF THESE CHANGES WOULD REQUIRE A CONSTITUTIONAL AMENDMENT.

SO WHAT EVER HAPPENED TO
SCHIP?

JUST AFTER THE INAUGURATION OF PRESIDENT BARACK OBAMA IN 2009, CONGRESS ADOPTED A BILL TO EXPAND MEDICAL CARE FOR KIDS,

NOW RENAMED *CHIP*.

BY SIGNING THIS, I ENSURE THE FUNDING OF CHIP THROUGH 2017.

AFTER MONTHS OF DELAY, CONGRESS EXTENDED CHIP IN EARLY 2018 FOR SIX YEARS.

PRESIDENT DONALD J. TRUMP THEN PROPOSED A BUDGET MANEUVER TO CUT $7 BILLION FROM THE PROGRAM.

NEVERTHELESS, CHILDREN RETAINED THEIR HEALTH INSURANCE.

4

majority rules—
except when it doesn't

supermajority rules

FALL 2010. CHICAGO, ILLINOIS.

CONGRATULATIONS, YOU HAVE BEEN SELECTED FOR THE DALLAS MORNING NEWS SUMMER INTERNSHIP PROGRAM!

LEEZIA DHALLA WAS A JOURNALISM MAJOR AT NORTHWESTERN UNIVERSITY.

SHE AND HER PARENTS HAD IMMIGRATED TO THE UNITED STATES FROM CANADA WHEN SHE WAS SIX YEARS OLD.

BUT DHALLA WAS NOT AN AMERICAN CITIZEN. TO RECEIVE THE SALARY THAT THE INTERNSHIP WAS OFFERING, SHE NEEDED A WORK PERMIT.

CANADA

PASSPORT PASSEPORT

SHE APPLIED FOR ONE BUT IT NEVER ARRIVED. THE EDITOR RESCINDED THE JOB OFFER.

I WAS CRUSHED.

I WANTED THAT INTERNSHIP MORE THAN ANYONE I KNEW.

LOSING THE JOB, THOUGH, TURNED OUT TO BE THE LEAST OF HER PROBLEMS.

MOM! DAD! I'M HOME! I—

DAD, WHAT'S WRONG?

YOU GOT A LETTER FROM THE DEPARTMENT OF HOMELAND SECURITY.

YOU ARE SUPPOSED TO APPEAR IN IMMIGRATION COURT.

THAT'S THE FIRST STEP IN GETTING DEPORTED.

BUT WHY? I'VE BEEN IN THE U.S. FOR SO LONG!

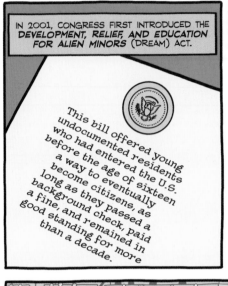

IN 2001, CONGRESS FIRST INTRODUCED THE **DEVELOPMENT, RELIEF, AND EDUCATION FOR ALIEN MINORS** (DREAM) ACT.

This bill offered young undocumented residents who had entered the U.S. before the age of sixteen a way to eventually become citizens, as long as they passed a background check, paid a fine, and remained in good standing for more than a decade.

POLLS SHOWED THAT MOST AMERICANS SUPPORTED THE LEGISLATION, BUT OPPONENTS CHARGED THAT THE BILL WOULD GIVE AMNESTY TO CRIMINALS.

ON DECEMBER 9, 2010, THE DREAM ACT PASSED THE HOUSE WITH 216 IN FAVOR AND 198 AGAINST.

FOLLOWING A WEEK OF DEBATE, FIFTY-FIVE SENATORS—MORE THAN HALF—VOTED FOR THE BILL.

A MAJORITY IN CONGRESS HAD SUPPORTED THE DREAM ACT.

YET, ON DECEMBER 18, IT **FAILED TO PASS**. HOW COULD A BILL THAT HAD THE SOLID SUPPORT OF THE MAJORITY OF BOTH HOUSES DIE?

The Senate's vote on the Act wasn't really on the bill itself. Under Senate rules, the group first had to vote on whether to end their debate and then vote on the bill.

A majority wanted to, but not a **supermajority**, which Senate rules required.

Debate was over. So were the DREAM Act and Dhalla's hopes of working in America without fear of deportation.

Meanwhile, back in 1787 . . .

SO IT WOULD BE BEST TO LET THE HOUSE AND THE SENATE EACH FIGURE OUT THEIR OWN RULES.

OTHERWISE, THIS CONSTITUTION WILL BE UNBEARABLY LONG AND CLOGGED.

AGREED!

YES!

MOST DEFINITELY!

THAT WAS SURPRISINGLY EASY.

CURRENTLY, THE SENATE HAS FORTY-FOUR STANDING RULES, COVERING SUBJECTS SUCH AS:

the order in which to read memorials about deceased citizens

circumstances when the sergeant at arms can compel the attendance of absent senators

and

ethical violations

THE HOUSE HAS TWENTY-NINE STANDING RULES, SUCH AS:

establishing committees to study bills

setting procedures for electing officers

determining the days of the week certain issues will be considered

and

limiting each member's speech to five minutes at a time, therefore prohibiting filibusters

AH! REMEMBER THE *FILIBUSTER*? OFTEN POLITELY REFERRED TO AS "EXTENDED DEBATE"!

IN 1957, SENATOR STROM THURMOND OF SOUTH CAROLINA, IN PROTEST OF THE CIVIL RIGHTS ACT, FILIBUSTERED FOR TWENTY-FOUR HOURS AND EIGHTEEN MINUTES.

I REALLY HAVE TO USE THE BATHROOM!

IN ADDITION TO PASSING—OR BLOCKING—A BILL, THE SENATE HAS OTHER IMPORTANT JOBS, LIKE APPROVING THE PRESIDENT'S NOMINEES FOR FEDERAL JUDGES.

SENATORS CAN FILIBUSTER JUST ABOUT ANYTHING THEY CHOOSE.

Just the threat of a filibuster can prevent a bill from coming up for a vote.

And with the two major political parties increasingly at odds, it has become nearly impossible to persuade three-fifths of the Senate to agree on anything controversial.

AN EXAMPLE OF THIS OCCURRED DURING PRESIDENT BARACK OBAMA'S ADMINISTRATION, WHEN REPUBLICANS REFUSED TO TAKE ACTION ON HIS NOMINEES TO THE SUPREME COURT AND TO LOWER COURTS.

IN 2013, DEMOCRATS, WHO WERE THE MAJORITY, VOTED TO CHANGE SENATE RULES.

WE WILL END THE FILIBUSTER FOR ALL PRESIDENTIAL NOMINEES, SAVE SUPREME COURT JUSTICES!

BUT FOUR YEARS LATER, REPUBLICANS WERE IN CHARGE.

NOW DEMOCRATS WON'T ALLOW PRESIDENT DONALD TRUMP'S SUPREME COURT NOMINEE TO BE VOTED ON?

FINE!

WE'LL WIPE THE SECTION OF RULE XXII REGARDING THAT COURT OFF THE BOOKS!

THE ACTION WAS SO DRAMATIC, IT WAS CALLED THE *NUCLEAR OPTION.*

THE FILIBUSTER REMAINS CONTROVERSIAL.

IT HELPS PREVENT TYRANNY OF THE MAJORITY!

NO! MAJORITY SHOULD RULE, NO MATTER WHAT!

CHANGE THE RULES NOW TO 51%....

OF COURSE, THERE ARE OTHER WAYS!

TWO DOZEN STATES REQUIRE A SUPERMAJORITY VOTE IN THEIR LEGISLATURES TO TAKE ACTION, BUT ONLY ON SPECIFIC ITEMS, GENERALLY RELATED TO BUDGETS OR TAXES.

YE$ YE$ NO

OTHERWISE, IN THOSE AND IN THE REMAINING STATES, MAJORITY VOTE IS SUFFICIENT TO CARRY OUT BUSINESS.

IN TEXAS, THE SENATE USED TO REQUIRE THAT TWO-THIRDS OF ITS MEMBERS MUST AGREE TO BRING A BILL UP FOR A VOTE; OTHERWISE IT WOULD BE SHELVED.

THIS GIVES CLOUT TO THE MINORITY PARTY. DO YOU WANT TO SHARE POWER?

NOT REALLY.

IN 2015, THEY ELIMINATED THAT REQUIREMENT.

ALTHOUGH NOT UNKNOWN, FILIBUSTERS AT THE STATE LEVEL ARE RARE.

IN MOST STATE LEGISLATURES, THE PARTY IN POWER CAN END DEBATE.

SOME STATES REQUIRE AN ABSOLUTE MAJORITY (A MAJORITY OF THE ENTIRE MEMBERSHIP) TO END DEBATE.

STOP !!!

PLEASE let's stop !

OTHERS ACCEPT A MAJORITY OF ONLY THOSE LEGISLATORS WHO ARE PRESENT AND VOTING.

IN OTHER COUNTRIES, A SUPERMAJORITY IS REQUIRED BY ONLY A HANDFUL OF NATIONS TO SUPPORT CERTAIN ACTIONS.

FOR INSTANCE, LEGISLATORS IN INDIA AND JAPAN CANNOT AMEND THEIR CONSTITUTIONS WITHOUT AGREEMENTS FROM AT LEAST TWO-THIRDS OF THEIR MEMBERS.

AS FOR FILIBUSTERS, SOME COUNTRIES ALLOW MEMBERS TO DELAY VOTES, BUT NOT TO BLOCK THEM ENTIRELY. IN JAPAN, RESISTERS CAN RESORT TO USHI ARUKI, OR "COW-WALKING."

I CAN TAKE HOURS TO GET FROM MY SEAT TO THE BALLOT BOX THAT'S ONLY TWENTY FEET AWAY.

BUT EVENTUALLY, I HAVE TO MAKE IT AND VOTE.

IN GREAT BRITAIN, THE PARLIAMENT ALLOWS MEMBERS TO SPEAK FOR A MAXIMUM OF FOUR HOURS.

AND THEY MUST STAY ON TOPIC!

U.S. SENATORS CAN STILL FILIBUSTER BILLS. BUT BY MAJORITY VOTE, THEY COULD DELETE THIS FINAL BIT OF RULE XXII.

THE SAME WAY WE ELIMINATED THE FILIBUSTER FOR JUDGESHIPS!

THEN, ORDINARY LEGISLATION COULD BE PASSED BY A MAJORITY OF THE SENATE RATHER THAN NEEDING A SUPERMAJORITY.

ALTERNATIVELY, THE CONSTITUTION COULD BE AMENDED.

THIS WOULD ALLOW THE SUPERMAJORITY REQUIREMENT TO STAND ONLY IN REGARD TO AREAS WHERE THE GOVERNMENT MIGHT WANT MORE THAN HALF OF THE ELECTED OFFICIALS TO AGREE BEFORE THEY TAKE EFFECT.

SO WHAT HAPPENED TO THE DREAM ACT?

IN 2012, PRESIDENT OBAMA ISSUED AN EXECUTIVE ORDER.

DEFERRED ACTION FOR CHILDHOOD ARRIVALS, OR DACA, WILL ALLOW CERTAIN UNDOCUMENTED IMMIGRANTS WHO ENTERED THE U.S. AS MINORS TO APPLY EVERY TWO YEARS TO POSTPONE DEPORTATION AND RECEIVE A WORK PERMIT!

ONE OF THE REQUIREMENTS IS THAT APPLICANTS MUST HAVE ARRIVED IN THE U.S. BEFORE THE PROGRAM WAS ANNOUNCED ON JUNE 15.

THAT WAS DHALLA'S GRADUATION DAY.

THANKS TO DACA, I'VE BEEN ABLE TO WORK LEGALLY. AND MY FOCUS HAS TURNED TO IMMIGRATION REFORM.

IN 2017, PRESIDENT TRUMP THREATENED TO END DACA, THOUGH CONGRESS DID NOT TAKE ACTION. A YEAR LATER, A FEDERAL COURT RULED THAT TRUMP CANNOT STOP DACA.

IT WILL LIKELY BE UP TO THE SUPREME COURT TO DECIDE WHETHER THE PROGRAM LIVES OR DIES.

IF DACA GETS RULED DOWN, I'D BE *DEPORTED* BACK TO CANADA—WHICH IS ESPECIALLY LIKELY, BECAUSE I AM MUSLIM.

I HAVEN'T BEEN IN CANADA SINCE I WAS SIX YEARS OLD.

★PART II:★

hello, can you hear me?

There are many ways in which our Constitution makes it difficult, sometimes even impossible, for citizens to participate in the democratic process.

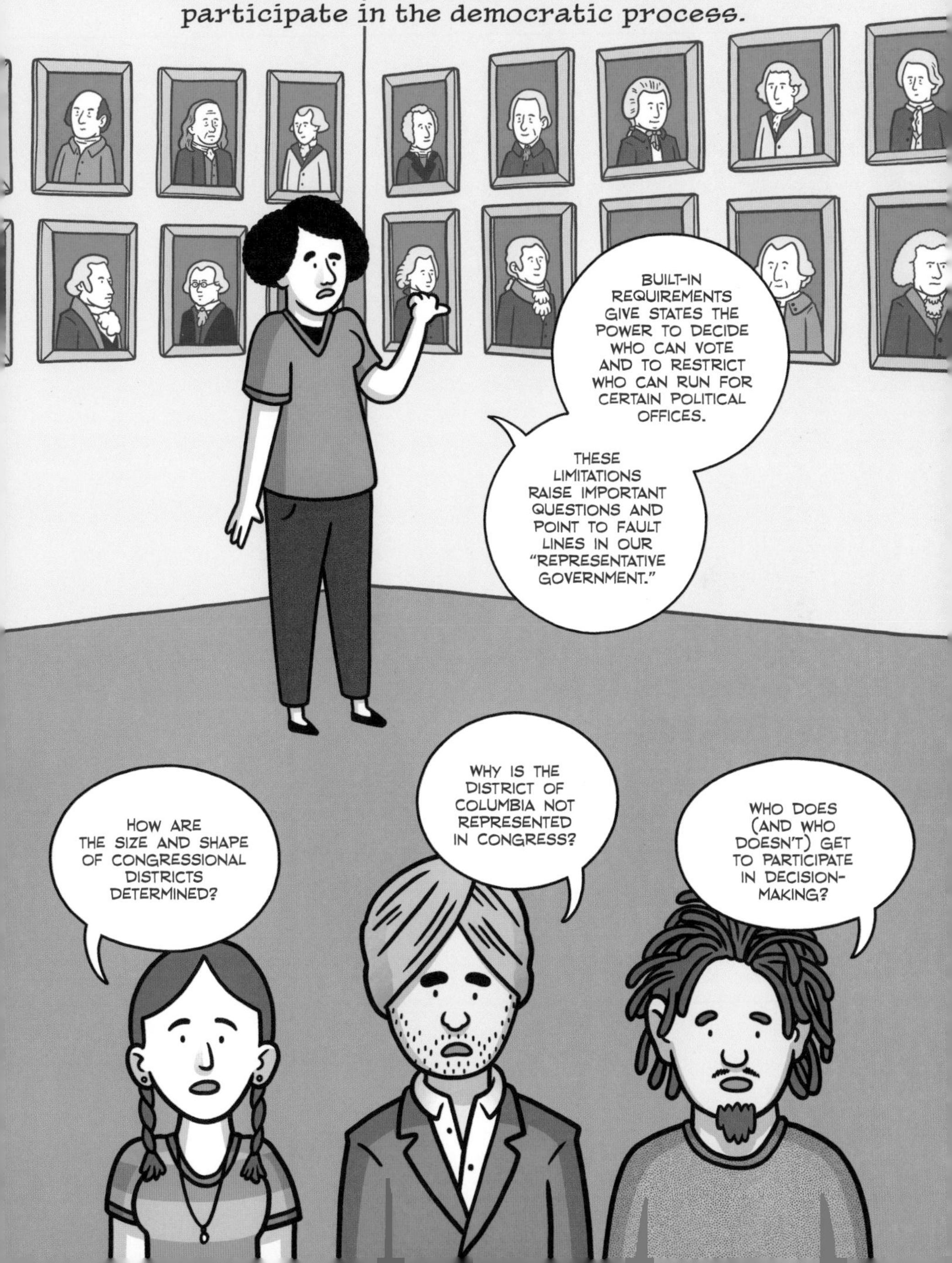

BUILT-IN REQUIREMENTS GIVE STATES THE POWER TO DECIDE WHO CAN VOTE AND TO RESTRICT WHO CAN RUN FOR CERTAIN POLITICAL OFFICES.
THESE LIMITATIONS RAISE IMPORTANT QUESTIONS AND POINT TO FAULT LINES IN OUR "REPRESENTATIVE GOVERNMENT."
HOW ARE THE SIZE AND SHAPE OF CONGRESSIONAL DISTRICTS DETERMINED?
WHY IS THE DISTRICT OF COLUMBIA NOT REPRESENTED IN CONGRESS?
WHO DOES (AND WHO DOESN'T) GET TO PARTICIPATE IN DECISION-MAKING?

5

how to
cherry-pick voters

gerrymandering

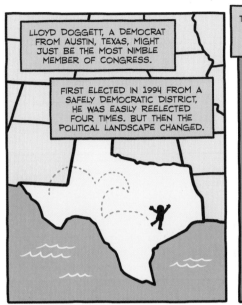

LLOYD DOGGETT, A DEMOCRAT FROM AUSTIN, TEXAS, MIGHT JUST BE THE MOST NIMBLE MEMBER OF CONGRESS.

FIRST ELECTED IN 1994 FROM A SAFELY DEMOCRATIC DISTRICT, HE WAS EASILY REELECTED FOUR TIMES. BUT THEN THE POLITICAL LANDSCAPE CHANGED.

THE CONSTITUTION LETS EVERY STATE DECIDE ON THE PROCESS FOR DETERMINING THE SHAPE AND LOCATION OF ITS FEDERAL CONGRESSIONAL DISTRICTS.

STATES GENERALLY DRAW THESE MAPS ONCE EVERY TEN YEARS, FOLLOWING THE MOST RECENT U.S. CENSUS.

WITH THIS, WE CAN DETERMINE HOW MANY RESIDENTS WE LOST AND GAINED, AND THEREFORE THE NUMBER OF REPRESENTATIVES WE CAN SEND TO CONGRESS.

U.S. CENSUS

IN MOST STATES, LIKE TEXAS, THE LEGISLATURE DRAWS THE MAPS FOR CONGRESSIONAL DISTRICTS, DETERMINING THE GEOGRAPHICAL BOUNDARIES OF EACH DISTRICT.

THAT MEANS WE CAN SHIFT THE BOUNDARY LINES TO INCLUDE—

AND EXCLUDE!

—CERTAIN POPULATIONS.

THE SUPREME COURT REQUIRES THAT EACH DISTRICT CONTAINS ROUGHLY THE SAME NUMBER OF INDIVIDUALS, BUT EACH DISTRICT'S SHAPE AND LOCATION ARE LEFT UP TO ELECTED STATE SENATORS AND REPRESENTATIVES.

SO, WE WANT TO KNOW WHETHER RESIDENTS IN A CERTAIN AREA ARE WELL-OFF OR POOR.

ANGLO, HISPANIC, OR AFRICAN AMERICAN.

AND MOST IMPORTANT, REGISTERED DEMOCRATS, REPUBLICANS, OR INDEPENDENTS.

THIS INFORMATION INDICATES HOW RESIDENTS ARE LIKELY TO VOTE IN UPCOMING ELECTIONS, AND STATE LEGISLATORS CAN USE IT TO CONTROL THE MAKEUP OF THEIR DISTRICTS.

FROM 1995 THROUGH 2002, MOST OF DOGGETT'S CONSTITUENTS WERE DEMOCRATS WHO LIVED IN *AUSTIN*.

THAT'S BECAUSE THE STATE LEGISLATORS WHO DREW THE DISTRICT MAPS WERE MOSTLY DEMOCRATS WHO HAD CONFIGURED THE DISTRICTS IN THEIR OWN FAVOR.

UP UNTIL 2000, THERE WAS A BALANCE OF POWER BETWEEN DEMOCRATS AND REPUBLICANS IN THE STATE.

BUT PUBLIC OPINION AND PARTY MEMBERSHIP SHIFTED DRAMATICALLY.

AFTER STATEWIDE ELECTIONS IN 2002, BOTH THE LEGISLATURE AND THE GOVERNOR'S MANSION WERE REPUBLICAN.

THE REPUBLICANS WANTED TO REPLACE DOGGETT, ALONG WITH NINE OTHER TEXAS DEMOCRATS.

KEEP AUSTIN WEIRD?! HOW ABOUT KEEP TEXAS REPUBLICAN!

AUSTIN

10TH CONGRESSIONAL DISTR

A MAP THAT RETURNS DOGGETT TO OFFICE IS UNACCEPTABLE.

THEY ALMOST SUCCEEDED IN TOSSING HIM OUT.

RATHER THAN RETAINING A DISTRICT COMPOSED MOSTLY OF DEMOCRATIC RESIDENTS IN AUSTIN, DOGGETT WAS PLACED IN A SKINNY NEW DISTRICT THAT INCLUDED A SLIVER OF AUSTIN AND ZIGZAGGED DOWN TO THE MEXICAN BORDER.

IT LOOKED LIKE A FAJITA STRIP!

MY ENEMIES ASSUMED VOTERS IN THE DISTRICT WOULD CHOOSE A HISPANIC CANDIDATE AND THAT ENOUGH REPUBLICANS LIVED THERE TO DEFEAT ANY DEMOCRAT IN THE GENERAL ELECTION.

EVEN WORSE, THE MAPMAKERS CARVED MY NEIGHBORHOOD OUT OF MY DISTRICT. I HAD TO MOVE TO A DIFFERENT PART OF TOWN TO LIVE IN THE DISTRICT I HOPED TO REPRESENT.

I STILL WON THE NEXT ELECTION—AND THE THREE AFTER THAT—BUT THE MAPS KEPT GETTING REDRAWN AND MY CONSTITUENTS KEPT CHANGING!

LLOYD DOGGETT'S DISTRICTS
1995-2017

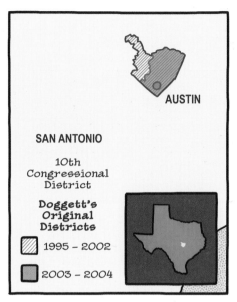

SAN ANTONIO

10th
Congressional
District

**Doggett's
Original
Districts**

1995 - 2002

2003 - 2004

AUSTIN

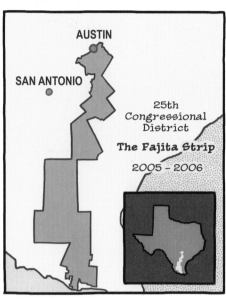

AUSTIN

SAN ANTONIO

25th
Congressional
District

The Fajita Strip

2005 - 2006

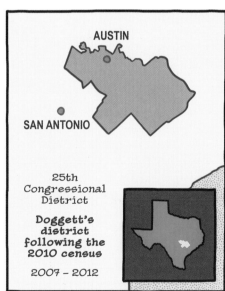

AUSTIN

SAN ANTONIO

25th
Congressional
District

**Doggett's
district
following the
2010 census**

2007 - 2012

AUSTIN

SAN ANTONIO

35th
Congressional
District

The **upside-down
elephant,**
the second
most "squiggly"
district in Texas

2013 - Present

This map was declared illegal by
the U.S. Supreme Court because
it discriminated against
minorities.

Doggett's house again fell
outside the distric (by three
blocks) but he didn't want to
move again . . . and therefore
wasn't allowed to vote
for himself.

MISCHIEVOUS MAPMAKERS: PACKING AND CRACKING

PEOPLE WHO DESIGN CONGRESSIONAL MAPS CAN USE COMPUTER SOFTWARE TO OBTAIN CERTAIN OUTCOMES FOR VARIOUS DISTRICT SHAPES AND SIZES.

CREATE YOUR DISTRICT:
- number of people within a district
- the electorate's race
- ethnicity
- income level
- political party membership

THIS INFORMATION CAN BE USED TO MANIPULATE A DISTRICT'S BOUNDARIES TO FAVOR ONE PARTY.

THAT'S CALLED *GERRYMANDERING*!

IN 1812, GOVERNOR ELBRIDGE GERRY WORKED WITH HIS ALLIES IN THE LEGISLATURE TO CRAFT A MASSACHUSETTS DISTRICT THAT LOOKED LIKE A SALAMANDER.

THE NAME STUCK!

ELBRIDGE *GERRY*? SALA*MANDER*? GET IT?!

I DON'T SEE THE RESEMBLANCE.

ONE METHOD IS CALLED *"PACKING"*: DRAWING DISTRICT BOUNDARIES SO THAT PEOPLE WHO BELONG TO A PARTICULAR POLITICAL PARTY ARE GROUPED IN AS FEW AREAS AS POSSIBLE.

IF CONSTITUENTS WERE REPRESENTED IN SEVERAL DISTRICTS, THEY COULD VOTE FOR MANY REPRESENTATIVES.

PACKED TOGETHER, THEY DON'T HAVE AS MUCH INFLUENCE.

ANOTHER METHOD IS CALLED *"CRACKING."* THIS TAKES THE OPPOSITE APPROACH: MEMBERS OF A PARTICULAR PARTY ARE SPREAD OUT SO THAT THEY'RE IN MULTIPLE DISTRICTS—BUT ALWAYS IN THE POLITICAL MINORITY.

THIS WAY, THE PERSON THEY VOTE FOR WILL LOSE EVERY TIME.

REGULAR CITIZENS CAN TRY OUT SOFTWARE, LIKE THE ONLINE PROGRAM AT *WWW.DISTRICTBUILDER.ORG*, TO COME UP WITH HYPOTHETICAL ALTERNATIVE MAPS. CHANGES TO DISTRICTS CAN ALSO BE VIEWED AT *WHAT-THE-DISTRICT.ACLU.ORG*.

Meanwhile, back in 1787...

SETTING UP THE BASICS OF GOVERNMENT WAS THE EASY PART.

NOW WE HAVE TO DEFINE WHAT WE MEAN BY "PERSONS."

WELL, FIRST WE NEED TO FIGURE OUT HOW MANY PEOPLE LIVE IN THE COUNTRY.

WE DON'T EVEN KNOW HOW MANY PEOPLE LIVE IN EACH STATE!

WE NEED TO HOLD A CENSUS. EVERY TEN YEARS, WE'LL VERIFY THE NUMBER OF INHABITANTS.

OF COURSE, THE CONSTITUTION MADE IT CLEAR THAT RESIDENTS WERE NOT MEANT TO BE COUNTED EQUALLY—AND SOME NOT AT ALL.

"INDIANS" WHO DIDN'T PAY TAXES—ALMOST ALL NATIVE AMERICANS—WEREN'T INCLUDED.

ENSLAVED PEOPLE, REFERRED TO AS "OTHER PERSONS," WERE COUNTED AS ONLY THREE-FIFTHS OF A PERSON.

BUT THE FRAMERS MOVED ON TO OTHER MATTERS, LIKE HOW TO DECIDE WHEN, WHERE, AND HOW REPRESENTATIVES WOULD BE ELECTED TO OFFICE.

I DON'T TRUST THE STATES TO BE IN CHARGE.

IF LEFT UP TO THE STATES, SOME MIGHT NEVER GET AROUND TO HOLDING ELECTIONS!

BUT I HAVE QUALMS ABOUT CONGRESS MAKING ALL THESE DECISIONS!

THAT WOULD LEAD TO THE UTTER EXTINCTION AND ABOLITION OF ALL STATE GOVERNMENTS!

YES, IT COULD REQUIRE VOTERS FROM PENNSYLVANIA TO TRAVEL ALL THE WAY TO PHILADELPHIA TO CAST A BALLOT.

THAT WOULDN'T BE FAIR TO THE HARDWORKING FARMERS WHO CAN'T TREK ALL THE WAY TO THE BIG CITY!

LET'S NOT GET INTO ARGUMENTS ABOUT THIS! THE STATES WILL PLAN HOW THEIR ELECTIONS WILL RUN.

AND CONGRESS CAN HAVE THE RIGHT TO PASS LAWS IN THE FUTURE TO REGULATE ELECTIONS. OKAY?

OKAY!

OKAY!

OKAY!

HOW MANY REPRESENTATIVES?

Early drafts of the Constitution directed that there should be one member of Congress for every 40,000 citizens.

The population is about a hundred times larger now than it was in 1787, and there are almost four times as many states. If the original provision had remained, the House of Representatives would hold about 11,000 members today!

Fortunately, James Madison predicted,

IF THE UNION SHOULD BE PERMANENT, THE NUMBER OF REPRESENTATIVES WOULD BE EXCESSIVE.

HOW ABOUT WE LIMIT IT TO NO MORE THAN ONE REPRESENTATIVE FOR EVERY 40,000 PEOPLE?

LET'S REDUCE IT TO 30,000. THE POPULACE WILL OBJECT TO A NUMBER AS HIGH AS 40,000.

Today many people feel unheard in Congress, where the average district contains more than 750,000 inhabitants.

AND WHAT ABOUT THE CENSUS?

THE DECENNIAL (EVERY TEN YEARS) CENSUS COLLECTS INFORMATION ABOUT INCOME AND RACE, WHICH IS IMPORTANT FOR PLANNING CONGRESSIONAL DISTRICTS AND PROGRAMS, BUT . . .

I'M AN UNDOCUMENTED IMMIGRANT. WHAT IF I'M DISCOVERED AND DEPORTED?

DO I HAVE TO MENTION HOW MUCH I EARN?

I'M LIVING ABROAD. I DON'T GET COUNTED AT ALL.

I IDENTIFY WITH MORE THAN ONE RACE . . .

EVEN TODAY, THE CENSUS REMAINS CONTROVERSIAL.

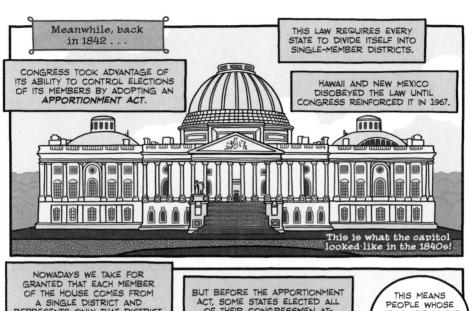

Meanwhile, back in 1842...

CONGRESS TOOK ADVANTAGE OF ITS ABILITY TO CONTROL ELECTIONS OF ITS MEMBERS BY ADOPTING AN *APPORTIONMENT ACT.*

THIS LAW REQUIRES EVERY STATE TO DIVIDE ITSELF INTO SINGLE-MEMBER DISTRICTS.

HAWAII AND NEW MEXICO DISOBEYED THE LAW UNTIL CONGRESS REINFORCED IT IN 1967.

This is what the capitol looked like in the 1840s!

NOWADAYS WE TAKE FOR GRANTED THAT EACH MEMBER OF THE HOUSE COMES FROM A SINGLE DISTRICT AND REPRESENTS ONLY THAT DISTRICT.

BUT BEFORE THE APPORTIONMENT ACT, SOME STATES ELECTED ALL OF THEIR CONGRESSMEN AT-LARGE, MEANING FROM ACROSS THE ENTIRE STATE.

THIS MEANS PEOPLE WHOSE VIEWS ARE IN THE MINORITY CAN BE FROZEN OUT ENTIRELY!

I VOTE FOR HIM!

WITH SINGLE-MEMBER DISTRICTS, SOME COULD BE COMPOSED OF RESIDENTS WHO HOLD DIFFERENT VIEWS FROM THOSE IN OTHER DISTRICTS.

THIS WAY, WE'LL HAVE A BETTER CHANCE OF ELECTING SOMEONE WHO AGREES WITH US!

THAT DID SOLVE THE PROBLEM FACING CONGRESS IN 1842, BUT 175 YEARS LATER, WE SEE THE PROBLEMS OF THE APPORTIONMENT ACT.

LIKE STATE LEGISLATORS DRAWING (AND REDRAWING) CONGRESSIONAL BOUNDARIES.

YOU KNOW, *GERRYMANDERING!*

73

SO WHAT ARE THE PROBLEMS?

USUALLY WE THINK OF ELECTIONS AS OPPORTUNITIES FOR VOTERS TO PICK THEIR LEADERS.

VOTE HERE →

BUT WHEN POLITICIANS HAVE THE POWER TO SHIFT DISTRICT BOUNDARY LINES, THEY CAN PRESELECT THE VOTERS WHO WILL PUT THEM INTO OFFICE.

LIKE IN TEXAS. AND THE RESULTS OF ONGOING GERRYMANDERING THERE HAS THE POTENTIAL TO AFFECT THE REST OF THE COUNTRY.

TEXAS SENDS THE COUNTRY'S SECOND HIGHEST NUMBER OF REPRESENTATIVES TO WASHINGTON.

SO EVEN IF A MAJORITY OF THE COUNTRY VOTED FOR DEMOCRATS, TEXAS ALONE COULD POSSIBLY HELP REPUBLICANS KEEP CONTROL OF CONGRESS.

AFTER THE 2010 CENSUS, REPUBLICANS DEVELOPED A PLAN TO WIN OVER AS MANY STATE LEGISLATURES AS POSSIBLE.

WE'LL CALL IT THE "REDISTRICTING THE MAJORITY PROJECT."

REDMAP.

THE STRATEGY SUCCEEDED: THE MAJORITY OF BOTH HOUSES IN TWENTY-FIVE STATES CHANGED FROM DEMOCRATIC BLUE TO REPUBLICAN RED.

In the 2012 House Election, Democrats got nearly 1,400,000 more votes than Republicans . . .

. . . but Republicans captured 33 more seats than Democrats, largely because of the way districts were configured.

As many as 90% of congressional districts are predictably either Democratic or Republican thanks in part to **gerrymandering**.

If one party gains control of both houses and the presidency, gridlock can be broken.

Assuming the party is united, lawmakers can pass legislation, confident the president will sign it.

THERE ARE OTHER WAYS!

SEVERAL STATES HAVE TAKEN THE POWER TO DRAW CONGRESSIONAL DISTRICT LINES AWAY FROM ELECTED STATE OFFICIALS.

Idaho

Iowa

Arizona

California

INSTEAD, INDEPENDENT, NONPARTISAN CITIZEN COMMISSIONS CREATE THE MAPS. SOME FOREIGN COUNTRIES, INCLUDING ALBANIA, AUSTRALIA, BOTSWANA, CANADA, AND ZIMBABWE, DO THIS, TOO.

ANOTHER POTENTIAL APPROACH IS TO REQUIRE STATE LEGISLATURES TO FOLLOW CERTAIN RULES WHEN THEY DEVISE DISTRICTS.

IN FLORIDA, MAPMAKERS MUST MAKE DISTRICTS AS COMPACT AS POSSIBLE AND MUST NOT DIVIDE UP COMMUNITIES, AS HAPPENED IN AUSTIN.

BUT THIS CAN BACKFIRE AND PACK DISTRICTS, SINCE PEOPLE WHO LIVE IN THE SAME NEIGHBORHOOD OFTEN HOLD SIMILAR OPINIONS.

IN SOME COUNTRIES, SYSTEMS HAVE SHIFTED AWAY FROM SINGLE-MEMBER DISTRICTS.

IN GERMANY AND NEW ZEALAND, FOR EXAMPLE, HALF THEIR PARLIAMENT IS ELECTED FROM SINGLE-MEMBER DISTRICTS; THE OTHER HALF IS ELECTED IN A NATIONWIDE VOTE.

VOTE FOR ME

WÄHLE MICH

COUNTRIES WITH MULTIMEMBER DISTRICTS FIND THAT CANDIDATES ARE MORE DIVERSE.

ALSO, THEY DON'T NEED TO REDRAW BOUNDARY LINES, EVEN IF THE POPULATION CHANGES, BECAUSE THE NUMBER OF REPRESENTATIVES CAN EASILY BE INCREASED OR DECREASED IN PROPORTION TO POPULATION SHIFTS.

GREAT! I WAS SO BAD AT CARTOGRAPHY.

THE U.S. CONSTITUTION GIVES CONGRESS THE POWER TO PASS LAWS ABOUT THE ELECTORAL PROCESS.

THEREFORE, CONGRESS COULD MANDATE A NUMBER OF FIXES TO THE PROBLEM OF GERRYMANDERING.

REQUIRE NONPARTISAN COMMISSIONS TO PLAN DISTRICTS!

MAKE ELECTION PROCEDURES CONSISTENT ACROSS THE COUNTRY!

REPEAL THE 1842 APPORTIONMENT ACT!

USE PROPORTIONAL REPRESENTATION!

AS FOR LLOYD DOGGETT, DESPITE LIVING OUTSIDE HIS OWN DISTRICT, HE KEPT HIS CONGRESSIONAL SEAT.

NOT ONLY IN THE 2012 ELECTION, BUT ALSO THROUGH THE NEXT THREE!

BUT THE REPUBLICANS PREVAILED IN ANOTHER WAY.

AUSTIN IS THE ELEVENTH LARGEST CITY IN THE COUNTRY. IT IS ALSO THE BIGGEST CITY NOT REPRESENTED BY A SINGLE CONGRESSPERSON.

BECAUSE OF HOW ITS DISTRICTS ARE SLICED AND DICED, FOUR OF ITS FIVE REPRESENTATIVES ARE REPUBLICANS—EVEN THOUGH A MAJORITY OF THE POPULACE LEANS STRONGLY DEMOCRATIC.

IN 2017, A FEDERAL COURT DECLARED THAT ELEVEN OF THE STATE'S DISTRICT MAPS, INCLUDING DOGGETT'S DISTRICT, DISCRIMINATED AGAINST HISPANIC AND BLACK VOTERS.

THE SUPREME COURT DISAGREED AND RULED THAT ONLY ONE DISTRICT—NOT DOGGETT'S—NEEDED TO BE REDRAWN.

6

taxation without representation

the district of columbia

APRIL 11, 2001. THE DISTRICT OF COLUMBIA.

MAYOR VINCENT GRAY AND THE CITIZENS OF DC ORGANIZE A PROTEST AT THE HART SENATE OFFICE BUILDING.

FREE DC!

NO TAXATION WITHOUT REPRESENTATION

WE CAN'T TAKE IT ANYMORE!

WE'RE FIGHTING FOR THE FREEDOM OF THE PEOPLE OF DC!

NO TAXATION WITHOUT REPRESENTATION

YOU ARE BEING PLACED UNDER ARREST FOR UNLAWFUL ASSEMBLY AND BLOCKING PASSAGE.

YOU HAVE THE RIGHT TO REMAIN SILENT . . .

NO TAXATION WITHOUT REPRESENTATION

FREE DC

NO TAXATION WITHOUT REPRESENTATION

THE MAYOR AND THE PROTESTORS WERE FIGHTING FOR THE RIGHT OF DC RESIDENTS TO DETERMINE HOW THE 5.5 BILLION DOLLARS IN ANNUAL TAXES THEY PAY TO THE CITY SHOULD BE SPENT AND HOW THE TOWN THEY LIVE IN SHOULD BE GOVERNED.

SEVERAL MONTHS EARLIER, THE CITY COUNCIL HAD DECIDED TO USE CITY TAX REVENUE TO PAY FOR PROGRAMS THAT PROVIDE ABORTION SERVICES FOR LOW-INCOME WOMEN.

CONGRESS RESPONDED WITH A BILL.

THIS WILL BAR THE CITY FROM SPENDING ITS FUNDS IN THIS WAY—OR ANY WAY IT SEES FIT.

ALL WE WANT TO DO IS SPEND OUR OWN MONEY.

Meanwhile, back in 1787 . . .

WE NEED TO FIGURE OUT WHERE OUR NATIONAL CAPITAL WILL PERMANENTLY BE!

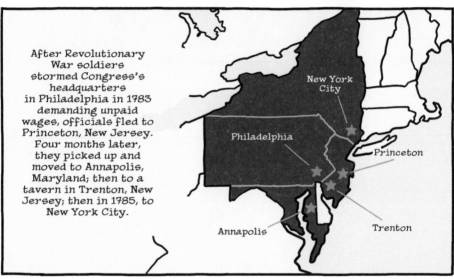

After Revolutionary War soldiers stormed Congress's headquarters in Philadelphia in 1783 demanding unpaid wages, officials fled to Princeton, New Jersey. Four months later, they picked up and moved to Annapolis, Maryland; then to a tavern in Trenton, New Jersey; then in 1785, to New York City.

New York City

Philadelphia

Princeton

Trenton

Annapolis

GEORGE WASHINGTON TOOK HIS FIRST OATH OF OFFICE HERE!

IT'S A FINE PLACE FOR THE CAPITAL CITY!

I DON'T KNOW ABOUT THAT.

I DON'T WANT NEW YORK TO DOMINATE THE WHOLE FEDERAL GOVERNMENT!

THE FRAMERS DECIDED THAT THE NATIONAL CAPITAL NEEDED TO BE LOCATED IN A SPECIAL AREA, NOT CONNECTED TO ANY PARTICULAR STATE.

BUT WHERE?

THE SOLUTION RESULTED FROM SECRET NEGOTIATIONS AMONG THOMAS JEFFERSON, JAMES MADISON, AND ALEXANDER HAMILTON.

NO ONE ELSE WAS IN THE ROOM.

WE VIRGINIANS WILL SUPPORT YOUR PROPOSAL THAT THE NATIONAL GOVERNMENT PAY OFF THE STATES' WAR DEBTS—

—INCLUDING MONEY OWED TO THE VETERANS OF THE REVOLUTION.

IN RETURN, OUR NEW FEDERAL TOWN WILL BE ESTABLISHED ALONG THE POTOMAC RIVER ON LAND DONATED BY MARYLAND AND VIRGINIA—

BUT BELONGING TO NO STATE.

THIS BECAME KNOWN AS THE COMPROMISE OF 1790.

BECAUSE CONGRESS WAS THE REASON FOR THE TOWN'S EXISTENCE, IT MADE SENSE TO THE FRAMERS THAT THIS BODY WOULD OVERSEE THE TOWN.

PLAN of the City of WASHINGTON

SO WHAT'S THE BIG PROBLEM?

JOHN ADAMS, THE SECOND PRESIDENT, BECAME THE FIRST TO LIVE IN WASHINGTON, THE DISTRICT OF COLUMBIA.

THE DISTRICT OF COLUMBIA IS A *TERRITORY*, NOT A STATE—IT'S NOT EVEN *IN* A STATE.

THEREFORE ITS RESIDENTS ARE NOT REPRESENTED BY SENATORS IN CONGRESS.

NOR CAN THEIR MEMBER OF THE HOUSE VOTE! I CAN SPEAK, BUT THAT'S ALL.

THE PEOPLE WHO LIVE IN DC HAVE NO ROLE IN MAKING THE NATION'S LAWS, INCLUDING HOW MUCH FEDERAL TAX THEY PAY.

DC RESIDENTS ELECT A MAYOR AND CITY COUNCIL, JUST AS RESIDENTS OF MOST OTHER CITIES DO. HOWEVER, CONGRESS HOLDS THE POWER TO OVERTURN EACH OF THEIR LAWS AND ACTIONS.

THAT IS WHY THE LICENSE PLATE OF EVERY CAR REGISTERED IN DC HOLDS THE SAME COMPLAINT THE COLONISTS MADE AGAINST ENGLAND BEFORE WINNING THE AMERICAN REVOLUTION.

TAXATION WITHOUT REPRESENTATION

ON TOP OF THAT, CONGRESS HAS ULTIMATE CONTROL OVER THE DISTRICT'S BUDGET.

WE CAN ONLY *HOPE* THE FEDERAL GOVERNMENT WILL LET US SPEND OUR MONEY AS WE WANT.

OBVIOUSLY, THAT DOESN'T ALWAYS HAPPEN.

UNTIL 1961, U.S. CITIZENS WHO LIVED IN DC COULDN'T EVEN VOTE IN PRESIDENTIAL ELECTIONS.

SOME OF US WORKED FOR THE CITY GOVERNMENT, WHICH REQUIRED US TO LIVE HERE.

SOME OF US EVEN WORKED FOR THE PRESIDENT! THANKFULLY, THE RATIFICATION OF THE 23RD AMENDMENT CHANGED THAT.

VOTE HERE

Because the 700,000 citizens of DC are not represented by a voting member in Congress, we can't even effectively complain about this state of affairs.

The District is the only democratic capital in the world without a vote in the national legislature.

TAXATION WITHOUT REP

FREE DC

FREE DC

FREE DC

FREE DC

FREE DC

WHAT ELSE DO DC RESIDENTS FACE?

Congress can pass any law it decides to impose on the District.

Inhabitants pay more per person in federal income taxes than the residents of any state.

Members of the military from the District risk their lives to establish democratic systems abroad but cannot participate in their nation's own system by voting when they return home.

When the federal government shut down for five weeks in 2019, DC picked up the government's trash and provided water— for free!

In 2014, voters approved an ordinance allowing residents to use small amounts of marijuana in private homes in DC.

Congress then passed a law preventing the city from taxing sales of the substance, funds that could've been used to update schools and bridges.

Every state is allowed to display two statues in the Capitol. The District does not have this right.

IN 1978, CONGRESS PROPOSED AN AMENDMENT TO GIVE THE DISTRICT REPRESENTATION IN THE HOUSE AND SENATE WITHOUT BEING DESIGNATED A STATE.

IT WAS APPROVED BY ONLY SIXTEEN STATES BEFORE THE SEVEN YEARS ALLOWED FOR RATIFICATION RAN OUT.

THE CLOSEST DC CAME TO REPRESENTATION WAS IN 2009.

LEADERS IN THE SENATE DEMANDED THAT THE DISTRICT ROLL BACK ITS RESTRICTIONS ON FIREARM POSSESSION IN EXCHANGE FOR A VOTING REPRESENTATIVE IN THE HOUSE.

DC REFUSED.

THERE ARE OTHER WAYS!

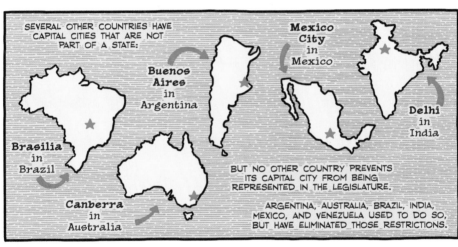

SEVERAL OTHER COUNTRIES HAVE CAPITAL CITIES THAT ARE NOT PART OF A STATE:

Buenos Aires in Argentina

Mexico City in Mexico

Delhi in India

Brasilia in Brazil

Canberra in Australia

BUT NO OTHER COUNTRY PREVENTS ITS CAPITAL CITY FROM BEING REPRESENTED IN THE LEGISLATURE.

ARGENTINA, AUSTRALIA, BRAZIL, INDIA, MEXICO, AND VENEZUELA USED TO DO SO, BUT HAVE ELIMINATED THOSE RESTRICTIONS.

CANBERRA HAS ONLY ONE DELEGATE TO THE HOUSE AND TWO SENATORS TO THE UPPER HOUSE, RATHER THAN THE TWELVE ASSIGNED TO EACH OF THE SIX AUSTRALIAN STATES.

STILL, CITIZENS OF THE CAPITAL HAVE A VOICE!

Nearly 86% of voters supported a referendum on statehood in 2016.

A state constitution was drafted in which the mayor would become governor, the city council would become unicameral, and local citizens could choose their members of congress.

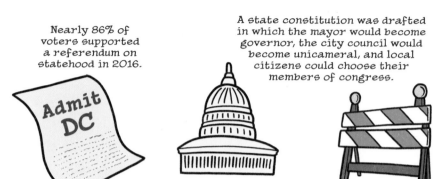

But because of the likelihood that DC's two senate seats would go to Democrats, statehood remains a non-starter among Republicans.

EVEN IF THE DISTRICT ISN'T ENTITLED TO TWO SENATORS, WE'D STILL LIKE TO HAVE A VOTING MEMBER OF THE HOUSE.

BUT THAT WOULD PROBABLY REQUIRE A CONSTITUTIONAL AMENDMENT.

ANOTHER POSSIBILITY WOULD BE TO SHRINK DISTRICT BOUNDARIES TO JUST THE AREA WHERE THE NATIONAL GOVERNMENT BUILDINGS ARE.

RESIDENTIAL NEIGHBORHOODS WOULD BE RETURNED TO VIRGINIA AND MARYLAND. THAT'S CALLED *RETROCESSION*. AND IT'S HAPPENED BEFORE.

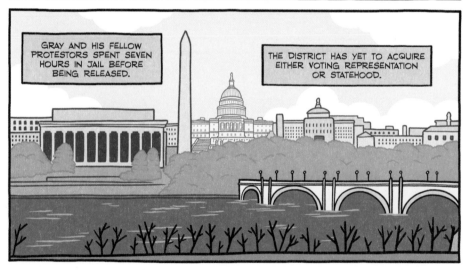

GRAY AND HIS FELLOW PROTESTORS SPENT SEVEN HOURS IN JAIL BEFORE BEING RELEASED.

THE DISTRICT HAS YET TO ACQUIRE EITHER VOTING REPRESENTATION OR STATEHOOD.

WHAT ABOUT PUERTO RICO?

The United States includes five territories whose status, like that of Washington, DC, is irregular.

American **Samoa, Guam,** and the **Northern Mariana Islands** (in the mid-Pacific Ocean)

Puerto Rico and the U.S. **Virgin Islands** (in the Caribbean)

Unlike Washingtonians, American citizens on these islands **cannot** vote for president. Like DC, they have only a nonvoting House representative, called **a delegate.**

The Constitution gives Congress the right to admit territories to the Union but doesn't lay out any criteria for membership.

Puerto Rico, which has a population of about 3.7 million, is the largest of these territories in both area and population. Understandably, Puerto Ricans have a variety of opinions about how they're governed.

IN 2012 APPROXIMATELY 45% OF PEOPLE SAID THEY WOULD LIKE THEIR ISLAND TO BECOME A FULL-FLEDGED STATE.

ANOTHER 45% SUPPORTED THE CURRENT ARRANGEMENT.

MOST OF THE REMAINDER SUPPORTED *INDEPENDENCE—* BECOMING A SEPARATE COUNTRY.

Five years later, 97% of those who voted supported statehood; however, most voters sat out the election, probably because they don't.

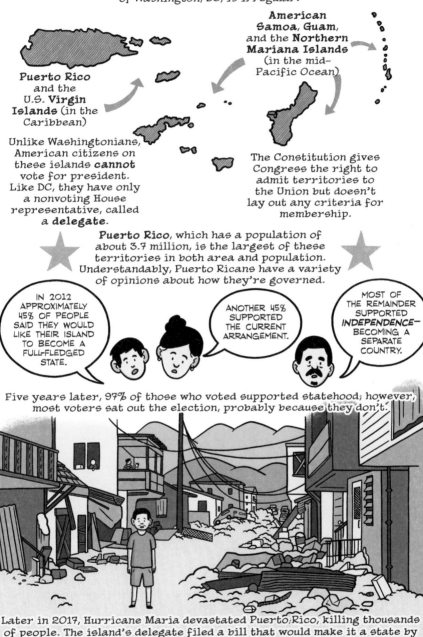

Later in 2017, Hurricane Maria devastated Puerto Rico, killing thousands of people. The island's delegate filed a bill that would make it a state by 2021. It was co-sponsored by thirty-five members of the House.

Meanwhile, the territory declared a form of bankruptcy, and its finances are supervised by a board on the mainland.

7

"i'll just do it myself!"
"oh, no, you won't."

direct democracy

1995. THIS IS JENNIFER GRATZ.

I HAVE GOOD GRADES, I'M IN A TON OF EXTRACURRICULARS . . .

I'LL DEFINITELY GET INTO THE UNIVERSITY OF MICHIGAN!

GRATZ HAD HER HEART SET ON ATTENDING U OF M'S FLAGSHIP CAMPUS IN ANN ARBOR.

WHAT? DEARBORN CAMPUS?!

...ulations!

...en accepted ...rsity of ...Dearborn!

SHE LATER LEARNED THAT THE ADMISSIONS OFFICE AWARDED EXTRA POINTS TO MINORITY APPLICANTS. FOLLOWING A POLICY CALLED *AFFIRMATIVE ACTION,* THE UNIVERSITY WANTED TO ENROLL A DIVERSE RANGE OF STUDENTS.

BUT THAT'S DISCRIMINATION! WHY SHOULD I BE REJECTED IN FAVOR OF SOMEONE WITH A LOWER GPA?

TY OF MICHIGAN
DEARBORN

IN 2003, SHE SUED THE UNIVERSITY IN A CASE THAT REACHED THE SUPREME COURT.

SHE WON.

BUT IN A SIMILAR CASE DECIDED THAT SAME DAY, A SLIGHTLY DIFFERENT VERSION OF AFFIRMATIVE ACTION WAS UPHELD AT THE U OF M LAW SCHOOL.

AFFIRMATIVE ACTION IS INAPPROPRIATE IN ALL CASES.

I PROPOSE AN AMENDMENT TO ELIMINATE IT FROM THE STATE CONSTITUTION!

MICHIGAN ALLOWS ORDINARY CITIZENS TO DO EXACTLY THAT IF THEY CAN SHOW WIDESPREAD SUPPORT FOR CHANGE.

WITH HELP FROM ORGANIZATIONS THAT ALSO OPPOSED AFFIRMATIVE ACTION, GRATZ COLLECTED MORE THAN 320,000 SIGNATURES ON A PETITION—

—MORE THAN ENOUGH TO MEET THE REQUIREMENT FOR HER PROPOSED AMENDMENT TO BE VOTED ON IN A STATEWIDE ELECTION.

PETITIO

WHEN **PROPOSAL** 2 CAME UP FOR A VOTE IN 2006, 58% OF VOTERS APPROVED.

REGIST
HERI

BY DIRECT ACTION, GRATZ, A PRIVATE, UNELECTED CITIZEN, SUCCEEDED IN CHANGING HER STATE'S CONSTITUTION.

Meanwhile, back in 1787 . . .

I CAN'T IMAGINE CITIZENS EVER DIRECTLY MAKING LAWS.

OR REVISING THE CONSTITUTION OF THEIR OWN INITIATIVE!

THE BASIS OF THE CONSTITUTION IS ITS TOTAL EXCLUSION OF THE PEOPLE IN ACTUALLY GOVERNING!

ONLY THE PEOPLE'S REPRESENTATIVES SHOULD BE ABLE TO MAKE ACTUAL DECISIONS ABOUT PUBLIC POLICIES, RIGHT?

SO WHAT'S THE BIG PROBLEM?

Although our Constitution was written in the name of **"We the People,"** the people themselves have **no explicit power** at the national level.

ARE THERE OTHER WAYS?

Like what happened in Michigan, almost all states allow for direct democracy. Since 1900, nearly **14,000** proposed measures have gone directly to voters!

EVERY STATE EXCEPT DELAWARE REQUIRES THAT A MAJORITY OF VOTERS APPROVE PROPOSED STATE CONSTITUTIONAL AMENDMENTS BEFORE THEY TAKE EFFECT. IN DELAWARE, THE STATE LEGISLATURE CAN AMEND THE CONSTITUTION WITHOUT ANY INVOLVEMENT BY THE PEOPLE.

MAINE AND OHIO ALLOW THE ELECTORATE TO CHALLENGE LAWS PASSED BY THE STATE LEGISLATURE. IF ENOUGH VOTERS SIGN PETITIONS, THE CHALLENGED LAWS ARE VOTED ON AT THE NEXT ELECTION.

MANY WESTERN STATES, INCLUDING ARIZONA, CALIFORNIA, OREGON, AND WASHINGTON, ALLOW THE ELECTORATE TO PUT PROPOSALS, INCLUDING STATE CONSTITUTIONAL AMENDMENTS, ON THE BALLOT. THEN A STATEWIDE VOTE DETERMINES WHETHER THEY SHOULD BE ADOPTED.

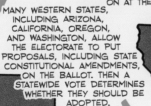

IN FOURTEEN STATES, THE ELECTORATE GETS TO DECIDE EVERY TEN OR TWENTY YEARS OR SO WHETHER TO HOLD A STATE CONSTITUTIONAL CONVENTION. IF A MAJORITY CALLS FOR IT, THE CITIZENRY HAS THE OPPORTUNITY TO FIX DEFECTS IN ITS EXISTING CONSTITUTION.

NEW HAMPSHIRE HAS HAD SEVENTEEN SUCH CONVENTIONS SINCE 1789!

AND SOME STATES CHOOSE TO REPLACE THEIR EXISTING CONSTITUTIONS WITH A BRAND NEW ONE DURING A CONSTITUTIONAL CONVENTION. IT THEN MUST GET APPROVAL FROM THE ELECTORATE.

IN OTHER COUNTRIES, *REFERENDA*—VOTES ON SPECIFIC ISSUES BY THE ELECTORATE—ARE INCREASINGLY COMMON.

IT'S COMMON IN SWITZERLAND, AUSTRALIA, AND NEW ZEALAND!

SOMETIMES A NATIONAL REFERENDUM EVEN GETS INTERNATIONAL ATTENTION. IN 2015, IRELAND, A LARGELY CATHOLIC COUNTRY, VOTED TO LEGALIZE SAME-SEX MARRIAGE.

AND IT WAS VOTED BY A LARGE MAJORITY, TOO!

IN 2016, A REFERENDUM IN BRITAIN INITIATED THAT COUNTRY'S EXIT FROM THE EUROPEAN UNION.

THIS WAS CALLED BREXIT!

PERHAPS U.S. CITIZENS SHOULD BE ABLE TO SIDE-STEP CONGRESS AND PASS OR ERASE CERTAIN LAWS ON THEIR OWN.

THIS PROCESS EXISTS IN A NUMBER OF STATES, SO WHY NOT AT THE NATIONAL LEVEL?

MAYBE IT'D BE GOOD TO AMEND THE CONSTITUTION TO GIVE CITIZENS A WAY OF PARTICIPATING IN THIS "REPRESENTATIVE GOVERNMENT"!

OPPONENTS CHALLENGED THE CONSTITUTIONALITY OF JENNIFER GRATZ'S AMENDMENT IN FEDERAL COURT, BUT THE SUPREME COURT UPHELD IT IN 2014 BY A VOTE OF 6 TO 2.

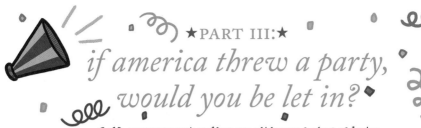

★PART III:★

*if america threw a party,
would you be let in?*

Self-government relies on citizens being able to
choose their leaders, generally through elections.

But the Constitution doesn't guarantee that all
citizens actually have the right to vote, nor does it
make it easy for citizens to run for certain offices.

States can control citizens' access to the polls,
depending on whether they want to decrease or
increase the number of voters. The percentage
of citizens who get to vote or who can do so
easily varies widely from state to state.

The Constitution makes it impossible for some
otherwise eligible candidates to run for public
office. That means voters lose the opportunity to
choose leaders whom they might like but who can't
run because of restrictions in the Constitution!
And one of these restrictions applies to the
president, the highest executive in the land.

Also, a president can't necessarily finish
the job he was elected to do.

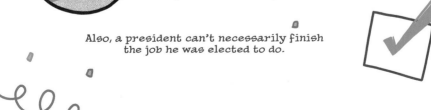

8

who can vote?
how do you know?

voting rights

JUNE 2015.

VOTE
for
MAYOR
of San
Antonio

THIS IS MARY LOU MILLER, AGE 101.

I'VE BEEN VOTING REGULARLY IN ALMOST EVERY ELECTION SINCE I TURNED TWENTY-ONE—

ONLY FOURTEEN YEARS AFTER THE 19TH AMENDMENT GAVE WOMEN THE RIGHT TO DO SO!

IT'S IMPORTANT TO BE INVOLVED IN POLITICS.

THAT'S WHY I TEACH CLASSES ABOUT THE CANDIDATES AND ISSUES.

I'VE EVEN DRIVEN PEOPLE TO THE POLLS!

I TRIED VOTING BY MAIL—TEXAS ALLOWS CERTAIN PEOPLE TO DO THAT. BUT I RECENTLY MOVED, AND THE POST OFFICE DOESN'T FORWARD BALLOTS.

TEXAS
ample Ballot

BUT REGISTERED VOTERS CAN CAST THEIR BALLOTS SEVERAL WEEKS BEFORE ELECTION DAY.

SO, I'M HERE TO VOTE EARLY IN PERSON!

I'M SORRY, MA'AM. YOU CAN'T VOTE TODAY.

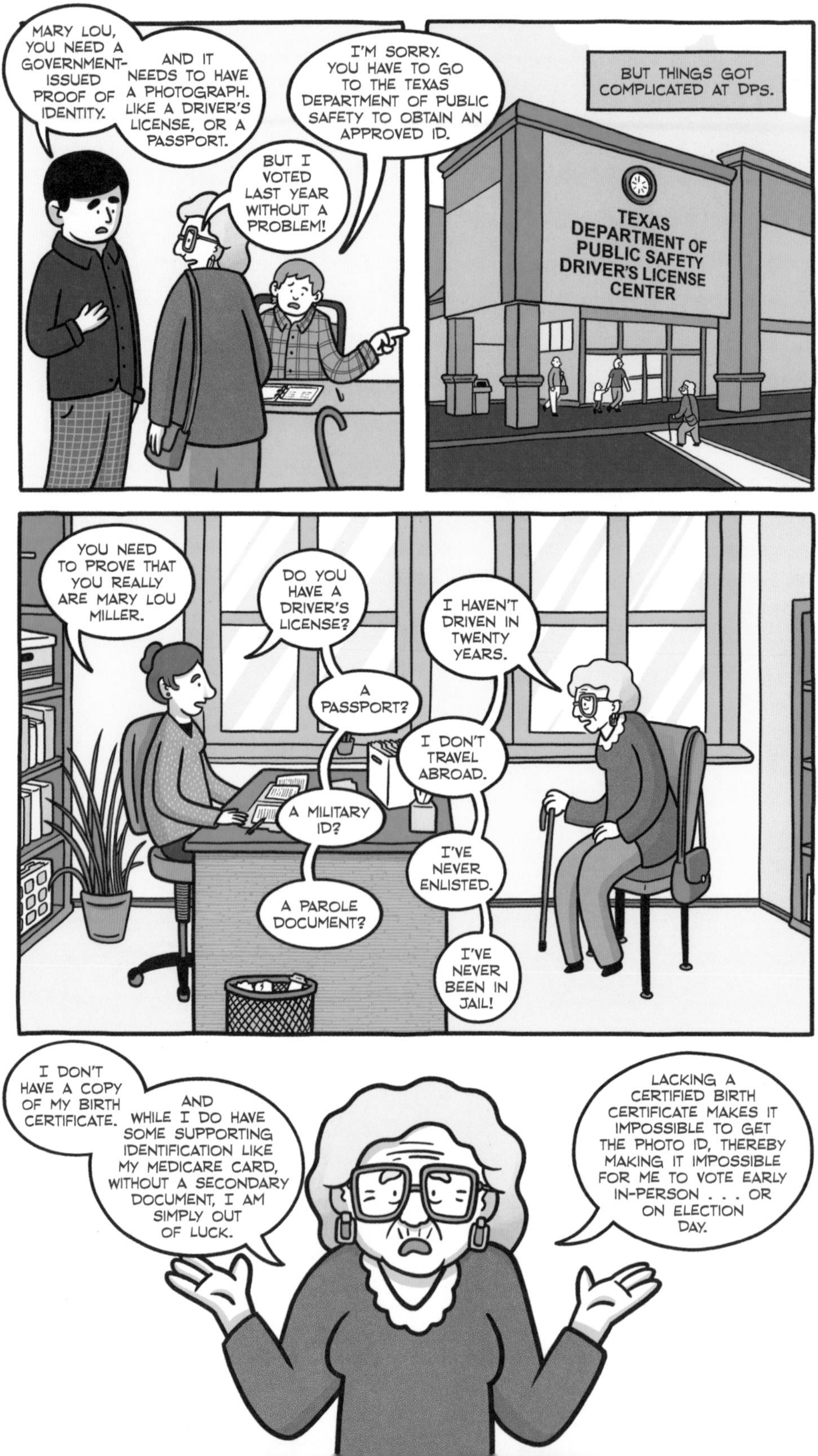
MARY LOU, YOU NEED A GOVERNMENT-ISSUED PROOF OF IDENTITY.
AND IT NEEDS TO HAVE A PHOTOGRAPH. LIKE A DRIVER'S LICENSE, OR A PASSPORT.
I'M SORRY. YOU HAVE TO GO TO THE TEXAS DEPARTMENT OF PUBLIC SAFETY TO OBTAIN AN APPROVED ID.
BUT I VOTED LAST YEAR WITHOUT A PROBLEM!
BUT THINGS GOT COMPLICATED AT DPS.
TEXAS DEPARTMENT OF PUBLIC SAFETY DRIVER'S LICENSE CENTER
YOU NEED TO PROVE THAT YOU REALLY ARE MARY LOU MILLER.
DO YOU HAVE A DRIVER'S LICENSE?
I HAVEN'T DRIVEN IN TWENTY YEARS.
A PASSPORT?
I DON'T TRAVEL ABROAD.
A MILITARY ID?
I'VE NEVER ENLISTED.
A PAROLE DOCUMENT?
I'VE NEVER BEEN IN JAIL!
I DON'T HAVE A COPY OF MY BIRTH CERTIFICATE.
AND WHILE I DO HAVE SOME SUPPORTING IDENTIFICATION LIKE MY MEDICARE CARD, WITHOUT A SECONDARY DOCUMENT, I AM SIMPLY OUT OF LUCK.
LACKING A CERTIFIED BIRTH CERTIFICATE MAKES IT IMPOSSIBLE TO GET THE PHOTO ID, THEREBY MAKING IT IMPOSSIBLE FOR ME TO VOTE EARLY IN-PERSON . . . OR ON ELECTION DAY.

Meanwhile, back in 1787 (and 1868, 1870, 1920, 1964, and 1971) . . .

WE DON'T NEED TO ADDRESS WHO HAS THE RIGHT TO VOTE, DO WE?

EH, THE STATES CAN SORT THAT OUT.

WHAT IF EACH STATE CONCOCTS AN ENTIRELY DIFFERENT PROCEDURE?

EVERYONE WILL HAVE ELECTIONS, AND EVERYONE WILL HAVE VOTERS.

WHAT ELSE DO WE NEED TO FIGURE OUT?

NOT SURPRISINGLY, THE STATES DID COME UP WITH DIFFERENT ANSWERS.

NEW JERSEY WAS THE ONLY STATE TO ALLOW WOMEN TO VOTE.

BUT ONLY WEALTHY, UNMARRIED WOMEN.

THAT'S BECAUSE ONLY PEOPLE WORTH FIFTY POUNDS HAD THE RIGHT TO VOTE.

AND WHEN WE GET MARRIED, OUR PROPERTY GOES TO OUR HUSBANDS.

EVEN THIS DIDN'T LAST LONG; IN 1807, WOMEN LOST THE RIGHT TO VOTE BECAUSE OF A DISPUTE BETWEEN THE MAJOR POLITICAL PARTIES.

SOME STATES REQUIRED THAT VOTERS OWN PROPERTY OR PAY TAXES.

AND ALL STATES LIMITED SUFFRAGE TO PERSONS OVER THE AGE OF TWENTY-ONE, THE AGE OF ADULTHOOD.

SOLD

NO STATE ALLOWED ENSLAVED PEOPLE TO VOTE.

SOME ALLOWED FREE BLACKS TO DO SO, BUT OTHERS DID NOT.

95

SOME OF THESE RESTRICTIONS WERE BARRED FOLLOWING THE CIVIL WAR.

IT HAS BEEN FIVE YEARS SINCE GENERAL LEE SURRENDERED TO GENERAL GRANT! WE ARE A REUNITED NATION.

IT IS TIME TO STOP MAKING IT IMPOSSIBLE FOR PEOPLE TO VOTE BECAUSE OF THEIR RACE . . .

. . . WITH THE *15TH AMENDMENT!*

"The right of citizens of the United States to vote shall not be denied or abridged by the United States or by any State on account of race, color, or previous condition of servitude.

"The Congress shall have power to enforce this article by appropriate legislation."

WE CAN STILL REQUIRE VOTERS TO PASS DIFFICULT LITERACY TESTS OR PAY POLL TAXES, THOUGH.

MEANING WE CAN STILL DENY MANY AFRICAN AMERICANS THE RIGHT TO VOTE.

THE WOMEN'S SUFFRAGE MOVEMENT HAD SPLIT OVER WHETHER TO SUPPORT THE 15TH AMENDMENT.

IF MEN OF ANY COLOR CAN VOTE, WHY NOT US?

SORRY, LADIES.

WE'RE GOING TO HAVE TO WAIT ANOTHER FIFTY YEARS BEFORE THE *19TH AMENDMENT* ADDS THAT THE RIGHT TO VOTE SHALL NOT BE DENIED "ON ACCOUNT OF SEX."

WHAT ABOUT THE POOR?

WE CAN'T AFFORD THE POLL TAXES THAT MANY STATES REQUIRE!

STATES WON'T STOP CHARGING POLL TAXES UNTIL 1964, WHEN THEY ADOPT THE *24TH AMENDMENT.*

SO WE SLOWLY FORGED MORE PATHS TO VOTING! IN 1971, THE *26TH AMENDMENT* CHANGED THE AGE OF ADULTHOOD FROM TWENTY-ONE TO EIGHTEEN.

AND EVEN THOUGH IT WAS ADOPTED IN 1868, VOTING-RIGHTS ACTIVISTS HAVE USED, AND ARE STILL USING, THE *14TH AMENDMENT* TO PREVENT STATES FROM RESTRICTING THE ABILITY TO VOTE. THIS AMENDMENT GUARANTEED ALL CITIZENS "EQUAL PROTECTION" UNDER THE LAW.

WHAT'S THE BIG PROBLEM?!

THE PROBLEM IS THAT VOTING RULES
ARE NOT NEUTRAL!

SOME STATES ARE EASING ACCESS TO THE POLLS, WHILE OTHERS ARE LIMITING IT.

RESIDENCE REQUIREMENTS

Some states refuse to count college students as residents or make it hard for them to vote at school. Undergrads at Prairie View A&M University in Texas sued in 2018 when county officials told them to register using an address in the wrong precinct.

Twenty-six states require residence ranging from ten days to thirty days before registering to vote. (The other twenty-four have no residence requirement.)

REGISTRATION PROCEDURES

Seventeen states and the District of Columbia allow automatic voter registration (AVR) when people renew their driver's licenses or get IDs at a motor vehicle office.

Seventeen states plus DC allow people to register when they show up at the polls on Election Day.

Thirty-four states and DC allow online registration. The other states require people to appear in advance at official sites, sometimes inconveniently located, with documentation to prove their identity and eligibility.

Only Maine and Vermont allow felons to vote while they're serving sentences. Nebraska automatically restores felons' right to vote two years after they're released.

Wyoming does so for those who have committed nonviolent crimes. Florida approved a referendum in 2018 that did the same, but the legislature tried to limit their eligibility.

More than six million people across the country have lost the right to vote because of their criminal record.

IDENTIFICATION REQUIREMENTS

Nineteen states do not require identification during voter registration.

Thirty-six states require voters to produce an ID when they show up at the polls.

Of these, seventeen say the ID must include a photograph. These types of IDs are often more expensive, making it harder for low-income people to obtain.

Some say it can be a hunting license, an electric bill, or a student ID.

And some allow voters who arrive without an ID to fill in a provisional ballot, which is only counted after other documents are produced.

POLLING HOURS

Thirty-eight states plus DC allow people to cast their ballots before Election Day. This time period ranges from less than two weeks beforehand to more than a month.

Three states require that all ballots be mailed.

The rest allow voting only on one day and only between certain limited hours, which vary from state to state.

Citizens' ability to register and vote continues to vary widely, and it's likely to keep changing.

In 2016 alone, **seventeen states** introduced new voter restrictions, right in time for that year's presidential elections.

These regulations matter!

States, such as Minnesota, that allow same-day voter registration have the highest turnout of voters. In 2016, nearly **75%** of eligible Minnesotans voted!

AS OF 2018, LEGISLATORS IN FORTY-ONE STATES INTRODUCED 514 BILLS TO **INCREASE** ACCESS TO VOTING.

LEGISLATORS IN TWENTY-SEVEN STATES DID THE **OPPOSITE**.

THERE ARE OTHER WAYS!

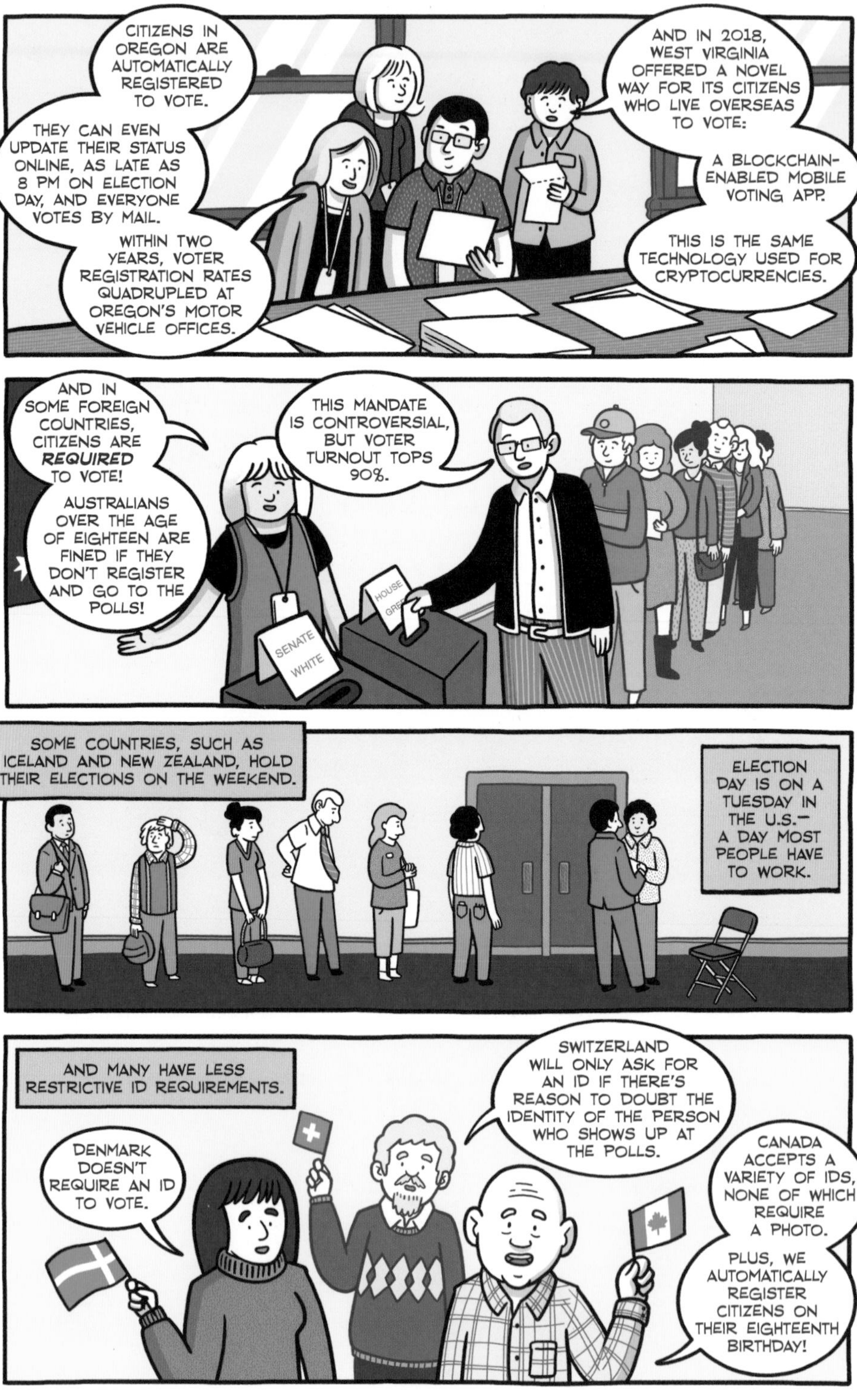

CITIZENS IN OREGON ARE AUTOMATICALLY REGISTERED TO VOTE.
THEY CAN EVEN UPDATE THEIR STATUS ONLINE, AS LATE AS 8 PM ON ELECTION DAY, AND EVERYONE VOTES BY MAIL.
WITHIN TWO YEARS, VOTER REGISTRATION RATES QUADRUPLED AT OREGON'S MOTOR VEHICLE OFFICES.
AND IN 2018, WEST VIRGINIA OFFERED A NOVEL WAY FOR ITS CITIZENS WHO LIVE OVERSEAS TO VOTE:
A BLOCKCHAIN-ENABLED MOBILE VOTING APP.
THIS IS THE SAME TECHNOLOGY USED FOR CRYPTOCURRENCIES.
AND IN SOME FOREIGN COUNTRIES, CITIZENS ARE ***REQUIRED*** TO VOTE!
AUSTRALIANS OVER THE AGE OF EIGHTEEN ARE FINED IF THEY DON'T REGISTER AND GO TO THE POLLS!
THIS MANDATE IS CONTROVERSIAL, BUT VOTER TURNOUT TOPS 90%.
HOUSE
SENATE WHITE
SOME COUNTRIES, SUCH AS ICELAND AND NEW ZEALAND, HOLD THEIR ELECTIONS ON THE WEEKEND.
ELECTION DAY IS ON A TUESDAY IN THE U.S.— A DAY MOST PEOPLE HAVE TO WORK.
AND MANY HAVE LESS RESTRICTIVE ID REQUIREMENTS.
DENMARK DOESN'T REQUIRE AN ID TO VOTE.
SWITZERLAND WILL ONLY ASK FOR AN ID IF THERE'S REASON TO DOUBT THE IDENTITY OF THE PERSON WHO SHOWS UP AT THE POLLS.
CANADA ACCEPTS A VARIETY OF IDS, NONE OF WHICH REQUIRE A PHOTO.
PLUS, WE AUTOMATICALLY REGISTER CITIZENS ON THEIR EIGHTEENTH BIRTHDAY!

IN THE U.S., JUST OVER HALF OF ELIGIBLE VOTERS VOTE IN PRESIDENTIAL ELECTIONS.

UP TO ONE-THIRD OF ELIGIBLE VOTERS AREN'T EVEN REGISTERED.

WE HAVE ONE OF THE LOWEST REGISTRATION RATES IN THE WORLD.

A SINGLE NATIONALLY RUN ELECTION SYSTEM COULD LIMIT THE CRAZY-QUILT ASPECT OF STATE ELECTION LAWS. CONGRESS HAS THE ABILITY TO MAKE THIS FIX, SIMPLY BY PASSING A LAW.

THIS PROBABLY WON'T HAPPEN, THOUGH.

CONGRESS WOULD FEAR THAT THE POLITICAL PARTY IN POWER WOULD GET THE BENEFIT IN THE SHORT RUN.

IN 2016, A FEDERAL APPEALS COURT RULED THAT TEXAS'S VOTER IDENTIFICATION LAW VIOLATED THE VOTING RIGHTS ACT BECAUSE IT DISCRIMINATED AGAINST MINORITIES.

VOTE for MAYOR of San Antonio

THE LAW IS STILL IN EFFECT.

STATE LAW IN TEXAS REQUIRES EVERY HIGH SCHOOL TO HAND OUT VOTER REGISTRATION MATERIALS TO EVERY ELIGIBLE STUDENT AT LEAST TWICE A YEAR, THOUGH ONLY ABOUT A THIRD OF THE SCHOOLS DO SO.

BUT THE COURT DIRECTED THE STATE TO HELP VOTERS OBTAIN THE NECESSARY FORMS OF IDENTIFICATION.

9

who gets to represent you?

restrictions on running for congress

MASSACHUSETTS. JULY 1780.

ALBERT GALLATIN, A SEAFARING ORPHAN FROM GENEVA, SWITZERLAND, ARRIVES AT THE AGE OF NINETEEN.

HOW MUCH TO BUY SOME LAND AND START A FARM?

MORE THAN YOU CAN AFFORD!

DETERMINED TO STAY, HE TRAVELED THROUGHOUT THE AMERICAN COLONIES, LEARNING ABOUT THE TERRAIN AND THE PEOPLE.

I EVEN JOINED A MILITIA TO BATTLE THE BRITISH IN MAINE!

IN 1785, I BECAME AN AMERICAN CITIZEN.

AFTER THE WAR, HE TAUGHT AT HARVARD COLLEGE.

WHEN HE INHERITED SOME MONEY, HE BOUGHT LAND AND BUILT A HOME IN WESTERN PENNSYLVANIA.

BUT WHAT I *REALLY* WANT TO DO IS ENTER *POLITICS*!

AT THE AGE OF TWENTY-SEVEN, GALLATIN SERVED ON A COMMITTEE TO EVALUATE THE U.S. CONSTITUTION.

I'M NOT A FAN OF THE DOCUMENT.

IT GIVES TOO MUCH POWER TO THE FEDERAL GOVERNMENT, AND NOT ENOUGH TO THE STATES!

HE LATER HELPED REVISE THE PENNSYLVANIA STATE CONSTITUTION AND WAS THEN ELECTED TO THE STATE'S HOUSE OF REPRESENTATIVES.

THIS GUY'S GOT TALENT!

WE NEED HIM TO REPRESENT PENNSYLVANIA IN THE U.S. SENATE!

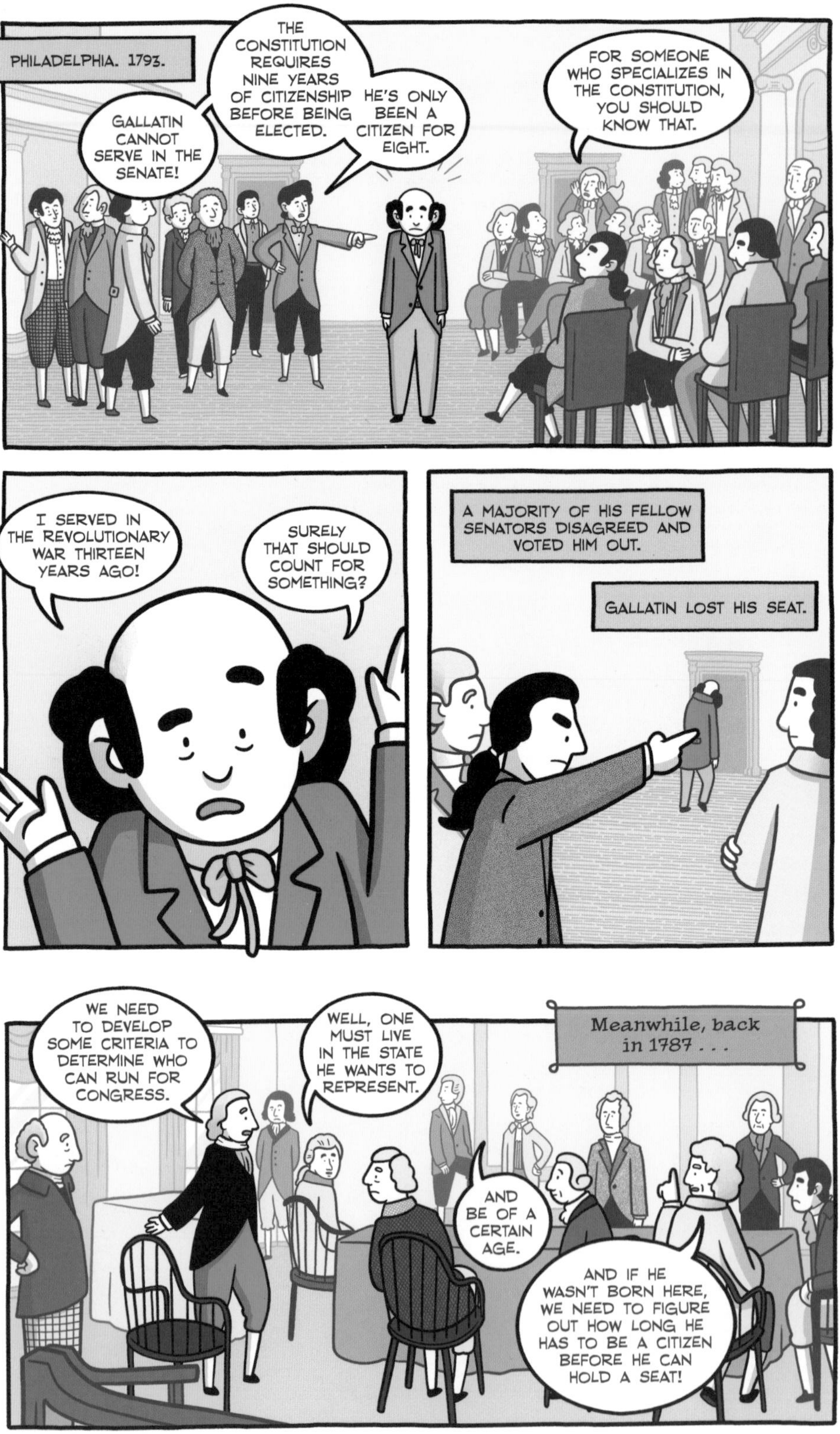
PHILADELPHIA. 1793.
GALLATIN CANNOT SERVE IN THE SENATE!
THE CONSTITUTION REQUIRES NINE YEARS OF CITIZENSHIP BEFORE BEING ELECTED.
HE'S ONLY BEEN A CITIZEN FOR EIGHT.
FOR SOMEONE WHO SPECIALIZES IN THE CONSTITUTION, YOU SHOULD KNOW THAT.
I SERVED IN THE REVOLUTIONARY WAR THIRTEEN YEARS AGO!
SURELY THAT SHOULD COUNT FOR SOMETHING?
A MAJORITY OF HIS FELLOW SENATORS DISAGREED AND VOTED HIM OUT.
GALLATIN LOST HIS SEAT.
Meanwhile, back in 1787 . . .
WE NEED TO DEVELOP SOME CRITERIA TO DETERMINE WHO CAN RUN FOR CONGRESS.
WELL, ONE MUST LIVE IN THE STATE HE WANTS TO REPRESENT.
AND BE OF A CERTAIN AGE.
AND IF HE WASN'T BORN HERE, WE NEED TO FIGURE OUT HOW LONG HE HAS TO BE A CITIZEN BEFORE HE CAN HOLD A SEAT!

THE FRAMERS DIDN'T DEFINE CITIZENSHIP OR EXPLAIN HOW SOMEONE BORN ELSEWHERE COULD BECOME A CITIZEN.

LET US DECIDE HOW LONG A CANDIDATE MUST BE A CITIZEN BEFORE RUNNING FOR OFFICE!

I THINK TWO YEARS FOR HOUSE MEMBERS AND FOUR FOR SENATORS.

BUT ALLOWING RECENT IMMIGRANTS TO HOLD OFFICE WOULD LET FOREIGNERS AND ADVENTURERS MAKE LAWS FOR US!

INCLUDING *BRITISH* ADVENTURERS!

IT SHOULD BE A MINIMUM OF FOURTEEN YEARS FOR BOTH HOUSES.

THAT WOULD PREVENT TOO MANY PEOPLE FROM RUNNING!

LET US COMPROMISE!

THEY SETTLED ON SEVEN YEARS FOR REPRESENTATIVES AND NINE FOR SENATORS.

WHAT ABOUT THE RESIDENCY REQUIREMENT?

CANDIDATES SHOULD LIVE AT LEAST SEVEN YEARS IN THE STATE THEY HOPE TO REPRESENT BEFORE THEY'RE EVEN CONSIDERED, I THINK!

IF SOMEONE FROM NEW ENGLAND JUST UP AND MOVES TO SOUTH CAROLINA, HE CAN VOTE HOWEVER HE WANTS, EVEN IF IT'S AGAINST THE BETTER INTERESTS OF CAROLINIANS!

WE'LL JUST SAY HE HAS TO "BE AN INHABITANT OF THAT STATE."

ENOUGH ARGUING!

EVERYONE HAPPY NOW?

WHAT ABOUT THE AGE REQUIREMENTS?

TWENTY-FIVE FOR REPRESENTATIVES AND THIRTY FOR SENATORS IS REASONABLE! LET'S MOVE ON!

SENATOR HIRAM REVELS?

Reverend Hiram Revels almost missed the honor of becoming our country's first African–American Senator.

Following the Civil War, members of the Republican Party set up governments in the defeated Southern States to try to guarantee that former slaves would receive the same rights as whites.

In 1870, Mississippi's new state senate elected Revels to the U.S. Senate. Democrats, however, didn't want a black man to represent the state in Congress.

SO, WE BLOCKED THE ELECTION!

AFTER ALL, THE CONSTITUTION MADE REVELS INELIGIBLE FOR OFFICE.

Even though he had been born in North Carolina forty-three years earlier, his opponents claimed he hadn't been an American citizen for nine years.

How could that be?

In an 1857 case called Dred Scott v. Sandford, the Supreme Court had ruled that people of African heritage were not citizens.

The 14th Amendment overturned that decision, but it was adopted only in 1868, two years before Revels's election.

HE'S BEEN A CITIZEN FOR ONLY TWO YEARS!

THAT'S . . . NOT HOW IT WORKS.

It was a clever argument, but they lost.

SO, IS THERE A PROBLEM HERE?

Does our Constitution demand unreasonable residency and age requirements to run for office?

By all accounts, Gallatin was a knowledgeable and patriotic American.

Should he have been denied the right to serve as a public official?

AMERICA IS OFTEN DESCRIBED AS A *NATION OF IMMIGRANTS.*

BUT BECOMING A CITIZEN IS A LENGTHY AND COMPLEX PROCESS!

BY LAW, MOST RESIDENT ALIENS HAVE TO LIVE IN THE U.S. FOR AT LEAST FIVE YEARS TO EVEN BE ELIGIBLE FOR CITIZENSHIP.

THAT MEANS A CANDIDATE FOR THE HOUSE CAN'T RUN UNTIL THEY HAVE LIVED HERE FOR AT LEAST TWELVE YEARS.

AND FOR SENATE CANDIDATES, IT'S FOURTEEN YEARS!

MINIMUM AGE REQUIREMENTS ARE ALSO HARD TO JUSTIFY.

THE CONSTITUTION STATES YOU MUST BE AT LEAST TWENTY-FIVE FOR THE HOUSE AND THIRTY FOR THE SENATE.

IF YOU CAN VOTE FOR YOUR REPRESENTATIVE AND SENATOR AT EIGHTEEN, WHY DO YOU HAVE TO WAIT ANOTHER SEVEN OR TWELVE YEARS BEFORE YOU CAN RUN FOR A SEAT?

AND CONSIDER THAT CONGRESS HAS THE POWER TO DECLARE WAR, AND AMERICANS CAN JOIN THE MILITARY AT AGE EIGHTEEN.

IF YOU'RE OLD ENOUGH TO SERVE, SHOULDN'T YOU BE OLD ENOUGH TO PARTICIPATE IN DECISIONS ABOUT YOUR DEPLOYMENT?

WHAT OTHER OPTIONS DO WE HAVE?

Massachusetts, Montana, North Dakota, Ohio, and Vermont have no minimum age requirements to run for the lower house of the state legislature.

(Massachusetts requires that candidates for the upper house merely be old enough to vote.)

California, Idaho, Kansas, New York, Ohio, Rhode Island, Washington, and Wisconsin allow eighteen-year-olds to run for some offices.

(In Kansas, that no longer includes governor or lieutenant governor.)

States have different requirements, or none at all, for residency.

Kansas, Michigan, and New Mexico require simply establishing residency. Rhode Island wants candidates to have lived in the state at least thirty days.

Other mandates range from one year of residence (Idaho) to seven years (New Hampshire).

In some countries, like Belgium and Ireland, any citizen can run for election, regardless of the source or length of their citizenship.

And in some others, like Australia, Britain, Iceland, and Germany, you can run for office if you're old enough to vote (though not usually for head of state).

Other countries allow their citizens to run for office a few years after they reach minimum voting age. In Austria, the period is two years. In Belgium, Ireland, and Luxembourg, it's three.

IN ORDER TO ELIMINATE CANDIDACY REQUIREMENTS, THE CONSTITUTION WOULD HAVE TO BE AMENDED.

SINCE THERE IS NO WIDESPREAD CALL TO DO SO, IT'D BE UP TO YOUNG PEOPLE AND NEWCOMERS TO PUSH FOR THIS CHANGE.

AFTER BEING OUSTED FROM THE SENATE, GALLATIN RAN FOR A SEAT IN THE HOUSE OF REPRESENTATIVES, WHICH REQUIRED ONLY SEVEN YEARS OF CITIZENSHIP.

HE WAS ELECTED IN NOVEMBER 1794.

NOW THAT I'M PRESIDENT, I'M NAMING YOU MY SECRETARY OF THE TREASURY.

HE BECAME AN IMPORTANT LEADER OF THE DEMOCRATIC-REPUBLICAN PARTY.

NOW THAT I'M PRESIDENT, I WANT YOU TO STAY ON AS SECRETARY!

GALLATIN CONTINUED TO SERVE UNTIL 1814.

HE HOLDS THE RECORD FOR HAVING SERVED THE LONGEST TERM AS SECRETARY OF THE TREASURY, ONE OF THE MOST IMPORTANT DEPARTMENTS WITHIN THE EXECUTIVE BRANCH.

10

who gets a shot at the oval office?

restrictions on running for president

JOHN SIDNEY MCCAIN III WAS BORN IN 1936 IN THE PANAMA CANAL ZONE, THEN A U.S. TERRITORY.

THE SON OF AN ACTIVE-DUTY, FOUR-STAR ADMIRAL, HE GREW UP ON NAVAL BASES IN AMERICA AND ABROAD. HE FOLLOWED IN FAMILY TRADITION BY ENROLLING IN THE NAVAL ACADEMY UPON GRADUATING HIGH SCHOOL.

IN 1966, MCCAIN VOLUNTEERED TO FLY BOMBING MISSIONS IN THE VIETNAM WAR.

A YEAR LATER, HIS PLANE WAS SHOT DOWN OVER HANOI, AND WITH A BROKEN LEG AND TWO BROKEN ARMS, HE WAS TAKEN PRISONER.

HE SPENT FIVE AND A HALF BRUTAL YEARS IN CAPTIVITY—THREE AND A HALF OF THEM IN SOLITARY CONFINEMENT.

HE WAS REGULARLY BEATEN AND TORTURED.

ALTHOUGH HIS CAPTORS REPEATEDLY OFFERED TO LET HIM GO, HE REFUSED.

THE MILITARY CODE OF CONDUCT DIRECTED THAT ANOTHER PILOT, IMPRISONED EARLIER, SHOULD BE RELEASED FIRST.

I JUST DIDN'T THINK IT WAS THE HONORABLE THING TO DO.

TWO MONTHS AFTER A CEASE-FIRE ENDED THE WAR IN 1973, MCCAIN FINALLY CAME HOME.

111

DESPITE MULTIPLE MILITARY HONORS, INJURIES WOULD'VE PREVENTED MCCAIN FROM ADVANCING IN HIS CAREER, SO HE LEFT THE MILITARY.

HE DECIDED TO SERVE HIS COUNTRY IN ANOTHER WAY.

McCain
for House
Representative
1982

AFTER SERVING TWO TERMS IN THE HOUSE, HE WAS ELECTED TO THE SENATE.

McCAIN
PALIN

McCAIN
★2008★

THEN HE DECIDED TO RUN FOR THE PRESIDENCY.

IT WASN'T CLEAR, HOWEVER, THAT HE WOULD BE ALLOWED TO SERVE IF HE WON.

THE CONSTITUTION REQUIRES THAT OUR EXECUTIVE BE A . . .

"natural born Citizen" and "fourteen years a resident of the United States."

UNFORTUNATELY, NO ONE KNOWS EXACTLY WHAT THOSE TERMS MEAN OR WHETHER THEY FIT SOMEONE BORN IN A U.S. TERRITORY, LIKE MCCAIN.

DURING HIS CAMPAIGN, MCCAIN ASKED PROMINENT CONSTITUTIONAL LAWYERS TO ANALYZE THE SITUATION.

WE BELIEVE YOU MEET THE DEFINITION OF "NATURAL-BORN CITIZEN,"

BUT OUR OPINION DOESN'T AMOUNT TO A BINDING DECISION.

YOUR OPPONENTS MIGHT CONTEST YOUR ELIGIBILITY TO BECOME PRESIDENT.

Meanwhile, back in 1787 . . .

THE FRAMERS DIDN'T JUST MAKE THE OBSTACLES FOR THE PRESIDENCY HIGHER THAN THOSE FOR CONGRESS.

THEY ALSO MADE THEM INCOMPREHENSIBLE.

THIS IS **JOHN JAY.** HE SERVED AS PRESIDENT OF THE CONTINENTAL CONGRESS BUT DID NOT ATTEND THE CONSTITUTIONAL CONVENTION.

CANDIDATES SHOULD BE OLD ENOUGH FOR VOTERS TO JUDGE THEIR TRUE CHARACTER. YOUNGER MEN MIGHT DECEIVE VOTERS WITH BRILLIANT APPEARANCES OF GENIUS AND PATRIOTISM, WHICH SOMETIMES MISLEAD AS WELL AS DAZZLE.

FURTHERMORE, PRESIDENTS SHOULD CONTINUE IN PLACE A SUFFICIENT TIME TO BECOME PERFECTLY ACQUAINTED WITH OUR NATIONAL CONCERNS.

AND THE COMMANDER IN CHIEF OF THE AMERICAN ARMY SHALL NOT BE GIVEN TO, NOR DEVOLVE ON, ANY BUT A NATURAL BORN CITIZEN.

SHORTLY AFTER SHARING THESE IDEAS WITH GEORGE WASHINGTON, THE PHRASE FOUND ITS WAY INTO THE CONSTITUTION . . .

. . . EVEN THOUGH IT STILL WASN'T CLEARLY DEFINED.

SO . . .
WHAT ARE WE SUPPOSED
TO MAKE OF THIS?

AMERICANS OFTEN SAY,

ANYONE CAN GROW UP TO BE PRESIDENT!

BUT THAT'S NOT NECESSARILY THE CASE.

THE U.S. PUTS MORE LIMITATIONS ON RUNNING FOR PRESIDENT THAN ANY OTHER DEMOCRATIC COUNTRY!

IN FACT, ONE-THIRD OF AMERICAN CITIZENS ARE INELIGIBLE TO BECOME PRESIDENT BECAUSE OF THE RESTRICTIONS IN OUR CONSTITUTION.

NATURALIZED CITIZENS (THOSE WHO WERE BORN ABROAD BUT BECAME LEGAL CITIZENS OF THE UNITED STATES) HAVE HELD MANY DIFFERENT GOVERNMENT POSITIONS.

THEY'VE SERVED IN CONGRESS, AS MEMBERS OF THE SUPREME COURT AND PRESIDENTIAL CABINETS, AND AS HEAD OF THE JOINT CHIEFS OF STAFF OF THE U.S. MILITARY.

Arnold Schwarzenegger, California governor, 2003–2011!

Born in Austria.

THE ONLY OFFICES BARRED TO THOSE WHO ARE NOT U.S. CITIZENS AT BIRTH ARE THE PRESIDENCY AND THE VICE PRESIDENCY, IN CASE THAT PERSON ULTIMATELY HAS TO SERVE AS PRESIDENT.

Jennifer Granholm, first female governor of Michigan.

Born in Canada.

AND THAT'S NOT EVEN COUNTING THE AGE RESTRICTIONS!

HOW DO OTHER PLACES DO IT?

Just as the president is the chief executive of the United States, the **governor** is the chief in every state. And states vary widely in their requirements for this office.

Residency Periods

– California, Louisiana, Maine, and Texas: 5 years

– Alabama and Florida: 7 years

– Missouri: 10 years

Citizenship requirements

– California: 5 years

– Georgia: 15 years

– New Jersey: 20 years

Age Requirements

– Thirty-five states, including Arkansas, Florida, and Pennsylvania: 30

– Five allow anyone who is old enough to vote to run

In most countries, any citizen can run for head of state.

However, Bhutan, Brazil, Mexico, Peru, the Philippines, Tunisia, Zambia, and several Latin American countries do require presidents to be natural-born citizens.

Most countries also set a minimum age, ranging from eighteen in Australia, France, and Britain to fifty in Italy.

France also mandates that a presidential candidate have a bank account!

Thirty countries stipulate that their leaders must belong to a particular religion.

Andorra and Lebanon: **Christian**

Bhutan and Thailand: **Buddhist**

Iran, Jordan, Morocco, Saudi Arabia, and Syria: **Muslim**

Of course, the Constitution would need to be amended to make any changes to the age and citizenship requirements in the U.S.

BACK IN 2008, MCCAIN FAILED TO WIN THE PRESIDENTIAL ELECTION, SO HIS STATUS AS A NATURAL-BORN CITIZEN WAS NOT TESTED IN COURT.

BUT THAT SAME YEAR, THE SENATE UNANIMOUSLY PASSED A RESOLUTION DECLARING MCCAIN A NATURAL-BORN CITIZEN.

THE PROBLEM AROSE AGAIN IN 2016, WHEN TEXAS SENATOR TED CRUZ RAN FOR THE REPUBLICAN PRESIDENTIAL NOMINATION.

2016
CRUZ
CRUZ 2016
CRUZ

CRUZ WAS BORN IN CANADA TO AN AMERICAN MOTHER AND CUBAN FATHER. ACCORDING TO FEDERAL LAW, HE WAS A CITIZEN AT BIRTH, SINCE HIS MOTHER HAD MET THE REQUIREMENTS FOR PASSING ON CITIZENSHIP.

CRUZ
CRUZ

BUT YOU'RE NOT "NATURAL-BORN" UNDER THE CONSTITUTION!

SINCE CRUZ FAILED IN HIS QUEST FOR THE NOMINATION, WE STILL DON'T KNOW FOR SURE WHETHER A CITIZEN BORN OUTSIDE THE TERRITORY OF THE UNITED STATES WOULD BE ELIGIBLE TO SERVE AS PRESIDENT.

11

time's up!

presidential term limits

IN 1939, GERMANY INVADED CZECHOSLOVAKIA, ITALY, POLAND, AND AUSTRIA.

BRITAIN AND FRANCE RESPONDED BY DECLARING WAR ON GERMANY.

THE FOLLOWING YEAR, THE NAZIS INVADED DENMARK, BELGIUM, LUXEMBOURG, THE NETHERLANDS, NORWAY, AND THE SOVIET UNION.

ON JUNE 14, PARIS FELL TO THE MARAUDING ENEMY.

MOST AMERICANS WERE STRUGGLING FROM THE GREAT DEPRESSION AND WANTED NOTHING TO DO WITH THE WAR IN EUROPE.

FREE DOUGHNUTS FOR

FREE SOUP

THESE ARE HARD TIMES.

WE'RE STILL DISILLUSIONED BY PRESIDENT WOODROW WILSON'S DECISION TO ENTER WORLD WAR I . . .

EVEN THOUGH HE HAD PROMISED NOT TO.

MANY PEOPLE WERE GLAD THAT PRESIDENT FRANKLIN DELANO ROOSEVELT WAS NEARING THE END OF HIS SECOND TERM.

THEY ASSUMED HE WOULDN'T RUN AGAIN.

BUT NO ONE ELSE KNOWS AS MUCH ABOUT THE COMPLEX ISSUES AT HOME AND ABROAD AS I DO!

IF GREAT BRITAIN GOES DOWN, ALL OF US IN ALL OF THE AMERICAS WOULD BE LIVING AT THE POINT OF A GUN.

BUT... WAIT!

AREN'T PRESIDENTS LIMITED TO TWO TERMS?

We tend to assume that, because something has been done a certain way for a long time, it has to be that way. For instance, we're used to seeing nine justices on the Supreme Court, even though the Constitution does not require that number. Nor does it stipulate that the president has to live in the White House.

AND IN 1940, THE CONSTITUTION DID NOT PROHIBIT A THIRD TERM FOR PRESIDENT.

I DIDN'T RUN FOR A THIRD TERM BECAUSE I DIDN'T WANT TO LOOK LIKE A MONARCH.

LET'S SEE WHAT HAPPENS WITH FDR . . .

JULY 15, 1940. DAY 1 OF THE DEMOCRATIC CONVENTION.

SENATOR ALBEN BARKLEY READS A STATEMENT TO THE CROWD:

PRESIDENT ROOSEVELT DOES NOT WANT TO CONTINUE AS PRESIDENT.

THE CONVENTION SHOULD FEEL FREE TO CHOOSE ANOTHER CANDIDATE.

WHAT?

HUH?

REALLY?

BUT I THOUGHT . . .

WE WANT ROOSEVELT.

A CHANT WAS STARTED BY THOMAS D. GARRY, CHICAGO'S SUPERINTENDENT OF SANITATION. IT WAS PIPED THROUGH THE LOUDSPEAKERS.

WE WANT ROOSEVELT.

WE WANT ROOSEVELT.

SOON ENOUGH . . .

WE WANT ROOSEVELT!

HUMANITY WANTS ROOSEVELT!

THE NEXT DAY.

YOU CANNOT TREAT THIS AS AN ORDINARY NOMINATION IN AN ORDINARY TIME.

WE PEOPLE IN THE UNITED STATES HAVE GOT TO REALIZE TODAY THAT WE FACE A GRAVE AND SERIOUS SITUATION!

AFTER FIRST LADY ELEANOR ROOSEVELT'S SPEECH, HER HUSBAND WON THE NOMINATION WITH SUPPORT FROM 86% OF THE DELEGATES.

ALTHOUGH MORE THAN TWENTY-TWO MILLION AMERICANS VOTED FOR WENDELL WILLKIE, THE REPUBLICAN NOMINEE . . .

ROOSEVEL FOR EX-PRESIDEN

STRIKE 3 YOU'RE OUT

NO 3RD ERM

. . . ROOSEVELT WON THE NOVEMBER ELECTION WITH NEARLY 55% OF THE VOTE.

FOUR MORE YEARS

Meanwhile, back in 1787 . . .

THE LENGTH OF THE PRESIDENT'S TERM AND THE NUMBER OF TIMES HE COULD BE REELECTED WERE ISSUES AS IMPORTANT TO THE FRAMERS AS HIS POWER.

ALLOW A MAN TO BE PRESIDENT FOR LIFE, HE MIGHT AS WELL BE KING. BUT TOO SHORT A TERM AND HE WON'T ACCOMPLISH ANYTHING.

WHY NOT HAVE THREE PRESIDENTS, EACH FROM DIFFERENT PARTS OF THE COUNTRY, SERVE TOGETHER FOR TWELVE YEARS?

ONE PRESIDENT. ONE TERM. NO POSSIBILITY FOR REELECTION.

MAYBE THE PRESIDENT SHOULD BE APPOINTED BY CONGRESS AND SERVE AS LONG AS HE SHOWS GOOD BEHAVIOR?

AFTER MONTHS OF NEGOTIATING, VOTING, DELAYING, AND DEBATING, THE FRAMERS FINALLY SETTLED ON THE TERM OF FOUR YEARS.

BUT THEY DID NOT DEAL WITH WHETHER THE PRESIDENT COULD BE REELECTED, LET ALONE FOR THE NUMBER OF TERMS.

HEY, WE HAD ENOUGH ON OUR PLATES!

IT WASN'T UNTIL 1947, WHEN CONGRESS PROPOSED THE *22ND AMENDMENT.*

ADOPTED IN RESPONSE TO MY WINNING A THIRD AND FOURTH TERM!

WHAT'S THE BIG DEAL HERE?

ROOSEVELT'S PROLONGED PRESIDENCY MIGHT HAVE BEEN EXACTLY WHAT SOME FRAMERS FEARED: A MONARCHY. THE 22ND AMENDMENT RESOLVED THAT, BUT IT COMES WITH A DOWNSIDE.

THIS LIMIT COULD HINDER US IN TIMES OF WAR OR OTHER CATASTROPHE.

AT THESE TIMES, WE MIGHT WELL NEED A KNOWLEDGEABLE AND EXPERIENCED LEADER—

—BUT WE MIGHT NOT BE ABLE TO KEEP THEM.

OTHER PRESIDENTS ALSO CONSIDERED RUNNING FOR MORE THAN TWO TERMS:

Ulysses S. Grant wanted to run for a third term in 1880, but his party refused to nominate him.

Theodore Roosevelt (FDR's distant cousin) ran unsuccessfully for a third term in 1912 as a third-party candidate after being out of office for four years.

JUSTICE FOR LIFE

The President loses his job after two terms.
Congresspeople can be thrown out at any
election. But judges are a different matter.

The
Constitution
states,

"Judges, both of
the supreme and
inferior Courts,
shall hold their
Offices during
good Behaviour."

The term **"good Behaviour"**
is not defined but is taken
to mean that judges cannot
be impeached simply
because they hand down
an unpopular decision.

This supports the idea of
judicial independence,
meaning that judges can
enforce the Constitution
however they see fit.

This provision is also generally
interpreted to mean that, once
they're appointed, judges can
stay on the bench as long as
they want.

Supreme Court Justice John
Paul Stevens, for example,
retired at age ninety after
serving for thirty-four years.

All but one state, Rhode Island, and almost all other countries force
judges to retire at a certain age or after a number of years on the job.

ONLY FOURTEEN STATES ALLOW THEIR CHIEF EXECUTIVES (GOVERNORS) TO SERVE AS LONG AS THE VOTERS WANT THEM TO STAY IN OFFICE.

IDAHO GOVERNOR FOR LIFE (OR AS LONG AS HE WANTS IT)

THE OTHER THIRTY-SIX STATES IMPOSE VARIOUS TERM LIMITS.

AND SOME BAR GOVERNORS FROM SERVING MORE THAN TWICE.

STATE OF ARKANSAS
PINK SLIP

ALMOST TWO DOZEN STATES, INCLUDING ALASKA, HAWAII, AND NEW MEXICO, ALLOW GOVERNORS TO SERVE MORE THAN TWO TERMS, BUT ONLY AFTER THEY'VE BEEN OUT OF OFFICE FOR AT LEAST ONE TERM.

GOVERNOR 2010

GOVERNOR 2014

VACATION

GOVERNOR 2018

AND INDIANA, MONTANA, WYOMING, AND A FEW OTHERS IMPOSE A LIMIT OF EIGHT YEARS OUT OF EVERY TWELVE OR SIXTEEN.

IN SOME COUNTRIES WITH DEMOCRACIES, LIKE ICELAND AND INDIA, THERE ARE NO PRESIDENTIAL TERM LIMITS.

IN OTHERS WITH PARLIAMENTARY SYSTEMS, SUCH AS GERMANY, ISRAEL, JAPAN, AND THE U.K., THE LEGISLATURE APPOINTS OR ELECTS THE HEAD OF GOVERNMENT.

NO CONFIDENCE!

HERE, THE PRIME MINISTER KEEPS THE JOB UNTIL DEFEATED IN AN ELECTION, RESIGNATION, OR THE PARLIAMENT VOTES THAT IT HAS "NO CONFIDENCE" IN THEM.

GET HIM OUTTA THERE!

James Callaghan, British Prime Minister. Received a vote of no confidence in 1979.

A vote of **"no confidence"** in parliamentary systems means that the legislature deems the head of government unfit or incompetent for the office.

No matter how long they've been in office, the leader is out of a job.

The Constitution doesn't allow for the same thing. If the president is suspected of committing a "high crime or misdemeanor," Congress can **impeach** them and hold a trial.

But if the commander in chief is merely reckless or incompetent or terrifying, **we have no way out.**

Richard Nixon, U.S. President. Resigned before being impeached, 1974.

IDEALLY, CONGRESS WOULD HAVE THE ABILITY TO SUSPEND THE TWO-TERM RULE—OR THE FOUR-YEAR-TERM RULE—UNDER EXCEPTIONAL CIRCUMSTANCES, PERHAPS BY A TWO-THIRDS VOTE.

THIS WOULD REQUIRE AMENDING THE CONSTITUTION.

WANTED A DECENT **JOB** A DECENT MAN - AGE 37 FAMILY WAR VET

WANTED A DECENT **JOB** FAMILY MAN AGE 44 3 YRS. FORD CO.

THE STORY CONTINUES . . .

FDR STAYED IN OFFICE UNTIL HIS DEATH IN 1945. BUT WITH THE PASSING OF THE 22ND AMENDMENT IN 1947, HE WAS THE FIRST—AND LAST—PRESIDENT TO BE ELECTED TO OFFICE FOUR TIMES.

"hurrah!

I'M 18. I CAN FINALLY VOTE FOR THE PRESIDENT!"

"not so fast."

Americans don't vote directly for their president.

Instead, we vote for individuals who represent our voting preferences (we hope) in an organization informally called the **Electoral College**.

STATE COLLEGE

NOPE! NOT A REAL COLLEGE.

We vote for the members of this group at the state level, but the number of members in each state does not exactly reflect the size of its population. Some states count more than others—literally.

States also handle the results of their Electoral College votes differently. Presidential elections can indicate which candidate voters across the country prefer. But the Electoral College sometimes doesn't let the more popular candidate become president.

There are reasons the Framers established a way to choose our commander in chief that differs from direct election, the way we elect other leaders.

Even when the Constitution was drafted, this process was controversial. But in the 21st century, reasons that seemed logical in 1787 do not necessarily make sense.

THIS IS ONE WHOPPER OF A FAULT LINE!

12

the college with no courses or credits

the electoral college

TUESDAY, NOVEMBER 7, 2000.

ELECTION NIGHT 2000

THIS IS VICE PRESIDENT AL GORE, JR.

TONIGHT, HE'S ALSO THE DEMOCRATIC NOMINEE FOR PRESIDENT OF THE UNITED STATES.

ELECTORAL VOTE
(270 NEEDED TO WIN)

EXIT POLLS ARE CURRENTLY SHOWING 49% SUPPORT FOR GORE, 48% FOR BUSH.

☆ ELECTIO

IN FACT, THIS JUST IN: WE CAN NOW PROJECT THAT THE STATE OF FLORIDA IS GOING TO BE WON BY AL GORE.

29 ELECTORAL VOTES

AL GORE (D) WINS

TWO HOURS LATER, NETWORKS ALSO CALLED NEW MEXICO FOR GORE. THAT PUT HIM OVER THE TOP!

EVEN THOUGH THE POLLS HADN'T YET CLOSED EVERYWHERE, IT APPEARED HE'D BE THE NEXT PRESIDENT.

SEVEN MINUTES LATER . . .

WE GOT A PROBLEM HERE.

SOME OF THE PRECINCTS IN FLORIDA WE THOUGHT WOULD GO TO US ACTUALLY FAVORED BUSH.

SINCE WE CAN'T COUNT ON WHAT WE PRESUMED WERE RELIABLY DEMOCRATIC PRECINCTS,

THIS RACE IS TOO CLOSE TO CALL BEFORE *EVERY SINGLE VOTE* IS COUNTED.

Projected Districts

THAT WARNING ENDED WHAT ONE SPOKESMAN CALLED THEIR "SEVEN-MINUTE PRESIDENCY."

BUSH WAS BEATING GORE IN FLORIDA BY ABOUT FIFTY THOUSAND VOTES.

FLORIDA

★ ☐ BUSH
★ ☐ GORE

BUT ACROSS THE COUNTRY, IT LOOKED AS IF GORE WAS BEATING BUSH BY ABOUT HALF A MILLION VOTES.

WHY WAS GORE'S STAFFER SO WORRIED?

GORE SHOULD WIN THE ELECTION NO MATTER WHICH WAY FLORIDA TILTED, RIGHT?

Roger Sherman

Elbridge Gerry and
Gunning Bedford

James Wilson

There was a somewhat understandable reason for this view. In 1787, roughly three and a half million Americans were dispersed across a vast terrain—as much territory as Britain, France, Germany, Ireland, and Italy combined.

HALLLOOOO

Fewer than a hundred newspapers were published in the country, and none was widely distributed. They also contained only four pages, half of which were advertisements.

THE SHARING OF NATIONAL NEWS WAS LIMITED.

THE PENNSYLVANIA PACKET and DAILY ADVERT

Now in South Carolina! Works While You Sleep! CURES CHRONIC CONSTIPATION

THE PIC

LET'S GO WITH SHERMAN'S IDEA AND LET CONGRESS FIGURE IT OUT.

WAIT! THAT GIVES CONGRESS TOO MUCH POWER. PEOPLE WILL NEVER RATIFY THE CONSTITUTION UNLESS THEY ARE SOMEHOW INVOLVED IN CHOOSING THEIR LEADER.

OH, COME NOW! LET'S JUST FIGURE THIS OUT ALREADY!

I HAVE A BETTER IDEA.

Madison wrote out a complicated alternative, calling for a system of presidential electors. Each state's legislature would decide how to select a group of trustworthy individuals.

THESE ELECTORS WILL THEN VOTE FOR THE PERSON THEY CONSIDER MOST WORTHY OF SERVING AS PRESIDENT.

EACH STATE WILL BE ALLOWED AS MANY ELECTORS AS THE SUM OF ITS REPRESENTATIVES PLUS ITS TWO SENATORS.

I'M CONFUSED . . . BUT LET'S ROLL WITH IT!

YEAH, I'M EXHAUSTED. LET'S CRANK OUT THE DETAILS AND GET THIS OVER WITH.

130

THE EXECUTIVE POWER SHALL BE VESTED IN A PRESIDENT OF THE UNITED STATES OF AMERICA.

HE SHALL HOLD HIS OFFICE DURING THE TERM OF FOUR YEARS, AND, TOGETHER WITH THE VICE-PRESIDENT CHOSEN FOR THE SAME TERM, BE ELECTED, AS FOLLOWS:

EACH STATE SHALL APPOINT, IN SUCH MANNER AS THE LEGISLATURE THEREOF MAY DIRECT, A NUMBER OF ELECTORS, EQUAL TO THE WHOLE NUMBER OF SENATORS AND REPRESENTATIVES TO WHICH THE STATE MAY BE ENTITLED IN THE CONGRESS:

BUT NO SENATOR OR REPRESENTATIVE, OR PERSON HOLDING AN OFFICE OF TRUST OR PROFIT UNDER THE UNITED STATES, SHALL BE APPOINTED AN ELECTOR.

IT SHALL BE CALLED THE *ELECTORAL COLLEGE!* EVENTUALLY.*

*THIS TERM WASN'T POPULARIZED UNTIL THE EARLY 19TH CENTURY.

THIS ARRANGEMENT WAS POPULAR WITH SMALL STATES.

WE STILL GET THREE ELECTORAL VOTES!

DELAWARE
POPULATION: SMALL

SLAVEHOLDING STATES ALSO LIKED IT.

UNDER THE THREE-FIFTHS COMPROMISE, WE GET TO COUNT THREE-FIFTHS OF OUR ENSLAVED PERSONS!

THAT MEANS MORE REPRESENTATION!

OF COURSE, NOT EVERYONE COULD VOTE.

AND THE PEOPLE WHO COULD VOTE DIDN'T NECESSARILY KEEP OUR BEST INTERESTS IN MIND!

The Framers decided on the following rules:

Electors in every state would meet on a day set by Congress and vote for their two favorite candidates. If no single candidate received a majority of the electoral votes, the House of Representatives would choose the president from the top five vote-getters, with each state casting one vote.

If the representatives from a state were evenly split in their choice, the state would be listed as abstaining. The Senate would choose the vice president.

The electors' votes from all the states would be compiled. A majority of the electors have to agree on a single candidate. The winner would become president; the runner-up would be vice-president.

BALLOT BOX

WE DID IT! HUH.

WE FINALLY FIGURED OUT HOW TO PICK A LEADER!

I DON'T KNOW, I'M SURE SOMETHING WILL GO WRONG . . .

DOESN'T THIS SYSTEM DEEM THE NUMBER OF VOTERS IN A GIVEN STATE IRRELEVANT?

BY 1796, POLITICAL PARTIES HAD BEGUN TO FORM, AND THE ELECTORS' TOP TWO FAVORITE CANDIDATES BELONGED TO DIFFERENT FACTIONS.

President
John Adams
(Federalist)

Runner-up
Vice President
Thomas Jefferson
(Democratic-Republican)

1

THIS WOULD BE LIKE HAVING A CONSERVATIVE MEMBER OF THE 21ST CENTURY REPUBLICAN PARTY AS PRESIDENT AND A LIBERAL DEMOCRAT AS VICE PRESIDENT.

THE VP, WHO PRESIDES OVER THE SENATE AND BREAKS TIE VOTES, MIGHT VOTE AGAINST THE PRESIDENT'S POLICIES.

AND THAT'S EXACTLY WHAT HAPPENED WITH JEFFERSON AND ADAMS.

THESE ACTS MAKE IT A CRIME TO CRITICIZE THE PRESIDENT!

WHAT ABOUT THE VICE PRESIDENT?!

NOPE, JUST THE PRESIDENT!

THE ALIEN AND SEDITION ACTS

THAT IS APPALLING!

WE MUST MAKE IT SO THAT STATE LEGISLATURES CAN DECLARE FEDERAL LAWS LIKE THAT UNCONSTITUTIONAL!

IN 1798, THE KENTUCKY LEGISLATURE DID JUST THAT: THEY ADOPTED THE SO-CALLED *KENTUCKY RESOLUTIONS*, WHICH TRIGGERED A DEBATE ABOUT WHO GETS TO DECIDE WHETHER A LAW IS CONSTITUTIONAL.

OF COURSE, THE ADAMS ADMINISTRATION DISAGREED.

AND THAT ISSUE HAS NEVER BEEN COMPLETELY RESOLVED!

JEFFERSON'S OWN ELECTION IN 1800 REVEALED ANOTHER FLAW IN THE ELECTORAL COLLEGE.

The candidates:

Thomas Jefferson

Aaron Burr

(both Democratic-Republicans)

John Adams

Charles Pinckney

(both Federalists)

WHEN THE VOTES WERE TALLIED, IT TURNED OUT THAT BOTH JEFFERSON AND BURR GOT A MAJORITY . . .

SO . . . THERE'S NO WINNER?

AND THEY WERE TIED.

THE CONSTITUTION DIRECTS THE HOUSE OF REPRESENTATIVES TO PICK THE PRESIDENT.

AND MANY OF THOSE HOUSE MEMBERS WERE FEDERALISTS.

EVEN THOUGH MOST OF THEM HAD BEEN VOTED OUT OF OFFICE, THEIR TERMS DIDN'T EXPIRE UNTIL INAUGURATION DAY.

OH GREAT, WE HAVE TO PICK OUT OF *THOSE* GUYS.

THE HOUSE VOTED THIRTY-SIX TIMES OVER SIX DAYS BEFORE AGREEING ON JEFFERSON.

THE 12TH AMENDMENT WAS RATIFIED IN TIME FOR THE ELECTION OF 1804.

THIS AMENDMENT CHANGED THE VOTING SYSTEM: ELECTORS WOULD NOW CAST TWO SEPARATE VOTES, ONE FOR PRESIDENT AND ONE FOR VICE PRESIDENT.

IF THE ELECTORAL COLLEGE DID NOT PRODUCE A MAJORITY WINNER, THEN THE HOUSE WOULD DETERMINE THE PRESIDENCY BY CHOOSING AMONG THE TOP THREE VOTE GETTERS, NOT THE TOP FIVE, AS BEFORE.

BUT TWENTY YEARS LATER, THE PROBLEMS WITH THIS SOLUTION BECAME CLEAR.

I BECAME THE FIRST CANDIDATE TO GET THE MOST POPULAR AND ELECTORAL VOTES . . . BUT STILL *LOSE* THE PRESIDENCY.

Andrew Jackson

NONE OF THE FOUR CONTENDERS RECEIVED A MAJORITY OF ELECTORAL VOTES.

SO, THE HOUSE GOT TO DECIDE.

John Quincy Adams

Henry Clay

William H. Crawford

BECAUSE CLAY CAME IN FOURTH, HE WAS INELIGIBLE. INSTEAD, HE LOBBIED THE REPRESENTATIVES TO PICK ADAMS . . .

WHICH THEY DID.

YOU KNOW WHAT, CLAY?

YOU CAN BE MY SECRETARY OF STATE.

THIS . . . THIS IS A *CORRUPT BARGAIN!!*

GET READY FOR SOME MATH!

$$
\begin{array}{c}
\text{538 Members of the Electoral College}
\end{array}
=
\begin{array}{c}
\text{435 (1 for each member of the House)}
\end{array}
+
\begin{array}{c}
\text{100 (1 for each member of the Senate)}
\end{array}
+
\begin{array}{c}
\text{3 (for DC, which were granted in the 23rd Amendment)}
\end{array}
$$

SO WHAT'S THE BIG PROBLEM WITH THIS SYSTEM?

Sometimes the national popularity of a presidential candidate in November has little to do with who becomes president in January.

To become president, a candidate needs to win the popular vote in the right combination of states–those whose Electoral College votes will add up to 270, a majority. Calculating ways to achieve this number can cause campaign shenanigans.

For example, you could win just **these 11 states** by extremely narrow margins and become president, even if you failed to get a single vote in any other state!

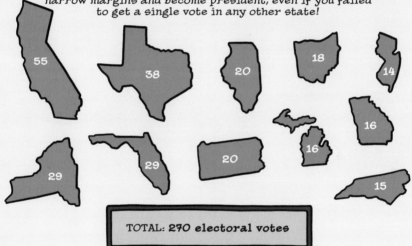

TOTAL: **270 electoral votes**

Nationwide, 26 states have a higher percentage of electoral votes than is warranted by their percentage of the population.

In 2016, for example, California was home to 39 million people–about 2 million more than the 21 smallest states plus DC combined.

Yet, California got 55 electoral votes while those other states and DC got a total of 95.

IN ALL BUT TWO STATES—MAINE AND NEBRASKA—THE CANDIDATE WHO WINS THE MOST POPULAR VOTES AMASSES ALL OF THAT STATE'S ELECTORAL COLLEGE VOTES.

BECAUSE OF THIS SYSTEM, INDIVIDUAL VOTERS DON'T MATTER AS MUCH AS STATES DO. AND NOT MANY STATES MATTER, AT THAT!

THE WINNER DOESN'T EVEN NEED TO GET A MAJORITY OF THE VOTES IN THE STATE—ONLY TO COME IN AHEAD OF EVERYONE ELSE.

CANDIDATES HAVE TO CALCULATE WHERE TO SPEND THEIR TIME AND MONEY CAMPAIGNING.

RATHER THAN FOCUSING ON STATES THEY'RE CONFIDENT THEY'LL WIN, CANDIDATES WILL PAY CLOSER ATTENTION TO STATES IN WHICH THE RESULTS ARE A TOSS-UP—THE BATTLEGROUND (OR SWING) STATES!

IN 1884, IF ONLY 575 NEW YORK RESIDENTS HAD SWITCHED THEIR VOTES, AMERICA WOULD HAVE BEEN LED BY PRESIDENT JAMES G. BLAINE INSTEAD OF GROVER CLEVELAND!

THIS INFLUENCES THE TOPICS THAT GET RAISED. FOR EXAMPLE, ONLY ONE OF THE COUNTRY'S TEN LARGEST CITIES, PHILADELPHIA, IS LOCATED IN A BATTLEGROUND STATE.

AS A RESULT, MANY ELIGIBLE VOTERS IN NON-BATTLEGROUND STATES MAY FEEL DISCOURAGED FROM GOING TO THE POLLS.

SO, DURING THE CAMPAIGN, CANDIDATES ADDRESS URBAN ISSUES FAR LESS OFTEN THAN MATTERS THAT CONCERN OTHER BATTLEGROUND STATES.

IF THEY DIDN'T GO OUT OF THEIR WAY TO ASK FOR MY VOTE, WHY SHOULD I CARE?

PHILADELPHIA WELCOMES GEORGE W. BUSH & AL GORE

AND IF PEOPLE DON'T GO TO THE POLLS, THE ELECTORATE AS A WHOLE ISN'T REPRESENTED.

In the 2016 presidential election, candidates spent almost all their time and money in only fourteen states.

Half of that was just in four battleground states.

Thirty-six states (2/3 of the population) were pretty much ignored.

Maybe that's why only 58% of registered voters voted in that election?

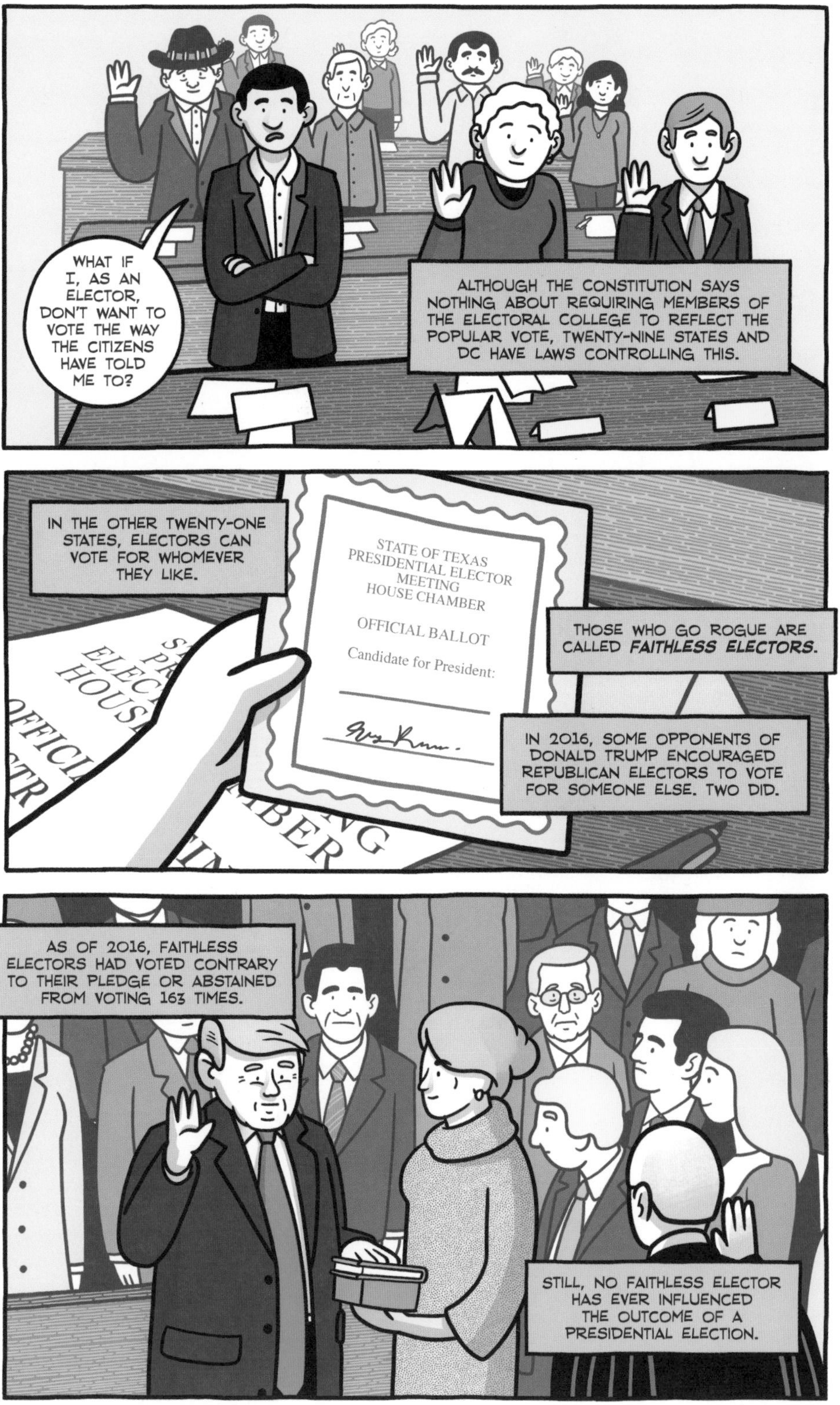
WHAT IF I, AS AN ELECTOR, DON'T WANT TO VOTE THE WAY THE CITIZENS HAVE TOLD ME TO?
ALTHOUGH THE CONSTITUTION SAYS NOTHING ABOUT REQUIRING MEMBERS OF THE ELECTORAL COLLEGE TO REFLECT THE POPULAR VOTE, TWENTY-NINE STATES AND DC HAVE LAWS CONTROLLING THIS.
IN THE OTHER TWENTY-ONE STATES, ELECTORS CAN VOTE FOR WHOMEVER THEY LIKE.
STATE OF TEXAS
PRESIDENTIAL ELECTOR
MEETING
HOUSE CHAMBER
OFFICIAL BALLOT
Candidate for President:
THOSE WHO GO ROGUE ARE CALLED ***FAITHLESS ELECTORS.***
IN 2016, SOME OPPONENTS OF DONALD TRUMP ENCOURAGED REPUBLICAN ELECTORS TO VOTE FOR SOMEONE ELSE. TWO DID.
AS OF 2016, FAITHLESS ELECTORS HAD VOTED CONTRARY TO THEIR PLEDGE OR ABSTAINED FROM VOTING 163 TIMES.
STILL, NO FAITHLESS ELECTOR HAS EVER INFLUENCED THE OUTCOME OF A PRESIDENTIAL ELECTION.

WHAT IF NO ONE WINS A MAJORITY?

As the Framers devised it, the **House** would then pick the president, and the **Senate** would choose the vice president. This sounds straightforward, but it could lead to exactly what happened in 1796.

JOHN ADAMS **VERSUS** THOMAS JEFFERSON

FEDERALIST — DEMOCRATIC-REP.

There is also the chance that the **Senate** could end up picking the president, too.

BALLOTS

When the House chooses the president, each state is entitled to cast one vote.

A majority of each state's representatives must agree on whom to vote for.

If a state's legislators are evenly divided between two candidates, then all the representatives from that state must abstain.

That state loses its right to vote.

ABSTAIN

In order to receive a majority, a candidate must receive the votes of 26 states.

If enough states abstain, the Senate's choice for VP would be promoted to president. This has never happened, but it could.

ARE THERE OTHER OPTIONS?

Every U.S. state allows its citizens to vote directly for its executives—the governor and lieutenant governor. And no other major country has anything like the Electoral College.

SO WHAT CAN WE DO?

Around six hundred amendments regarding the Electoral College have been proposed, but they have all been either defeated or abandoned. The last time this strategy was tried was in 1969, but the proposal passed in the House and failed in the Senate.

So if the Electoral College is here to stay . . .

. . . then what?

Option 1:	Option 2:
Eliminate winner-take-all.	**Adopt the National Popular Vote plan.**
Electors' votes could be allocated proportionately to the citizens' votes. If 52% of voters favor a particular candidate, then 52% of that state's Electoral College votes would do the same.	This proposal consists of an agreement among states to cast their Electoral College votes for the winner of the popular vote.
Or, as is already the case in Maine and Nebraska, votes could be allocated by congressional district, with the statewide winner getting the two bonus votes.	In order for this to go into effect, states that have a combined total of 270 electoral votes would have to accept it.
This still gives the advantage to states with low populations: their electoral votes would reflect the boost they get from having two senators. There's also no guarantee that any candidate would win a majority. And allocating by district would raise issues related to gerrymandering.	It's not clear that enough states would agree to this, especially if the results were close, the winner failed to get a majority of votes, or there were suspicions that votes were suppressed to tilt the election.

THE ELECTORAL COLLEGE HANDED THE WHITE HOUSE TO THE LESS POPULAR CANDIDATE FOUR TIMES AFTER JACKSON.

In 1876,
Samuel Tilden
got 250,000 more
votes than
Rutherford B. Hayes.

In 1888,
Grover Cleveland
got 90,000 more
votes than
Benjamin Harrison.

In 2000,
Al Gore, Jr.
got 500,000 more
votes than
George W. Bush.

And in 2016,
Hillary Rodham Clinton got
2,800,000 more
votes than
Donald J. Trump.

SO WHAT EVER HAPPENED WITH GORE?

TWO DAYS AFTER THE ELECTION, FLORIDA'S VOTES WERE FINALLY COUNTED, BUT THE RESULTS WERE MICROSCOPICALLY CLOSE:

BUSH LED GORE BY ONLY THREE HUNDRED BALLOTS OUT OF SIX MILLION CAST.

EACH SIDE CHALLENGED THE OTHER FOR WEEKS ON END.

THE TALLY WASN'T CONDUCTED CORRECTLY!

THE BALLOTS WERE CONFUSING!

THE RECOUNT SHOULD BE FOR THE WHOLE STATE!

NO! JUST FOR CERTAIN COUNTIES!

THE LAW STATES THAT ELECTORS MUST VOTE ON THE FIRST MONDAY AFTER THE SECOND WEDNESDAY IN DECEMBER, AND THE CONSTITUTION SETS JANUARY 20 AS INAUGURATION DAY.

THE PRESSURE WAS ON.

ON DECEMBER 12, 2000—A WEEK BEFORE THE ELECTORS MUST VOTE—THE SUPREME COURT STEPPED IN.

THE RECOUNT MUST END!

THIS DECISION LEFT BUSH THE WINNER IN FLORIDA . . .

. . . AND BECAUSE OF THEIR ELECTORAL COLLEGE VOTES, THE WINNER FOR THE COUNTRY.

can the president really do that?!

The three-part government the Framers established means that the president shares power with Congress and the federal courts in a variety of ways. This arrangement is known as

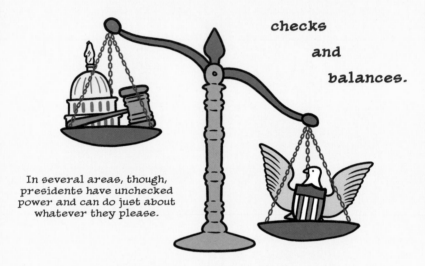

checks

and

balances.

In several areas, though, presidents have unchecked power and can do just about whatever they please.

For example . . .

Presidential Pardons

The president's ability to grant pardons or lessen the punishment for people who are convicted of or who might have committed a federal crime

GET OUT OF
JAIL FREE

The Unitary Executive

The president's control over the entire executive branch of the government

The Framers gave these areas less explanation than other issues they grappled with during the Convention. They just weren't as high a priority.

This lapse allows presidents the opportunity to make the most of these powers.

13

pardon me?

presidential pardons

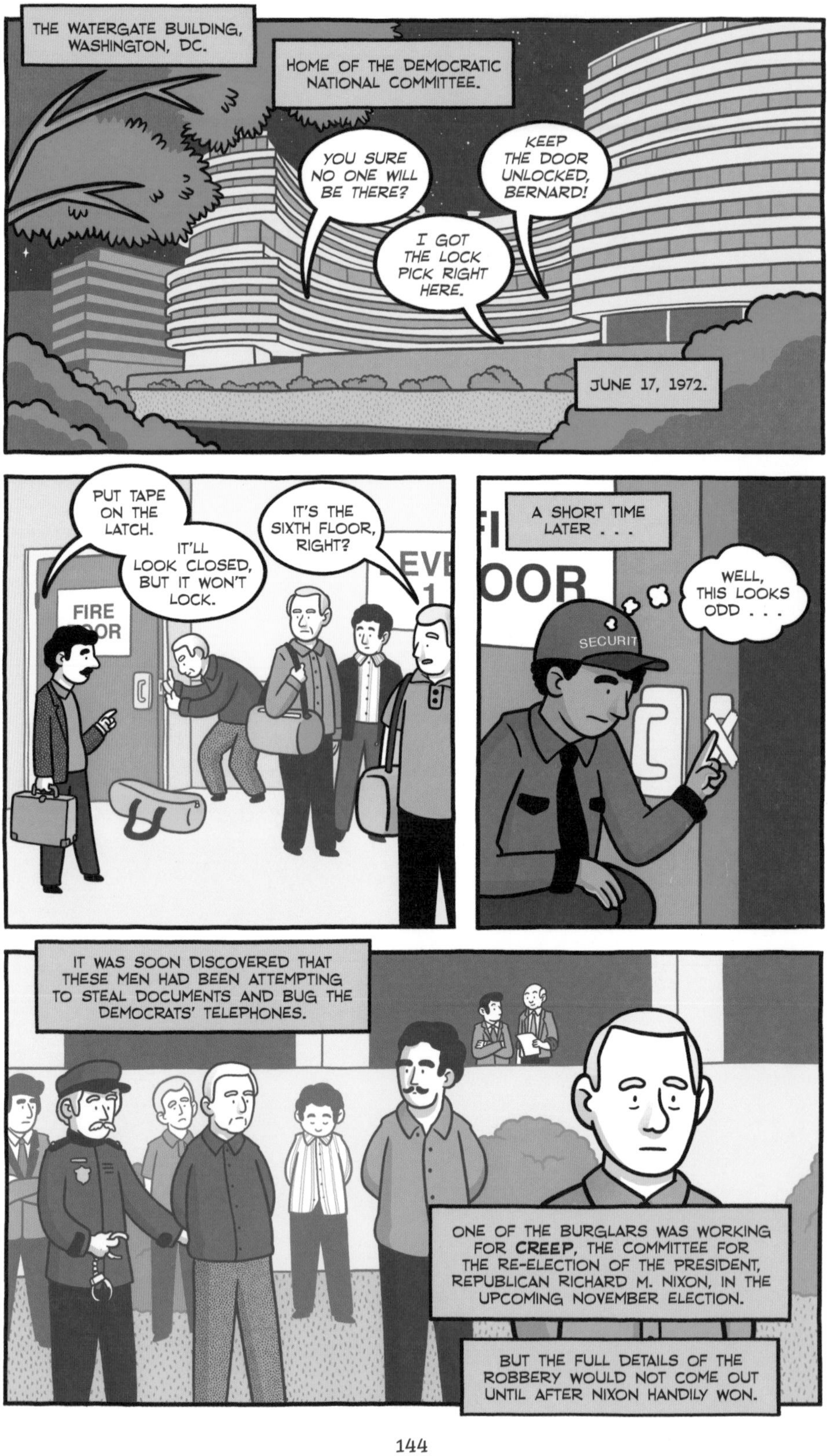
THE WATERGATE BUILDING, WASHINGTON, DC.
HOME OF THE DEMOCRATIC NATIONAL COMMITTEE.
YOU SURE NO ONE WILL BE THERE?
KEEP THE DOOR UNLOCKED, BERNARD!
I GOT THE LOCK PICK RIGHT HERE.
JUNE 17, 1972.
PUT TAPE ON THE LATCH.
IT'LL LOOK CLOSED, BUT IT WON'T LOCK.
IT'S THE SIXTH FLOOR, RIGHT?
FIRE
OR
A SHORT TIME LATER . . .
OOR
WELL, THIS LOOKS ODD . . .
SECURIT
IT WAS SOON DISCOVERED THAT THESE MEN HAD BEEN ATTEMPTING TO STEAL DOCUMENTS AND BUG THE DEMOCRATS' TELEPHONES.
ONE OF THE BURGLARS WAS WORKING FOR **CREEP**, THE COMMITTEE FOR THE RE-ELECTION OF THE PRESIDENT, REPUBLICAN RICHARD M. NIXON, IN THE UPCOMING NOVEMBER ELECTION.
BUT THE FULL DETAILS OF THE ROBBERY WOULD NOT COME OUT UNTIL AFTER NIXON HANDILY WON.

OVER THE NEXT TWO YEARS, JOURNALISTS BOB WOODWARD AND CARL BERNSTEIN INVESTIGATED THE BURGLARY.

SO DID A SENATE COMMITTEE HEADED BY SENATOR SAM ERVIN AND SPECIAL PROSECUTOR ARCHIBALD COX.

TESTIMONIES REVEALED THAT THE BURGLARS HAD BEEN PAID HUNDREDS OF THOUSANDS OF DOLLARS TO KEEP QUIET ABOUT CREEP'S INVOLVEMENT.

THE PRESIDENT RECORDED ALL CONVERSATIONS IN THE OVAL OFFICE.

SENATE WATERGATE COMMITTEE
CBS LIVE
ALEXANDER BUTTERFIELD
Deputy Assistant to President Nixon

PRESIDENT NIXON, WE NEED THOSE TAPES!

I REFUSE TO RELEASE THEM!

AND YOU KNOW WHAT, COX, YOU'LL BE FIRED!

THIS RASH ACT TRIGGERED WHAT WAS CALLED *THE SATURDAY NIGHT MASSACRE.* RATHER THAN OBEY NIXON'S DEMAND . . .

WE RESIGN!

Attorney General Elliot Richardson

Deputy Attorney General William Ruckelshaus

THE SUPREME COURT RULED THAT NIXON HAD TO TURN OVER THE TAPES, WHICH CONFIRMED THAT HE NOT ONLY KNEW ABOUT THE BURGLARY BUT HAD ALSO ATTEMPTED TO HIDE IT.

THIS AMOUNTS TO OBSTRUCTION OF JUSTICE . . .

THAT'S AN IMPEACHABLE OFFENSE!

AND ODDLY, EIGHTEEN MINUTES OF THE TAPES HAD SOMEHOW BEEN ERASED.

I AM NOT A CROOK.

MEANWHILE, THE COURTS FOUND MORE THAN A DOZEN ASSOCIATES AND MEMBERS OF NIXON'S STAFF GUILTY OF VARIOUS WATERGATE-RELATED CRIMES.

NIXON RECOGNIZED THAT HE WOULD PROBABLY BE IMPEACHED AND CONVICTED.

ON AUGUST 8, 1974, HE CHOSE TO RESIGN—THE FIRST PRESIDENT TO DO SO.

VICE PRESIDENT GERALD FORD WAS SWORN INTO OFFICE THE NEXT DAY.

SIX WEEKS LATER.

I GRANT HIM A FULL, FREE, AND ABSOLUTE PARDON FOR ALL CRIMES HE COMMITTED OR MAY HAVE COMMITTED WHILE IN THE WHITE HOUSE.

RICHARD NIXON HAS SUFFERED ENOUGH.

Meanwhile, back in 1787 . . .

WE HAVE TO BALANCE THE POWERS OF THE PRESIDENT WITH THOSE GIVEN TO BOTH CONGRESS AND THE FEDERAL COURTS.

YES! THE COURTS WILL DETERMINE WHETHER PEOPLE ACCUSED OF CRIMES ARE GUILTY, AND IF SO, HOW THEY SHOULD BE PUNISHED.

SO, ONE WAY TO LIMIT THE INFLUENCE OF THE COURTS WOULD BE TO LET THE PRESIDENT PARDON GUILTY PARTIES.

WOULD THE PRESIDENT BE ABLE TO PARDON ALL KINDS OF CRIMES AND MISDEEDS, OR JUST SOME?

AND WOULD HE NEED TO GET APPROVAL FROM CONGRESS BEFORE ISSUING SUCH A PARDON?

PERHAPS THIS CHIEF EXECUTIVE SHOULD HAVE THE SAME PARDON POWER THAT BRITISH MONARCHS TRADITIONALLY HAVE: THE ABILITY TO PARDON IN ALL CASES.

WITH AN EXCEPTION FOR IMPEACHMENT OF ANY OFFICER, HOWEVER.

THIS DEBATE LED TO THE **PARDON CLAUSE**, WHICH GRANTS THE PRESIDENT WIDE-OPEN POWERS TO PARDON, EXCEPT WHEN IMPEACHMENT IS INVOLVED.

THE PRESIDENT CAN ALSO COMMUTE, OR SHORTEN, A SENTENCE.

In 1795, **George Washington** pardoned grain farmers in western Pennsylvania who had been sentenced to death for taking up arms against U.S. tax collectors during the Whiskey Rebellion.

John Adams issued an amnesty in 1800 for other tax resisters convicted of treason during Fries's Rebellion.

Amnesty is the term sometimes used for pardons when lots of people are involved.

And in 1801, Thomas Jefferson pardoned prisoners convicted of disobeying the Alien and Sedition Acts.

THESE LAWS ARE UNCONSTITUTIONAL!

SO WHAT'S THE BIG PROBLEM?

THE PRESIDENT'S POWER TO GRANT PARDONS IS SO BROAD THAT THEY CAN ERASE A CRIMINAL CONVICTION AS IF IT HAD NEVER HAPPENED . . .

. . . REGARDLESS OF THE NATURE OF THE CRIME OR THE RATIONALE FOR THE PARDON!

BARKER 261422 6 17 72

GONZALEZ 261419 6 17 72

McCORD JR. 261423 6 17 72

STURGIS 261420 6 17 72

MARTINEZ 261421 6 17 72

PARDONING BEHAVIOR THAT IS POSSIBLY TRAITOROUS IS ALLOWED BUT CONTROVERSIAL.

DURING THE CIVIL WAR, VICE PRESIDENT ANDREW JOHNSON REFERRED TO SECESSIONISTS:

THE TRAITORS MUST BE IMPOVERISHED.

BUT WHEN HE BECAME PRESIDENT AFTER THE ASSASSINATION OF ABRAHAM LINCOLN . . .

TO THE TENS OF THOUSANDS OF CONFEDERATES, I GRANT AMNESTY AND PARDON!

THIS WAS PARTLY BECAUSE HE BELIEVED IN WHITE SUPREMACY, THE VIEW THAT WHITE PEOPLE ARE BETTER THAN PEOPLE OF COLOR AND SHOULD CONTINUE TO OVERSEE THEM.

I ALSO WANTED TO FULLY RESTORE CONFIDENCE AND FRATERNAL FEELING AMONG THE WHOLE PEOPLE!

AMERICANS WHO AGREED WITH THE OLD JOHNSON WERE APPALLED.

BETWEEN 1964 AND 1973, MANY YOUNG MEN FLED THE U.S. TO AVOID BEING DRAFTED INTO THE ARMED FORCES. SOME SAW THIS ACT AS TRAITOROUS.

BUT THE WAR IN VIETNAM IS IMMORAL!

DRAFT CARD

IN 1977, ON PRESIDENT JIMMY CARTER'S SECOND DAY IN OFFICE, HE PARDONED AS MANY AS TWO HUNDRED THOUSAND OF THOSE MEN.

THIS WILL HELP HEAL OUR COUNTRY!

NOT EVERYONE AGREED. REACTIONS RANGED FROM RELIEF TO OUTRAGE.

THIS WILL DIVIDE THE COUNTRY INSTEAD!

THE AMERICAN LEGION

US

PRESIDENTS CAN GIVE PARDONS IN SEVERAL WAYS AND FOR MANY REASONS . . . AND NEVER HAVE TO EXPLAIN THEM.

BILL CLINTON CLEARED HIS BROTHER OF DRUG CHARGES (ALTHOUGH ACTIONS ON BEHALF OF FAMILY MEMBERS ARE UNUSUAL.)

RONALD REAGAN PARDONED JUNIOR JOHNSON, A PROFESSIONAL SPORTS CAR RACER WHO COMMITTED A FELONY BY OPERATING A MOONSHINE STILL.

AND DONALD TRUMP PARDONED SHERIFF JOE ARPAIO OF MARICOPA COUNTY, ARIZONA, WHO HAD BEEN CONVICTED OF CONTEMPT OF COURT FOR USING RACIST PRACTICES AGAINST MEXICAN AMERICANS.

ARPAIO WAS PARDONED BEFORE HE HAD BEEN JAILED.

FURTHERMORE, PRESIDENTS CAN PARDON SOMEONE WHO HAS NOT EVEN BEEN INDICTED, TRIED, OR CONVICTED OF ANYTHING.

THIS IS HOW PRESIDENT FORD HANDLED NIXON'S SITUATION.

IT ALLOWED THE DISGRACED FORMER PRESIDENT TO AVOID EVEN THE PROSPECT OF A TRIAL.

It turns out that George Mason had a good point when he wondered if the president might use the pardon power preemptively to protect himself.

ON DECEMBER 24, 1992, GEORGE H. W. BUSH PARDONED PEOPLE WHO HAD PARTICIPATED IN A SCANDAL CALLED THE IRAN-CONTRA AFFAIR.

IN AN EFFORT TO SUPPORT REBELS IN NICARAGUA AND SECURE THE RELEASE OF AMERICAN HOSTAGES HELD IN LEBANON, GOVERNMENT OFFICIALS SECRETLY SOLD MISSILES TO IRAN.

IN EXCHANGE, IRAN FREED THE HOSTAGES, AND THE UNITED STATES SENT THE MONEY EARNED FROM THE ARMS SALES TO THE REBELS.

THERE WERE AT LEAST TWO PROBLEMS WITH THIS ARRANGEMENT.

FIRST, THE U.S. HAD A TRADE EMBARGO WITH IRAN.

THE GOVERNMENT WASN'T SUPPOSED TO SELL THEM ANYTHING, MUCH LESS ARMS.

IRAN

NICARAGUA

SECONDLY, CONGRESS HAD BARRED SHIPPING CASH OR OTHER RESOURCES TO NICARAGUAN INSURGENTS.

BUSH HAD BEEN VICE PRESIDENT WHEN BOTH TRANSACTIONS WERE CARRIED OUT. MANY PEOPLE VIEWED HIS PARDONS AS AN ATTEMPT TO PROTECT HIMSELF.

I ISSUED THE PARDONS JUST WEEKS BEFORE I LEFT OFFICE.

AND BECAUSE WE WERE PARDONED,

WE WERE UNDER NO PRESSURE TO OFFER EVIDENCE OF BUSH'S POSSIBLE ROLE IN THE ILLEGAL ARRANGEMENTS!

A MORE DRAMATIC EXAMPLE AROSE DURING WATERGATE, WHEN AMERICANS WONDERED WHETHER NIXON WOULD TRY TO PARDON HIMSELF. THE DEPARTMENT OF JUSTICE STEPPED IN.

NO PERSON CAN BE THE JUDGE OF HIS OWN CASE.

BUT THAT WAS ONLY ONE OPINION.

SOME LAWYERS INTERPRET THE PARDON CLAUSE TO ALLOW THE POSSIBILITY OF SELF-PARDON. THIS QUESTION AROSE DURING DONALD TRUMP'S PRESIDENCY.

ROBERT MUELLER, A SPECIAL PROSECUTOR, LOOKED INTO THE POSSIBILITY THAT RUSSIA HAD BEEN INVOLVED IN TRUMP'S CAMPAIGN DURING THE 2016 ELECTION.

SOME OF THE PRESIDENT'S ACTIONS SEEMED TO SUGGEST HE WAS OBSTRUCTING JUSTICE BY INTERFERING WITH THE ELECTION.

HE WAS ABLE TO PARDON ANYONE CAUGHT UP IN THE INQUIRY OR WHO WAS FOUND GUILTY; BUT HE ALSO DECLARED THAT HE COULD PARDON HIMSELF.

ALTHOUGH I WOULDN'T NEED TO, BECAUSE I DIDN'T DO ANYTHING WRONG!

WOULD CONGRESS CONSIDER A PRESIDENT'S SELF-PARDON TO BE AN ABUSE OF POWER WARRANTING IMPEACHMENT? IT REMAINS UNCLEAR!

GET OUT OF JAIL FREE

HOW TO GET A GET-OUT-OF-JAIL-FREE CARD

There are two routes to requesting a pardon from the president.

Typically, wrongdoers submit a petition to the Office of Pardon Attorney at the Department of Justice. Then, they follow a multistep process, including a five-year waiting period.

OR

Wrongdoers can ask someone who knows the president to lobby for a pardon on their behalf.

Either way, the petitioner might get good news from the president . . . or no response at all.

And the recipient of a pardon can always refuse it!

THERE ARE OTHER WAYS!

Every state has adopted legislation regarding procedures for pardons.

More than half require that the judge who sentenced the person applying be allowed to comment on whether the applicant deserves the pardon.

After that, pardon power varies from state to state.

Twenty-nine states allow **governors** to grant pardons. In most of these states, including Alaska, California, New York, and Ohio, an advisory board makes recommendations, though the governor is not bound to accept them.

Nine states, including Connecticut, Georgia, Idaho, and Utah, appoint a **clemency board**, such as a Board of Pardons and Parole, to make the decisions.

The remaining twelve states, including Arizona, Florida, Louisiana, and Texas, **divide the power** between the governor and a board.

No state has specified whether governors can pardon themselves.

However, in 1856, Isaac Stevens, the territorial governor of the Pacific Northwest, pardoned himself.

He had ordered farmers who had married Native Americans to leave the territory, and when the court system investigated the legality of the order, Stevens closed the courts down, declared martial law, and had the judges arrested.

Another court fined him for contempt . . . but he was able to avoid the punishment with a self-pardon.

Some countries work similarly to the U.S.

In France and Germany, the **president** can grant pardons. However, only the legislature in Germany can grant amnesty to a group.

The British **monarch** can grant pardons, but she does so on the advice of the Home Secretary.

In Canada, the **Parole Board of Canada** makes the decision, and a Canadian pardon does not erase the original conviction.

In Japan, the **Cabinet** does the job.

The Israeli **president** grants pardons based on recommendations by the Minister of Justice. In 2018, President Reuven Rivlin expanded the number of pardons.

IN HONOR OF THE SEVENTIETH ANNIVERSARY OF ISRAEL AS A COUNTRY, I DO THIS FOR THE SAKE OF MERCY AND KINDNESS!

AMERICANS MIGHT BENEFIT FROM A MORE ORDERLY PROCESS FOR PRESIDENTIAL PARDONS GIVEN TO INDIVIDUALS FOR REASONS OF MERCY.

THIS COULD INCLUDE REVIEW AND RECOMMENDATIONS BY THE DEPARTMENT OF JUSTICE OR AN INDEPENDENT BOARD.

THE RIGHT TO BESTOW AMNESTIES ON A NUMBER OF PEOPLE IN ORDER TO PRESERVE DOMESTIC TRANQUILITY COULD BE RETAINED BY THE PRESIDENT, AS WOULD PARDONS GIVEN FOR POLITICAL REASONS.

DRAFT CARD

THE STORY CONTINUES . . .

AFTER RESIGNING, NIXON RETURNED TO HIS HOME IN CALIFORNIA.

FORD ADDRESSED THE SITUATION IN HIS SPEECH TO CONGRESS UPON TAKING THE OATH OF OFFICE.

OUR LONG NATIONAL NIGHTMARE IS OVER.

FORD WAS WIDELY CRITICIZED FOR PARDONING NIXON.

HE LOST HIS RACE FOR ELECTION IN 1976.

AFTER HE DIED IN 2006, HOWEVER, MANY EDITORIALISTS SUGGESTED HE HAD DONE THE RIGHT THING, THAT JAILING A FORMER PRESIDENT WOULD NOT HAVE CONTRIBUTED TO NATIONAL HEALING.

14

"you're hired! (maybe.) you're fired!"

the unitary executive

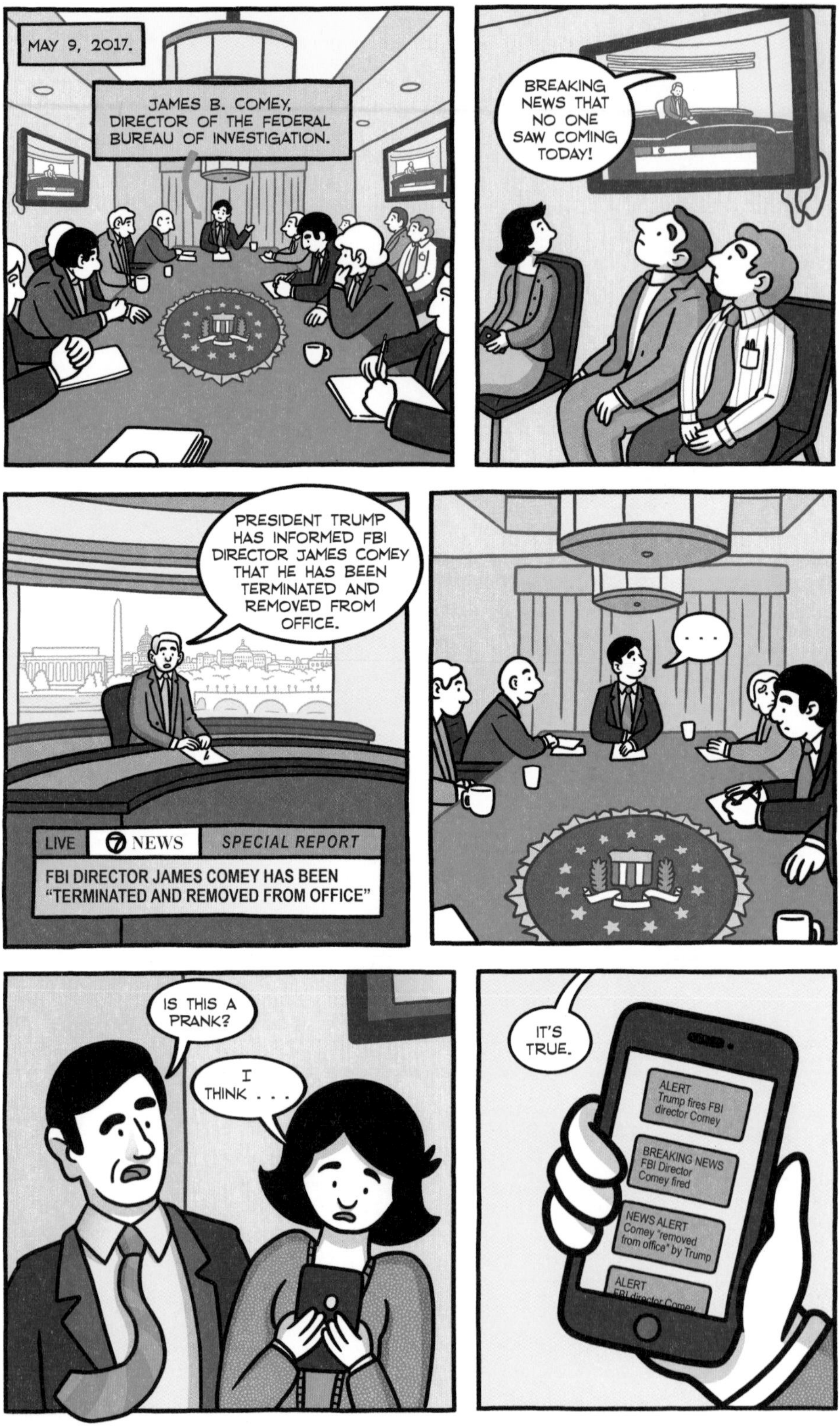
MAY 9, 2017.
JAMES B. COMEY, DIRECTOR OF THE FEDERAL BUREAU OF INVESTIGATION.
BREAKING NEWS THAT NO ONE SAW COMING TODAY!
PRESIDENT TRUMP HAS INFORMED FBI DIRECTOR JAMES COMEY THAT HE HAS BEEN TERMINATED AND REMOVED FROM OFFICE.
LIVE
NEWS
SPECIAL REPORT
FBI DIRECTOR JAMES COMEY HAS BEEN "TERMINATED AND REMOVED FROM OFFICE"
. . .
IS THIS A PRANK?
I THINK . . .
IT'S TRUE.
ALERT Trump fires FBI director Comey
BREAKING NEWS FBI Director Comey fired
NEWS ALERT Comey "removed from office" by Trump
ALERT

COMEY MISHANDLED THE INVESTIGATIONS INTO HILLARY RODHAM CLINTON'S USE OF A PRIVATE EMAIL SERVER WHILE SHE WAS SECRETARY OF STATE.

HE SAID SHE BEHAVED IRRESPONSIBLY BUT THERE WAS NOT SUFFICIENT REASON TO CHARGE HER WITH A CRIME.

I DISAGREED WITH COMEY.

SO, I HAD TO FIRE HIM.

IT SOON CAME OUT, HOWEVER, THAT TRUMP PROBABLY HAD ANOTHER REASON TO FIRE COMEY.

THE FBI HAD STARTED LOOKING INTO EFFORTS BY THE RUSSIAN GOVERNMENT TO INTERFERE WITH THE 2016 PRESIDENTIAL ELECTION.

THE INQUIRY INCLUDED POSSIBLE COMMUNICATIONS BETWEEN RUSSIANS AND SOME TRUMP CAMPAIGN STAFFERS AND FAMILY MEMBERS.

UNITED STATE

THIS IS A MADE-UP STORY!

COMEY IS NOT ABLE TO EFFECTIVELY LEAD THE BUREAU!

A REPUBLICAN APPOINTED BY PRESIDENT BARACK OBAMA TO HEAD THE FBI IN 2013, COMEY HAD SERVED IN THE DEPARTMENT OF JUSTICE UNDER PRESIDENT GEORGE W. BUSH.

CONGRESS HAD ESTABLISHED A TEN-YEAR TERM TO PROTECT THE FBI DIRECTOR FROM POLITICAL PRESSURE.

SINCE ONLY ONE DIRECTOR HAD EVER BEEN FIRED, I ANTICIPATED THAT I WOULD LEAD THE FBI FOR ANOTHER SIX YEARS.

EXIT

BUT I ALSO WAS AWARE THAT MY RELATIONSHIP WITH TRUMP HAD BEEN DETERIORATING.

I DIDN'T RESPOND WHEN HE SUGGESTED I STOP INVESTIGATING CONTACTS BETWEEN RUSSIA AND MICHAEL FLYNN, THE WHITE HOUSE NATIONAL SECURITY ADVISOR.

SOON, TRUMP TALKED OPENLY OF FIRING COMEY.

I DON'T ADVISE IT, THOUGH.

IT'D LOOK SUSPICIOUS!

HE'S A NUTJOB.

HE'S FIRED.

COMEY IMMEDIATELY RETURNED TO WASHINGTON, DC TO CLEAN OUT HIS DESK.

EXIT

Meanwhile, back in 1787 (and 1789) . . .

WITHIN TWO WEEKS OF GETTING TO WORK, THE FRAMERS AGREED THAT THE COUNTRY SHOULD HAVE ONLY ONE PRESIDENT AT A TIME.

RIGHT, HE SHOULD HAVE OFFICERS TO ASSIST IN EXECUTING HIS PLANS!

BUT WHO SHOULD SELECT THE OFFICERS: THE PRESIDENT OR THE LEGISLATURE?

HIS JOB WILL BE TO IMPLEMENT WHATEVER LAWS GET PASSED.

BUT HE'LL NEED HELP, OF COURSE.

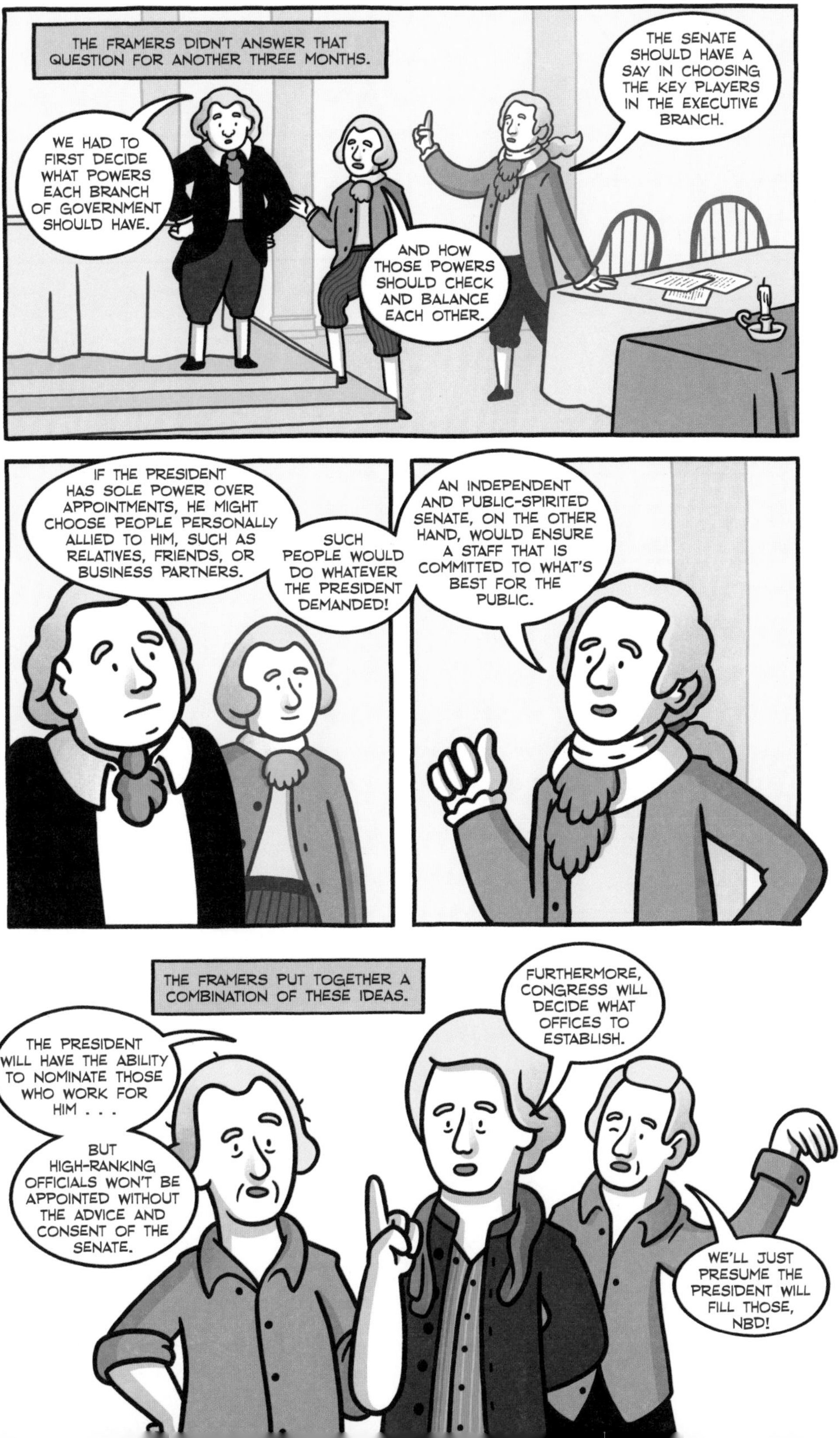
THE FRAMERS DIDN'T ANSWER THAT QUESTION FOR ANOTHER THREE MONTHS.
WE HAD TO FIRST DECIDE WHAT POWERS EACH BRANCH OF GOVERNMENT SHOULD HAVE.
AND HOW THOSE POWERS SHOULD CHECK AND BALANCE EACH OTHER.
THE SENATE SHOULD HAVE A SAY IN CHOOSING THE KEY PLAYERS IN THE EXECUTIVE BRANCH.
IF THE PRESIDENT HAS SOLE POWER OVER APPOINTMENTS, HE MIGHT CHOOSE PEOPLE PERSONALLY ALLIED TO HIM, SUCH AS RELATIVES, FRIENDS, OR BUSINESS PARTNERS.
SUCH PEOPLE WOULD DO WHATEVER THE PRESIDENT DEMANDED!
AN INDEPENDENT AND PUBLIC-SPIRITED SENATE, ON THE OTHER HAND, WOULD ENSURE A STAFF THAT IS COMMITTED TO WHAT'S BEST FOR THE PUBLIC.
THE FRAMERS PUT TOGETHER A COMBINATION OF THESE IDEAS.
THE PRESIDENT WILL HAVE THE ABILITY TO NOMINATE THOSE WHO WORK FOR HIM . . .
BUT HIGH-RANKING OFFICIALS WON'T BE APPOINTED WITHOUT THE ADVICE AND CONSENT OF THE SENATE.
FURTHERMORE, CONGRESS WILL DECIDE WHAT OFFICES TO ESTABLISH.
WE'LL JUST PRESUME THE PRESIDENT WILL FILL THOSE, NBD!

TWO DAYS LATER.

WE ARE DONE HERE!

I THINK . . .

LET US SIGN THIS, OUR CONSTITUTION, AND GO HOME!

IN THEIR RUSH TO GET OUT THE DOOR, THOUGH, THEY NEGLECTED TO CONSIDER:

HOW COULD THE PRESIDENT DISMISS SOMEONE HE HAD APPOINTED? COULD HE FIRE THE PERSON HIMSELF, OR DID THE SENATE HAVE TO APPROVE THE REMOVAL?

SO, IN 1789, DURING A CRISIS EARLY IN GEORGE WASHINGTON'S FIRST TERM, CONGRESS MADE THE DECISION THAT THE FRAMERS HAD IGNORED.

WE MUST ESTABLISH DEPARTMENTS TO HELP RUN THE GOVERNMENT.

THE HEADS OF THESE DEPARTMENTS WOULD BECOME THE PRESIDENT'S CABINET.

THE HOUSE OF REPRESENTATIVES CONSIDERED A BILL CREATING THE DEPARTMENT OF FOREIGN AFFAIRS. (TODAY, IT'S CALLED THE STATE DEPARTMENT.)

IT IS TO BE LED BY A SECRETARY WHO WOULD BE REMOVABLE FROM OFFICE BY THE PRESIDENT!

SOUNDS SIMPLE ENOUGH!

HOWEVER . . .

SINCE THE SENATE IS INVOLVED IN APPOINTMENTS, IT SHOULD APPROVE OR DISAPPROVE DISMISSALS AS WELL!

BUT THE ELECTORAL COLLEGE WILL GUARANTEE WE HAVE UPSTANDING PRESIDENTS!

THEY WOULD NEVER FIRE SOMEONE WITHOUT GOOD REASON!

THE ISSUE AT STAKE WAS THE POWER OF THE **PRESIDENCY** VERSUS THE POWER OF THE **LEGISLATURE**.

This system of an executive branch led by a single person at the top who oversees major employees below is called a **unitary executive**.

Because the executive chooses the underlings and doesn't have to get permission before firing them, the president has a lot of power.

IN 1867, PRESIDENT ANDREW JOHNSON FEUDED WITH HIS SECRETARY OF WAR, EDWIN STANTON, OVER RECONSTRUCTION POLICIES.

CONCERNED THAT JOHNSON WOULD GET RID OF STANTON, THE 39TH CONGRESS UNDID THE DECISION OF THE 1ST CONGRESS BY PASSING THE TENURE OF OFFICE ACT.

IT IS NOW LAW THAT THE PRESIDENT MUST GET SENATE APPROVAL BEFORE KICKING OUT CERTAIN OFFICEHOLDERS!

JOHNSON FIRED STANTON ANYWAY.

SO, THE HOUSE MOVED TO IMPEACH THE PRESIDENT.

JOHNSON WAS SAVED BY ONE VOTE IN THE SENATE.

THE ACT, WHICH MANY LAWYERS CONSIDERED UNCONSTITUTIONAL TO BEGIN WITH, WAS REPEALED IN 1887.

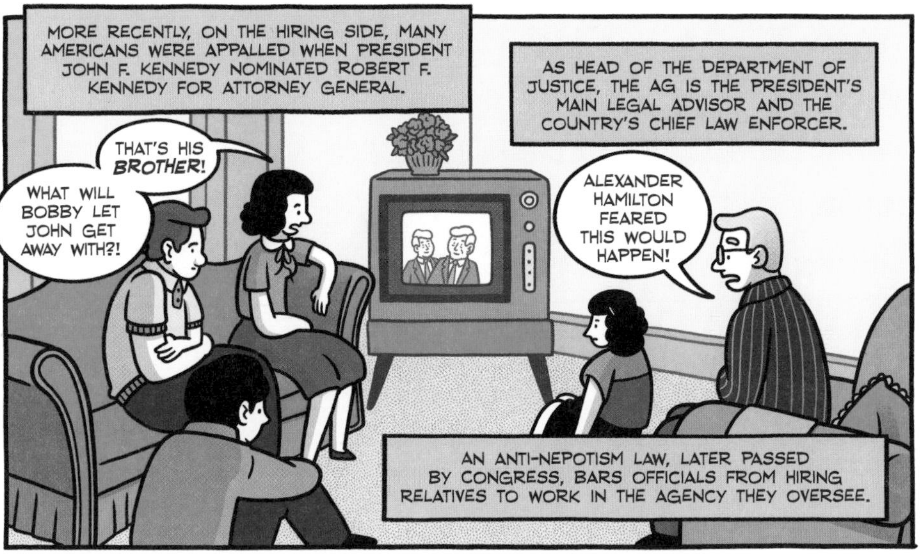
MORE RECENTLY, ON THE HIRING SIDE, MANY AMERICANS WERE APPALLED WHEN PRESIDENT JOHN F. KENNEDY NOMINATED ROBERT F. KENNEDY FOR ATTORNEY GENERAL.
AS HEAD OF THE DEPARTMENT OF JUSTICE, THE AG IS THE PRESIDENT'S MAIN LEGAL ADVISOR AND THE COUNTRY'S CHIEF LAW ENFORCER.
WHAT WILL BOBBY LET JOHN GET AWAY WITH?!
THAT'S HIS *BROTHER*!
ALEXANDER HAMILTON FEARED THIS WOULD HAPPEN!
AN ANTI-NEPOTISM LAW, LATER PASSED BY CONGRESS, BARS OFFICIALS FROM HIRING RELATIVES TO WORK IN THE AGENCY THEY OVERSEE.

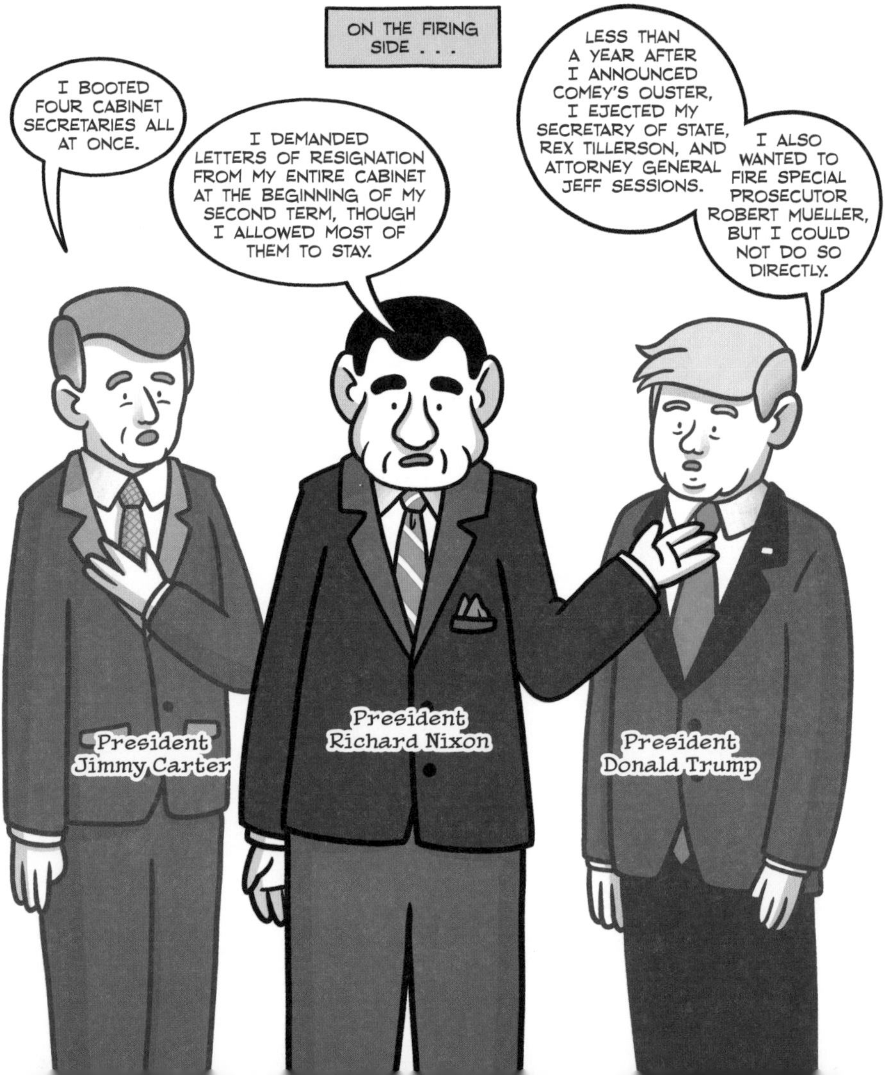
ON THE FIRING SIDE . . .
I BOOTED FOUR CABINET SECRETARIES ALL AT ONCE.
I DEMANDED LETTERS OF RESIGNATION FROM MY ENTIRE CABINET AT THE BEGINNING OF MY SECOND TERM, THOUGH I ALLOWED MOST OF THEM TO STAY.
LESS THAN A YEAR AFTER I ANNOUNCED COMEY'S OUSTER, I EJECTED MY SECRETARY OF STATE, REX TILLERSON, AND ATTORNEY GENERAL JEFF SESSIONS.
I ALSO WANTED TO FIRE SPECIAL PROSECUTOR ROBERT MUELLER, BUT I COULD NOT DO SO DIRECTLY.
President Jimmy Carter
President Richard Nixon
President Donald Trump

MUELLER WAS APPOINTED BY DEPUTY ATTORNEY GENERAL ROD ROSENSTEIN AFTER SESSIONS RECUSED HIMSELF—THAT IS, HE TOOK HIMSELF OFF THE CASE—WHEN IT CAME OUT THAT HE, TOO, HAD COMMUNICATED WITH RUSSIANS DURING THE PRESIDENTIAL CAMPAIGN.

DOJ RULES STATE THAT ONLY I CAN LET MUELLER GO.

DEPARTMENT OF JUSTICE

ROSENSTEIN RESIGNED IN 2019, BUT WHAT IF TRUMP HAD ORDERED HIM TO GET RID OF MUELLER BEFOREHAND?

IF THE DEPUTY AG REFUSED, TRUMP COULD HAVE REPLACED HIM WITH SOMEONE WHO WOULD COMPLY WITH HIS DEMAND.

THE PRESIDENT CHOSE NOT TO FIRE ROSENSTEIN, PARTLY BECAUSE REPUBLICAN SENATORS WARNED THE PRESIDENT THAT IT WOULD BE POLITICALLY DISASTROUS.

NOPE.

IN ADDITION TO OFFICES THAT REQUIRE SENATE CONFIRMATION, CONGRESS HAS CREATED MORE THAN THREE HUNDRED OTHER POSITIONS THAT THE PRESIDENT CAN FILL WITHOUT THEIR APPROVAL.

LIKE THE PRESS SECRETARY!

THE WHITE HOUSE
WASHINGTON

THE MOST IMPORTANT OF THESE MAY BE THE NATIONAL SECURITY ADVISOR, WHO COUNSELS THE PRESIDENT ON FOREIGN POLICY.

UNLIKE THE SECRETARY OF STATE, WHO ALSO ADVISES AND CARRIES OUT FOREIGN POLICY, THE NSA REPORTS ONLY TO THE PRESIDENT.

NSAS NEVER HAVE TO EXPLAIN OR EVEN REVEAL THEIR ACTIONS TO CONGRESS OR THE PUBLIC.

NIXON'S NSA, HENRY KISSINGER, UPENDED U.S. POLICY WITH CHINA BY SECRETLY ARRANGING A MEETING WITH CHAIRMAN MAO TSE-TUNG IN BEIJING IN 1972. THEIR FACE-TO-FACE TALK WAS GROUNDBREAKING BUT ELECTED LAWMAKERS HAD BEEN LEFT IN THE DARK.

SO WAS SECRETARY OF STATE WILLIAM ROGERS.

These unconfirmable positions are just one way the executive branch has swelled since 1789. During Washington's two terms, Congress authorized four cabinet departments and a couple of hundred positions to staff them.

Trump, on the other hand, oversaw fifteen cabinet members, more than a hundred federal agencies, and more than three million employees. Most work in the Department of Defense.

THE SENATE IS CHARGED WITH CONFIRMING OR REJECTING ABOUT 1,200 HIGH-RANKING OFFICIALS ONCE THEY ARE NOMINATED. THE PRESIDENT ALSO APPOINTS HUNDREDS OF OTHERS AND CAN DISMISS ALMOST ALL OF THEM.

THIS ARRANGEMENT GIVES MODERN-DAY PRESIDENTS A LOT OF SWAY.

WE MUST HOPE THEY ARE WORTHY OF THE JOB!

THERE ARE OTHER WAYS . . .

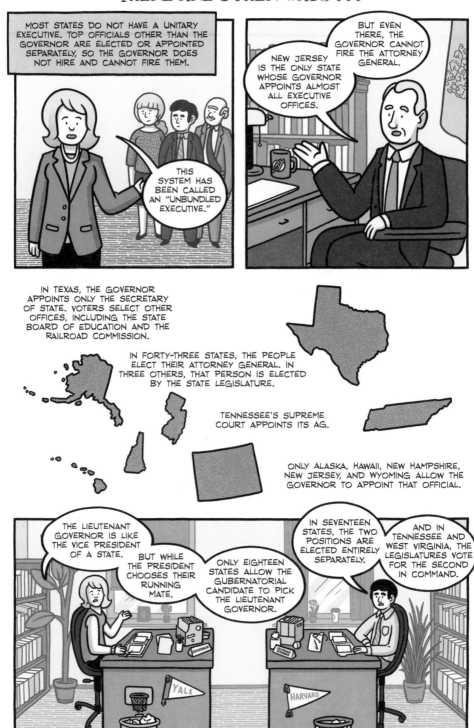

MOST STATES DO NOT HAVE A UNITARY EXECUTIVE. TOP OFFICIALS OTHER THAN THE GOVERNOR ARE ELECTED OR APPOINTED SEPARATELY, SO THE GOVERNOR DOES NOT HIRE AND CANNOT FIRE THEM.

THIS SYSTEM HAS BEEN CALLED AN "UNBUNDLED EXECUTIVE."

NEW JERSEY IS THE ONLY STATE WHOSE GOVERNOR APPOINTS ALMOST ALL EXECUTIVE OFFICES.

BUT EVEN THERE, THE GOVERNOR CANNOT FIRE THE ATTORNEY GENERAL.

IN TEXAS, THE GOVERNOR APPOINTS ONLY THE SECRETARY OF STATE. VOTERS SELECT OTHER OFFICES, INCLUDING THE STATE BOARD OF EDUCATION AND THE RAILROAD COMMISSION.

IN FORTY-THREE STATES, THE PEOPLE ELECT THEIR ATTORNEY GENERAL. IN THREE OTHERS, THAT PERSON IS ELECTED BY THE STATE LEGISLATURE.

TENNESSEE'S SUPREME COURT APPOINTS ITS AG.

ONLY ALASKA, HAWAII, NEW HAMPSHIRE, NEW JERSEY, AND WYOMING ALLOW THE GOVERNOR TO APPOINT THAT OFFICIAL.

THE LIEUTENANT GOVERNOR IS LIKE THE VICE PRESIDENT OF A STATE.

BUT WHILE THE PRESIDENT CHOOSES THEIR RUNNING MATE,

ONLY EIGHTEEN STATES ALLOW THE GUBERNATORIAL CANDIDATE TO PICK THE LIEUTENANT GOVERNOR.

IN SEVENTEEN STATES, THE TWO POSITIONS ARE ELECTED ENTIRELY SEPARATELY.

AND IN TENNESSEE AND WEST VIRGINIA, THE LEGISLATURES VOTE FOR THE SECOND IN COMMAND.

GOVERNOR

LIEUTENANT GOVERNOR

YALE

HARVARD

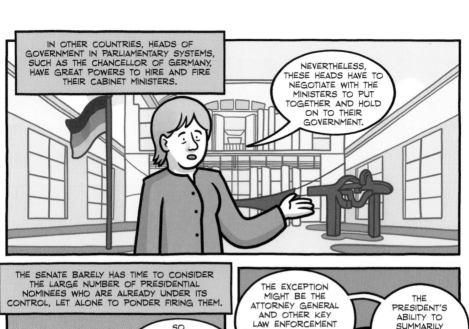

IN OTHER COUNTRIES, HEADS OF GOVERNMENT IN PARLIAMENTARY SYSTEMS, SUCH AS THE CHANCELLOR OF GERMANY, HAVE GREAT POWERS TO HIRE AND FIRE THEIR CABINET MINISTERS.

NEVERTHELESS, THESE HEADS HAVE TO NEGOTIATE WITH THE MINISTERS TO PUT TOGETHER AND HOLD ON TO THEIR GOVERNMENT.

THE SENATE BARELY HAS TIME TO CONSIDER THE LARGE NUMBER OF PRESIDENTIAL NOMINEES WHO ARE ALREADY UNDER ITS CONTROL, LET ALONE TO PONDER FIRING THEM.

SO, CONGRESS'S DECISION IN 1789 CONTINUES TO MAKE SENSE!

THE EXCEPTION MIGHT BE THE ATTORNEY GENERAL AND OTHER KEY LAW ENFORCEMENT PERSONNEL, INCLUDING THE HEAD OF THE FBI.

THE PRESIDENT'S ABILITY TO SUMMARILY DISMISS THESE OFFICERS CAN BE DANGEROUS.

THE NUMBER AND IMPORTANCE OF OTHER PRESIDENTIAL APPOINTEES WITHIN THE WHITE HOUSE HAS EXPANDED.

PERHAPS THEY SHOULD BE CONFIRMABLE AS WELL.

MORE IMPORTANT, CONGRESS SHOULD HAVE AUTHORITY TO QUESTION THEM, HOLDING THEM PUBLICLY ACCOUNTABLE FOR THEIR ACTIONS,

JUST AS IT DOES OTHER HIGH-LEVEL OFFICERS WHO ARE CONFIRMED BY THE SENATE.

THE STORY CONTINUES

PRESIDENT TRUMP WAS FURIOUS AT JEFF SESSIONS FOR RECUSING HIMSELF, PROBABLY BECAUSE HE HAD COUNTED ON THE AG TO STIFLE THE RUSSIAN PROBE.

HE FIRED SESSIONS IN 2018 AND NOMINATED WILLIAM BARR TO THE POST. THE SENATE CONFIRMED BARR IN 2019.

Hon. William P. Barr

MEANWHILE, TRUMP DECLINED TO NOMINATE HUNDREDS OF THE 1,200 POSITIONS THAT CONGRESS ESTABLISHED TO RUN THE GOVERNMENT.

LESS THAN HALF OF THOSE AT THE DEPARTMENT OF JUSTICE WERE FILLED, AND THE STATE DEPARTMENT WAS DESCRIBED AS EMPTY.

TRUMP BLAMED DEMOCRATS.

PART VI:
who's running america?

Accidents happen. So do acts of terrorism.
Our Constitution, however, doesn't make
provisions for such events if they result in
a need to replace our national leadership.
It lays out guidelines for succession
should a president die in office, but it
doesn't cover other important details.

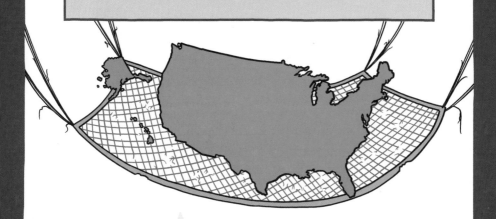

What happens when
representatives
and senators are
unable to finish
their terms?

What if the president
is unable to complete
his or her term—and
doesn't realize it?

What happens to
a new president
if the outgoing
president leaves
a mess just before
leaving office?

The Constitution could fail us when we need it
most, at times of frightening situations.

15

knock, knock.
is anybody there?

continuity in government

SEPTEMBER 11, 2001.

TOM BURNETT REACHED NEWARK, NEW JERSEY'S INTERNATIONAL AIRPORT EARLY ENOUGH TO NAB A SEAT ON A MORNING FLIGHT TO SAN FRANCISCO.

WE HAVE YOU ON UA 93, SET TO LEAVE THE GATE AT 8 AM.

GREAT, I'LL GET HOME EARLIER THAN PLANNED!

AROUND THE SAME TIME, REPRESENTATIVE JIM MATHESON, A DEMOCRAT FROM UTAH, WAS MEETING WITH HIS STAFF AT THE CAPITOL.

WHAT'S ON THE AGENDA FOR THIS BUDGET COMMITTEE MEETING?

8:42 AM

APOLOGIES FOR THE DELAY, FOLKS. WE'LL HAVE YOU AIRBORNE SHORTLY.

8:45 AM

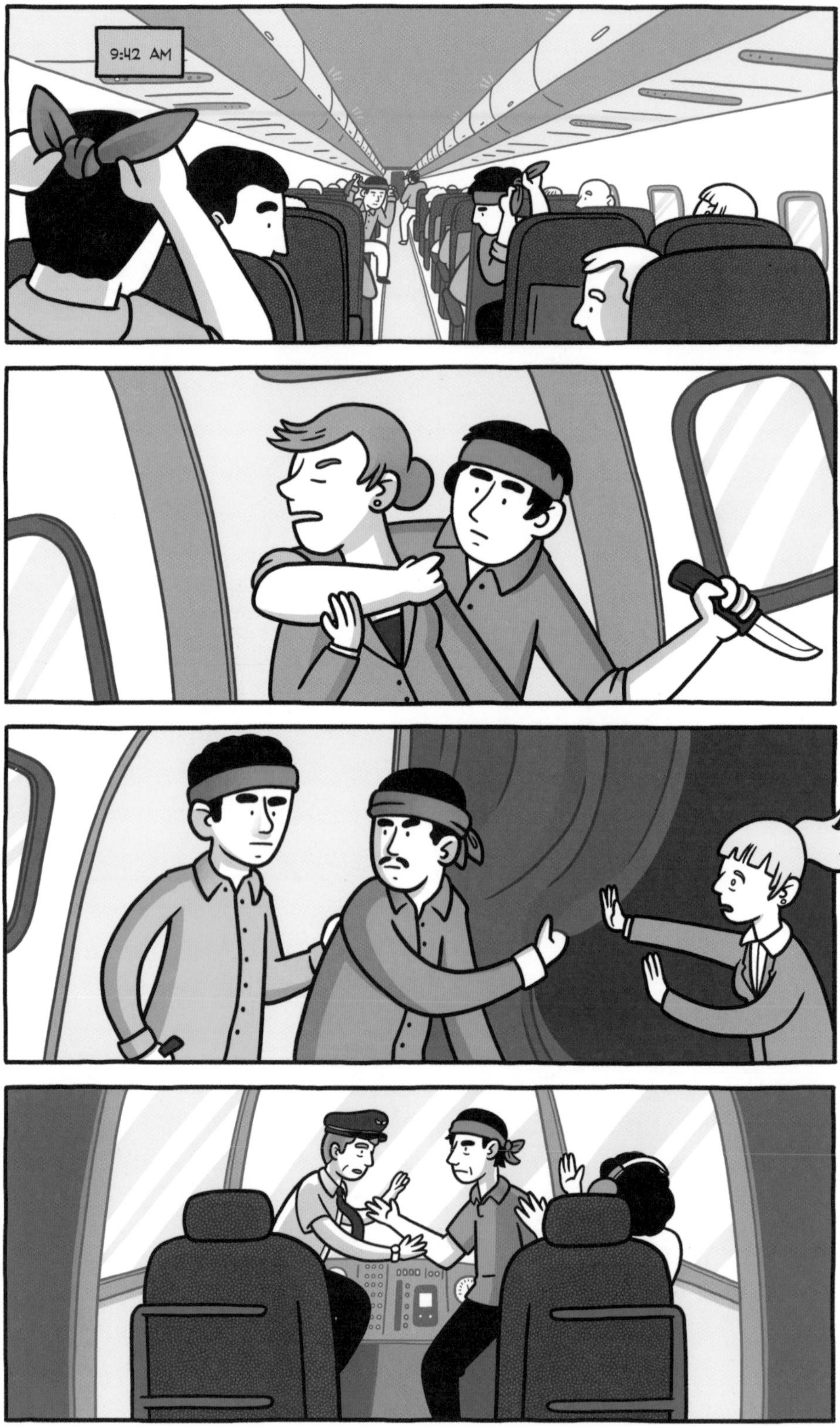
9:42 AM

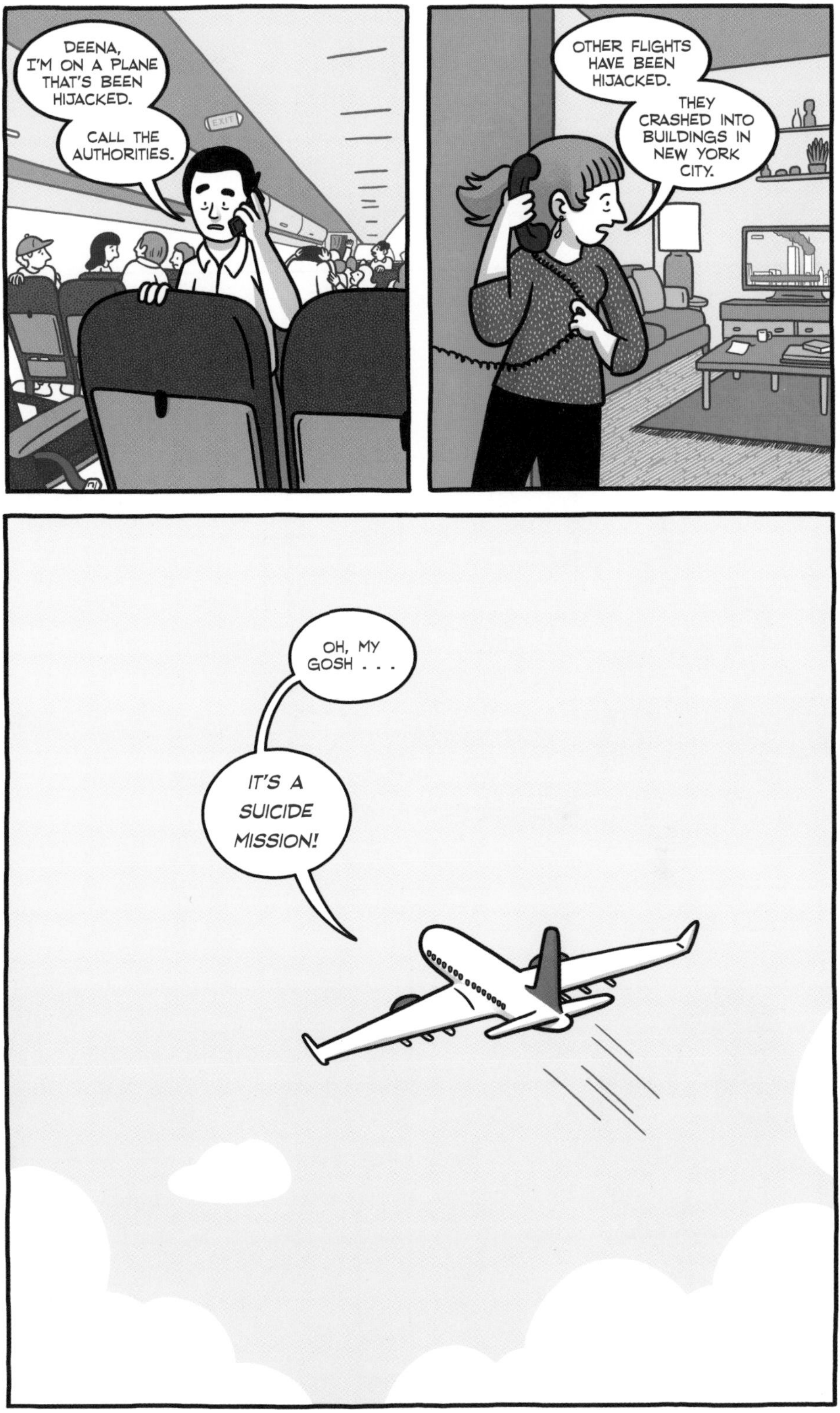
DEENA, I'M ON A PLANE THAT'S BEEN HIJACKED.
CALL THE AUTHORITIES.
OTHER FLIGHTS HAVE BEEN HIJACKED.
THEY CRASHED INTO BUILDINGS IN NEW YORK CITY.
OH, MY GOSH . . .
IT'S A SUICIDE MISSION!

GOOD MEETING, EVERYONE.

I'VE GOT TO HEAD BACK TO MY OFFICE FOR THAT CONSTITUENT MEET-AND-GREET.

A SHORT TIME LATER . . .

JIM . . .

TWO JETS JUST CRASHED INTO THE WORLD TRADE CENTER.

EVACUATE THE BUILDING! *EVACUATE THE BUILDING!*

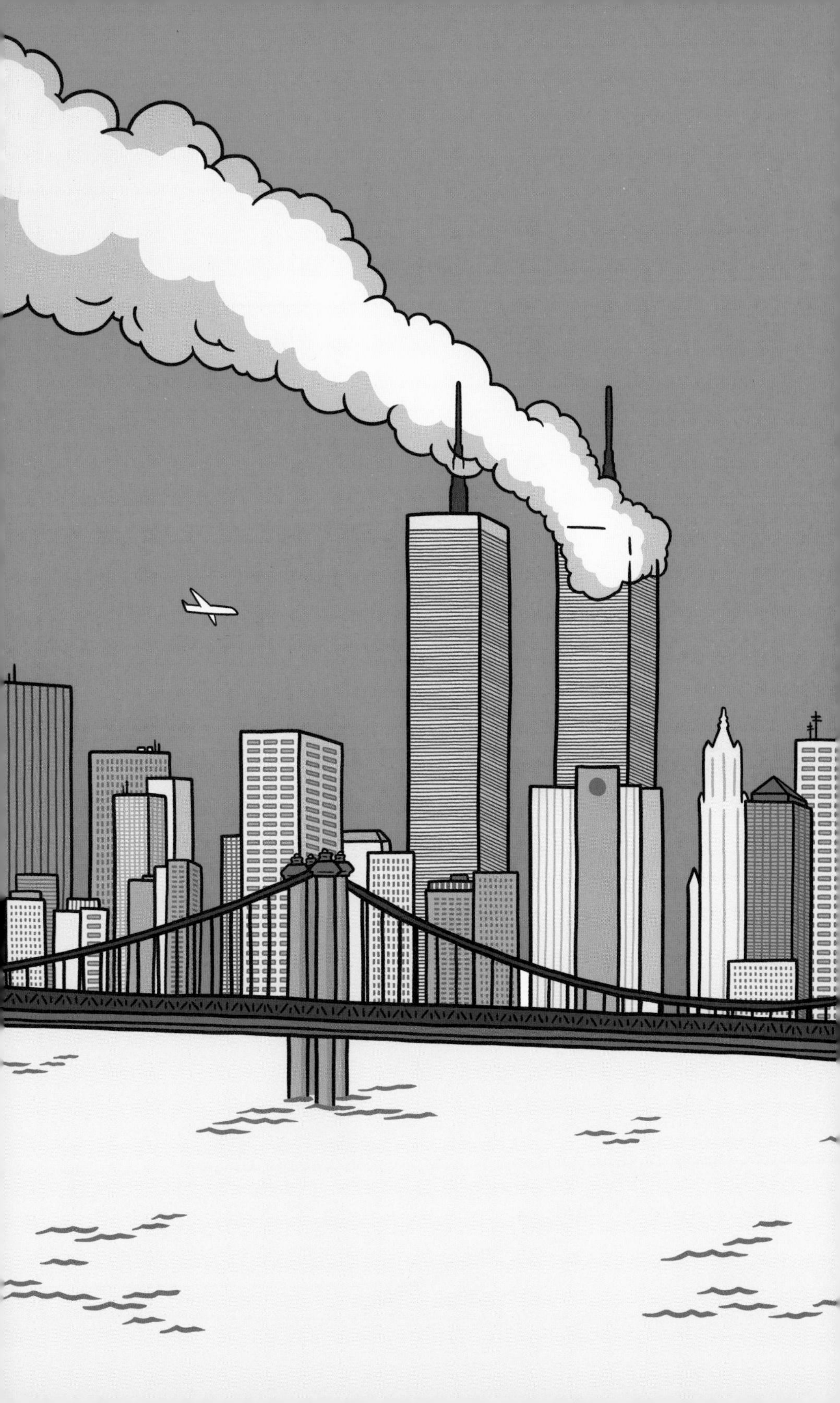

10 AM

BURNETT AND THE OTHER PASSENGERS COULDN'T GET CONTROL OF THE COCKPIT, BUT THEIR ATTEMPTS CONVINCED THE HIJACKERS THAT THEY WOULDN'T REACH THEIR TARGET.

AS BURNETT HAD SUSPECTED, UA 93 WAS ON A MURDER-SUICIDE MISSION, BUT WAS CUT SHORT NEAR SHANKSVILLE, PENNSYLVANIA, A TWENTY-MINUTE FLIGHT AWAY FROM THE CAPITOL.

THE TARGET WAS MOST LIKELY THE UNITED STATES CAPITOL COMPLEX, WHICH HELD THE OFFICES OF MATHESON AND EVERY OTHER U.S. REPRESENTATIVE AND SENATOR.

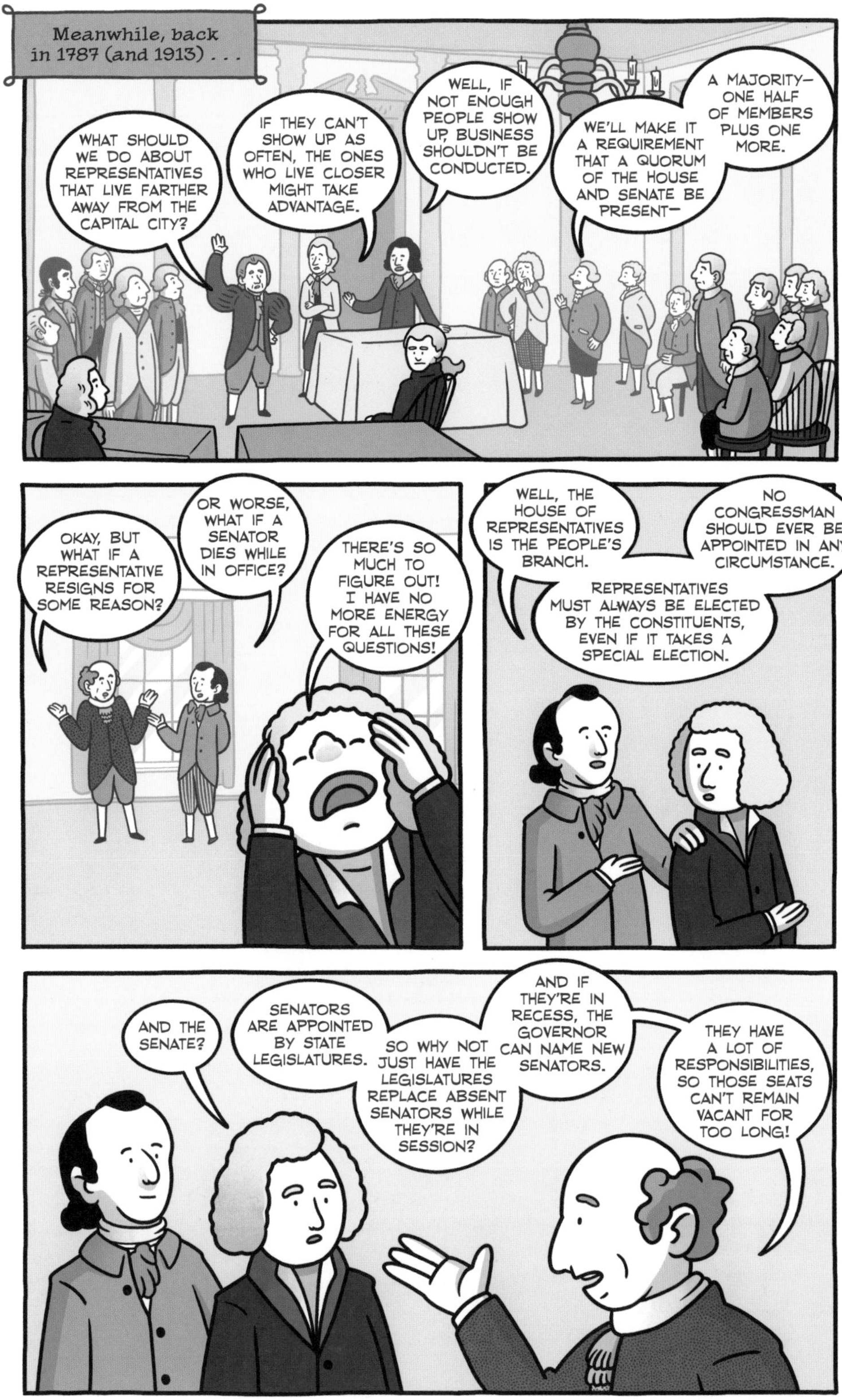

Meanwhile, back in 1787 (and 1913) . . .
WHAT SHOULD WE DO ABOUT REPRESENTATIVES THAT LIVE FARTHER AWAY FROM THE CAPITAL CITY?
IF THEY CAN'T SHOW UP AS OFTEN, THE ONES WHO LIVE CLOSER MIGHT TAKE ADVANTAGE.
WELL, IF NOT ENOUGH PEOPLE SHOW UP, BUSINESS SHOULDN'T BE CONDUCTED.
WE'LL MAKE IT A REQUIREMENT THAT A QUORUM OF THE HOUSE AND SENATE BE PRESENT—
A MAJORITY—ONE HALF OF MEMBERS PLUS ONE MORE.
OKAY, BUT WHAT IF A REPRESENTATIVE RESIGNS FOR SOME REASON?
OR WORSE, WHAT IF A SENATOR DIES WHILE IN OFFICE?
THERE'S SO MUCH TO FIGURE OUT! I HAVE NO MORE ENERGY FOR ALL THESE QUESTIONS!
WELL, THE HOUSE OF REPRESENTATIVES IS THE PEOPLE'S BRANCH.
NO CONGRESSMAN SHOULD EVER BE APPOINTED IN ANY CIRCUMSTANCE.
REPRESENTATIVES MUST ALWAYS BE ELECTED BY THE CONSTITUENTS, EVEN IF IT TAKES A SPECIAL ELECTION.
AND THE SENATE?
SENATORS ARE APPOINTED BY STATE LEGISLATURES.
SO WHY NOT JUST HAVE THE LEGISLATURES REPLACE ABSENT SENATORS WHILE THEY'RE IN SESSION?
AND IF THEY'RE IN RECESS, THE GOVERNOR CAN NAME NEW SENATORS.
THEY HAVE A LOT OF RESPONSIBILITIES, SO THOSE SEATS CAN'T REMAIN VACANT FOR TOO LONG!

APPOINT ME!
I MEAN, VOTE FOR ME.

THE SITUATION FINALLY GOT THE SENATORS' ATTENTION IN 1912.

WE CALL FOR A SECOND CONSTITUTIONAL CONVENTION!

TWENTY-SEVEN STATES PETITIONED FOR THIS. IF ANOTHER FOUR STATES JOINED THEM, A SECOND CONVENTION WOULD HAVE HAPPENED.

OKAY, OKAY! WE'LL DRAFT AN AMENDMENT!

WITH THE RATIFICATION OF THE **17TH AMENDMENT** IN 1913, ARRANGEMENTS CHANGED.

INSTEAD OF BEING PICKED BY STATE LEGISLATURES, SENATORS WOULD BE ELECTED DIRECTLY BY THE PEOPLE.

IT ALSO CHANGED THE WAY SENATORS WOULD BE REPLACED.

"When vacancies happen in the representation of any State in the Senate, the executive authority of such State shall issue writs of election to fill such vacancies:

"Provided, That the legislature of any State may empower the executive thereof to make temporary appointments until the people fill the vacancies by election as the legislature may direct."

With rare exceptions, states always have senators representing them, whether elected or appointed by governors.

They do not necessarily have a full delegation of representatives, however, if there is a lag between a congressperson's departure and the election of a new one.

SO, WHAT'S THE BIG ISSUE?

TURN THE PAGE!

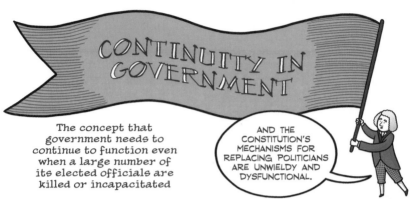

CONTINUITY IN GOVERNMENT

The concept that government needs to continue to function even when a large number of its elected officials are killed or incapacitated

AND THE CONSTITUTION'S MECHANISMS FOR REPLACING POLITICIANS ARE UNWIELDY AND DYSFUNCTIONAL.

WHAT IF UA 93 HADN'T BEEN DELAYED?

WHAT IF BURNETT'S PHONE COULDN'T GRAB A SIGNAL?

WHAT IF THE PASSENGERS HADN'T TRIED TO WREST THE PLANE FROM THE HIJACKERS?

WHAT IF UA 93 HAD HIT THE CAPITOL?

UNFORTUNATELY OUR ENEMIES DON'T NEED TO COMMANDEER A JETLINER TO CAUSE SUCH A CATASTROPHE.

IN 2012, A PHYSICIST TRIED TO FLY MODEL PLANES PACKED WITH GRENADES INTO GOVERNMENT BUILDINGS.

DRONES, POISONS, AND ENGINEERED VIRUSES CAN ALL ACCOMPLISH THE SAME THING.

NATURAL DISASTERS OR DISEASES COULD ALSO WIPE OUT MANY GOVERNMENT OFFICIALS—ALONG WITH THE REST OF US.

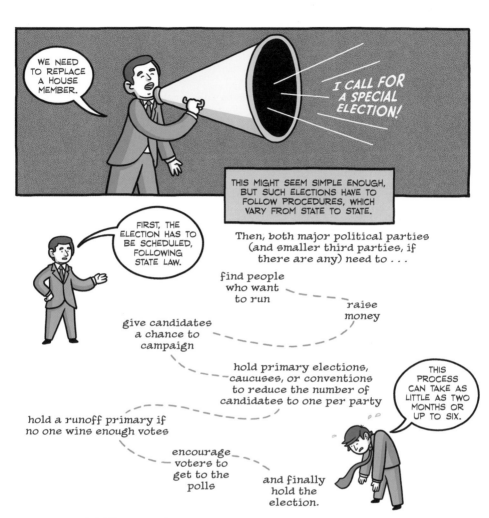

WE NEED TO REPLACE A HOUSE MEMBER.

I CALL FOR A SPECIAL ELECTION!

THIS MIGHT SEEM SIMPLE ENOUGH, BUT SUCH ELECTIONS HAVE TO FOLLOW PROCEDURES, WHICH VARY FROM STATE TO STATE.

FIRST, THE ELECTION HAS TO BE SCHEDULED, FOLLOWING STATE LAW.

Then, both major political parties (and smaller third parties, if there are any) need to . . .

find people who want to run

raise money

give candidates a chance to campaign

hold primary elections, caucuses, or conventions to reduce the number of candidates to one per party

THIS PROCESS CAN TAKE AS LITTLE AS TWO MONTHS OR UP TO SIX.

hold a runoff primary if no one wins enough votes

encourage voters to get to the polls

and finally hold the election.

THE MISSING REPRESENTATIVE'S STAFF MEMBERS CAN CARRY OUT SOME JOBS, BUT NO ONE ELSE CAN HOLD COMMITTEE HEARINGS OR VOTE ON BILLS.

THAT MEANS THE CONSTITUENTS BACK HOME ARE LITERALLY UNREPRESENTED!

The constitutional process to replace
a senator can take even longer since the
election is **statewide**, not just within
a single congressional district.

In all, 301 senators and 817 members of the House have died in office—three of them between their election and swearing-in ceremony. An additional twenty have been expelled.

Spencer Darwin Pettis, the first member of Congress killed in office. He died in a duel in 1831 after he criticized the president of the Bank of the United States.

YOU OFFENDED MY BROTHER!

NOW, I CHALLENGE YOU!

His opponent, Thomas Biddle, was so nearsighted that he chose to shoot pistols at short range—such short range that the shooters killed each other.

Elected officials also leave for reasons other than death.

Senators **John F. Kennedy** and **Barack Obama** moved into the White House as president.

Senators **Hillary Rodham Clinton** and **John Kerry** became Secretaries of State under President Obama, and several other senators also joined his administration.

President Donald J. Trump named Alabama Senator Jeff Sessions to serve as Attorney General, Kansas Representative Mike Pompeo to head the Central Intelligence Agency, Montana Representative Ryan Zinke to be Secretary of the Interior, and Georgia Representative Tom Price to head the Department of Health and Human Services.

There are drawbacks to the requirement for a quorum. For one, the Constitution is fuzzy about what "quorum" means. Furthermore, to pass a law, you need a majority of the quorum to do it.

How does that work?

Congress is composed of 100 senators and 435 representatives.

If "a Majority of each" means a majority of each body, here's a possible scenario:

If 50 senators or 218 representatives are alive but unable to appear on the floor for a vote because of a disaster, there would not be enough people to make a quorum.

In that case, Congress would not have enough members to pass legislation.

THE GOVERNMENT WOULD COME TO A STANDSTILL.

But if "a Majority of each" means a majority of those congresspeople who remain alive and are able to get to work, the scenario is entirely different.

If, say, 39 senators and 199 representatives are able to show up after a calamity, a quorum would be 20 senators plus 100 representatives.

And a majority of that quorum—that is, 11 senators and 51 representatives—could pass or defeat laws for the entire country.

HOW ARE WE SUPPOSED TO DEFINE "A MAJORITY OF EACH"?

"ALIVE AND ABLE TO GET TO WORK" WOULD'VE BEEN BETTER.

AND WHAT ABOUT A DOOMSDAY SCENARIO?

IF ONLY THREE REPRESENTATIVES IN THE HOUSE EMERGE FROM A CATASTROPHE, THEN TWO OF THEM COULD PASS WHATEVER BILL THEY WANT.

THE REPLACEMENTS FOR THE REMAINING 432 MEMBERS COULD NOT BE ELECTED FOR A BARE MINIMUM OF TWO MONTHS!

AND IF THERE ARE SURVIVORS BUT THEY ARE INJURED, INTELLECTUALLY IMPAIRED, OR COMATOSE, REPLACEMENTS CANNOT BE APPOINTED.

THESE SENATORS WOULD KEEP THEIR SEATS UNTIL THEY VOLUNTARILY LEAVE OFFICE.

DURING EACH STATE OF THE UNION ADDRESS, ALMOST ALL CHIEF FIGURES IN THE FEDERAL GOVERNMENT ASSEMBLE AT THE CAPITOL.

ONE CABINET MEMBER, THE **DESIGNATED SURVIVOR**, IS ORDERED NOT TO ATTEND SO THAT SOMEONE CAN STEP INTO THE PRESIDENCY SHOULD DISASTER STRIKE.

BUT THEY WOULDN'T BE ABLE TO ACCOMPLISH MUCH WITH NO OTHER ELECTED OR APPOINTED OFFICIALS TO CARRY OUT THEIR JOBS.

QUICK, HIDE ME!

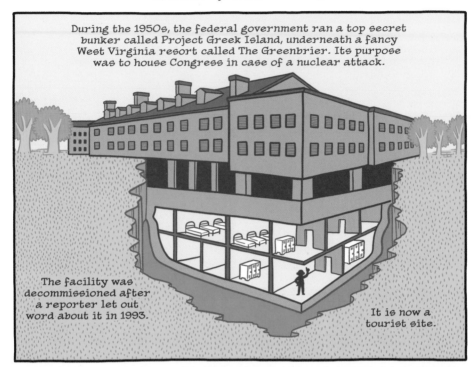

During the 1950s, the federal government ran a top secret bunker called Project Greek Island, underneath a fancy West Virginia resort called The Greenbrier. Its purpose was to house Congress in case of a nuclear attack.

The facility was decommissioned after a reporter let out word about it in 1993.

It is now a tourist site.

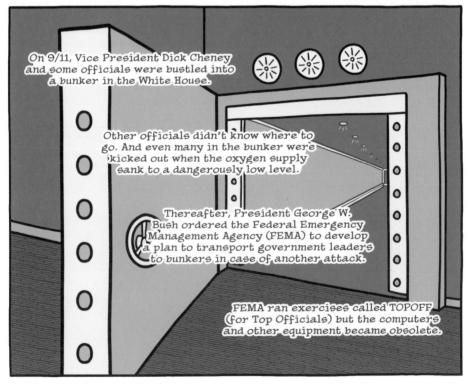

On 9/11, Vice President Dick Cheney and some officials were bustled into a bunker in the White House.

Other officials didn't know where to go. And even many in the bunker were kicked out when the oxygen supply sank to a dangerously low level.

Thereafter, President George W. Bush ordered the Federal Emergency Management Agency (FEMA) to develop a plan to transport government leaders to bunkers in case of another attack.

FEMA ran exercises called TOPOFF (for Top Officials) but the computers and other equipment became obsolete.

ARE THERE OTHER WAYS?

Few governments have tackled the enormity of this situation, and none has ever needed to. But some have basic provisions in place.

IN CALIFORNIA, THE GOVERNOR IS REQUIRED TO CALL FOR AN ELECTION TO FILL A LEGISLATIVE VACANCY IMMEDIATELY.

BUT THAT DOESN'T ADDRESS A POTENTIAL WHOLESALE LOSS OF MEMBERS.

THE FRENCH AND SOUTH AFRICAN CONSTITUTIONS AUTHORIZE NATIONAL LEGISLATION TO PROVIDE WAYS TO FILL VACANCIES.

BUT THESE LEGISLATURES HAVE NEVER PASSED APPROPRIATE LAWS.

LA CONSTITUTIO FRANÇAISE

THE CONSTITUTION OF THE REPUBLIC OF SOUTH AFRICA

In the U.S., the Constitution would have to be amended to change procedures for filling vacancies.

FROM THE END OF WORLD WAR II IN 1945 THROUGH THE CUBAN MISSILE CRISIS IN 1962 AND THROUGH THE COLD WAR, MANY AMERICANS WERE TERRIFIED THAT THE SOVIET UNION MIGHT DETONATE NUCLEAR WEAPONS IN WASHINGTON, DC.

OKAY, KIDS, DUCK AND COVER!

MOST OF THESE ALLOWED GOVERNORS TO MAKE INTERIM APPOINTMENTS.

DURING THAT TIME, CONGRESS PROPOSED MORE THAN THIRTY CONSTITUTIONAL **AMENDMENTS** THAT LAID OUT WAYS TO FILL SEATS QUICKLY IN THE HOUSE.

THE HOUSE, HOWEVER, DIDN'T TAKE ACTION ON ANY POSSIBLE MEASURES TO REPLACE ITSELF.

THREE PROPOSALS PASSED THE SENATE BY WIDE MARGINS.

AFTER 9/11, NEARLY A DOZEN ADDITIONAL AMENDMENTS WERE INTRODUCED TO RESOLVE ISSUES OF CONTINUITY IN GOVERNMENT.

SOMETHING MUST BE DONE!

NO PLAN WAS ADOPTED.

THE HOUSE OF REPRESENTATIVES DID PASS A BILL THAT WOULD REQUIRE EXPEDITED ELECTIONS IN CASE MORE THAN A HUNDRED MEMBERS ARE KILLED.

BUT THE BILL DID NOT ADDRESS DISABLED MEMBERS.

NOR DID IT MOVE THROUGH THE SENATE.

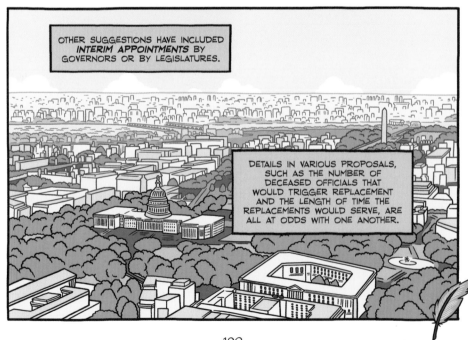

OTHER SUGGESTIONS HAVE INCLUDED *INTERIM APPOINTMENTS* BY GOVERNORS OR BY LEGISLATURES.

DETAILS IN VARIOUS PROPOSALS, SUCH AS THE NUMBER OF DECEASED OFFICIALS THAT WOULD TRIGGER REPLACEMENT AND THE LENGTH OF TIME THE REPLACEMENTS WOULD SERVE, ARE ALL AT ODDS WITH ONE ANOTHER.

16

is there a leader in the room?

presidential succession

MARCH 31, 1981. TWO MONTHS AFTER RONALD REAGAN'S INAUGURATION.

DON'T THREATEN OUR JOBS!

DON'T CUT THE FEDERAL BUDGET!

BOO!

HE'S GIVING A SPEECH TO LABOR UNION LEADERS.

NEVERTHELESS, HE WAS A GENERALLY POPULAR PRESIDENT.

Hilton

POP POP POP POP POP POP

192

SEEING REAGAN SITTING UP, WITNESSES ASSUMED HE REMAINED UNHURT.

BUT A .22 CALIBER BULLET HAD STRUCK HIS SEVENTH RIB AN INCH FROM HIS HEART AND PENETRATED HIS LEFT LUNG, COLLAPSING IT.

EMERGENCY

HONEY, I FORGOT TO DUCK.

WHO'S MINDING THE STORE?

A GOOD QUESTION!

VICE PRESIDENT GEORGE H. W. BUSH WAS IN TEXAS, PREPARING TO TALK TO STATE LEGISLATORS. ALTHOUGH HE BOARDED A PLANE TO WASHINGTON IMMEDIATELY, CABINET MEMBERS WERE LEFT TO FIGURE THINGS OUT AT THE WHITE HOUSE.

IN SUCH A CASE, WHAT IS THE LINE OF SUCCESSION?

THE NORMAL COMMAND STRUCTURE

When the president and then the vice president are incapacitated, the secretary of state becomes commander in chief. This system takes effect by a majority vote of the cabinet.

THE NATIONAL COMMAND AUTHORITY

When the military is involved, the secretary of defense takes charge.

SINCE THE CABINET HAD ASSEMBLED IN THE SITUATION ROOM, A MILITARY POST, WEINBERGER PRESUMED THAT HE OUTRANKED HAIG.

NO ONE KNEW WHAT ACTION THEY WERE AUTHORIZED TO TAKE. IT WASN'T CLEAR WHO HAD ULTIMATE AUTHORITY. THE COUNTRY WAS, IN EFFECT, *PRESIDENTLESS!*

CONGRESS HAS PASSED A SERIES OF SUCH LAWS, MOST RECENTLY
THE *PRESIDENTIAL SUCCESSION ACT OF 1947*,
WHICH LISTS THE ORDER OF SUCCESSION FOR SEVENTEEN POSSIBLE PRESIDENTS AFTER
THE VICE PRESIDENT.

SPEAKER OF THE HOUSE OF REPRESENTATIVES
PRESIDENT PRO TEMPORE OF THE SENATE
SECRETARY OF STATE
SECRETARY OF THE TREASURY
SECRETARY OF DEFENSE
ATTORNEY GENERAL
SECRETARY OF THE INTERIOR
SECRETARY OF AGRICULTURE
SECRETARY OF COMMERCE
SECRETARY OF LABOR
SECRETARY OF HEALTH AND HUMAN SERVICES
SECRETARY OF HOUSING AND URBAN DEVELOPMENT
SECRETARY OF TRANSPORTATION
SECRETARY OF ENERGY
SECRETARY OF EDUCATION
SECRETARY OF VETERANS AFFAIRS
SECRETARY OF HOMELAND SECURITY

AND IN 1967, THE 25TH AMENDMENT LAID OUT
WHO TAKES OFFICE UNDER VARIOUS INSTANCES.

SO WHAT'S THE BIG PROBLEM?

FOUR PRESIDENTS DIED WHILE IN OFFICE.

WILLIAM HENRY HARRISON (HE WAS ONLY IN OFFICE ONE MONTH)

ZACHARY TAYLOR

WARREN G. HARDING

FRANKLIN DELANO ROOSEVELT

FOUR WERE ASSASSINATED.

ABRAHAM LINCOLN

JOHN F. KENNEDY

JAMES A. GARFIELD

WILLIAM MCKINLEY

PRESIDENTS ALSO GET SICK.

WOODROW WILSON INSISTED ON REMAINING IN OFFICE UNTIL THE END OF HIS TERM IN 1921, EVEN AFTER SUFFERING A SERIOUS STROKE IN 1919 THAT LEFT HIM PHYSICALLY AND MENTALLY DEBILITATED.

DWIGHT D. EISENHOWER SUFFERED BOTH A HEART ATTACK AND A STROKE WHILE PRESIDENT. HE BUCKED HIS DOCTOR'S ADVICE NOT TO RUN FOR RE-ELECTION IN 1956. HE WON. FORTUNATELY, HIS HEALTH DID NOT DETERIORATE.

THE COUNTRY WOULD FACE A CONSTITUTIONAL CRISIS IF THE VICE PRESIDENT AND CABINET SECRETARIES DECIDE A PRESIDENT IS UNFIT BUT THAT PRESIDENT RESISTS REMOVAL FROM OFFICE.

HOW RUDE!

UNDER THOSE CIRCUMSTANCES, CONGRESS WOULD HAVE TWENTY-ONE DAYS TO CHOOSE:

I'M FIT!

NO, YOU'RE NOT!

THE PRESIDENT STAYS IN OFFICE, UNLESS A TWO-THIRDS VOTE IN BOTH HOUSES OF CONGRESS AGREES WITH THE VICE PRESIDENT AND CABINET.

WHO'S GOT THE BALL?

A hypothetical scenario was prepared by the Brookings Institution and the American Enterprise Institute to demonstrate the chaos that would result from a disaster hitting right before the swearing-in ceremonies on Inauguration Day.

According to the scenario, terrorists detonate a small nuclear device on Pennsylvania Avenue between the White House and the Capitol.

Everyone at those locations and in between is killed or immobilized. Without an incoming president, vice president, speaker of the house, or president pro tempore, the presidency should pass to a member of the cabinet—but which one?

The president-elect hasn't taken office or confirmed a cabinet. An outgoing cabinet officer who hasn't resigned and wasn't at the White House could get the job. Possibly the secretary of veterans affairs could step unsteadily into the presidency. *

Or, if no one in the constitutional line of succession is alive, a number of generals, undersecretaries, and governors might claim they are in charge. Undoubtedly, bitter arguments and political feuds would result. And Americans might not accept the person who gains power as a legitimate official.

* The president pro tempore is the most senior senator in the majority party and presides over the Senate when the vice president is absent.

EAGLE HORIZON

In 1977, preparing for a possible nuclear war, **President Jimmy Carter** announced, "my intention is to stay here at the White House as long as I live to administer the affairs of government." He planned to send Vice President **Walter Mondale** to a secure location.

On 9/11, while Vice President Dick Cheney hunkered down in the White House, President Bush flew around on Air Force One, whose communications systems were inadequate. A reporter wrote that Bush was "less informed than a normal civilian sitting at home watching the cable news."

These days, Eagle Horizon exercises carry out scenarios for nuclear accidents, chemical and cyberattacks, earthquakes, hurricanes, and other forms of mass destruction. These involve evacuating the president and other leadership as well as testing the preparedness of emergency teams.

THERE ARE OTHER WAYS!

MANY STATES HAVE DETAILED RULES FOR SUCCESSION IN OFFICE, EVEN FOR POSITIONS BELOW THE EXECUTIVE BRANCH.

SEVEN OF THEM STOP WITH THE INITIAL SUCCESSOR TO THE GOVERNOR.

the governor

the lieutenant governor

CALIFORNIA EXPLICITLY STATES THAT THE LIEUTENANT GOVERNOR CAN TAKE OVER IN THE CASE OF A "TEMPORARY DISABILITY."

WHAT DOES THAT MEAN?

IT'S NOT REALLY DEFINED.

THE MONTANA CONSTITUTION PROVIDES THAT THE LIEUTENANT GOVERNOR BECOMES THE "ACTING GOVERNOR" IF AN ILLNESS OR DISABILITY RENDERS THE GOVERNOR INCAPABLE OF PERFORMING THE OFFICE, AS WELL AS WHENEVER THE GOVERNOR HAS BEEN ABSENT FROM OFFICE FOR FORTY-FIVE DAYS.

YOU CAN'T FIND HIM, EITHER?

GUESS YOU'RE GOVERNOR NOW!

TWENTY STATES, INCLUDING CALIFORNIA AND NEW YORK, REQUIRE THE GOVERNOR TO TRANSFER POWER TO THE NEXT OFFICIAL IN LINE WHEN LEAVING THE STATE, EVEN BRIEFLY.

I'M JUST HEADING OUT FOR THE WEEKEND, NO BIG D—

SIR, WE'VE GOT THIS.

IN CONTRAST, THE PRESIDENT OF THE UNITED STATES IS ALWAYS FULLY EMPOWERED, REGARDLESS OF HOW FAR THEY ARE FROM HOME.

MANY COUNTRIES HAVE A LINE OF SUCCESSION, BUT THE CIRCUMSTANCES ARE NO MORE SPELLED OUT THAN THEY ARE IN THE U.S., AND THE LINE IS GENERALLY SHORTER.

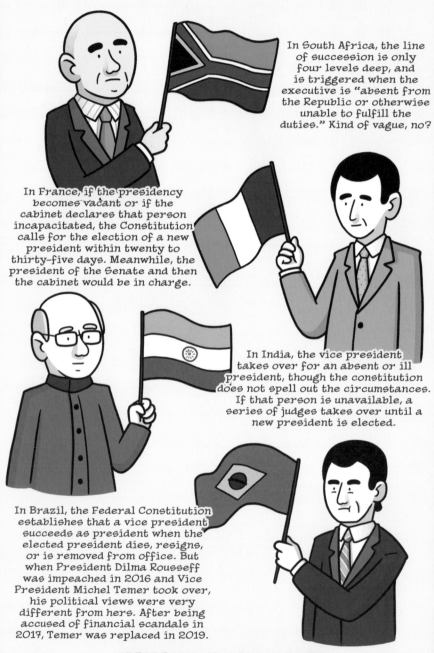

In South Africa, the line of succession is only four levels deep, and is triggered when the executive is "absent from the Republic or otherwise unable to fulfill the duties." Kind of vague, no?

In France, if the presidency becomes vacant or if the cabinet declares that person incapacitated, the Constitution calls for the election of a new president within twenty to thirty-five days. Meanwhile, the president of the Senate and then the cabinet would be in charge.

In India, the vice president takes over for an absent or ill president, though the constitution does not spell out the circumstances. If that person is unavailable, a series of judges takes over until a new president is elected.

In Brazil, the Federal Constitution establishes that a vice president succeeds as president when the elected president dies, resigns, or is removed from office. But when President Dilma Rousseff was impeached in 2016 and Vice President Michel Temer took over, his political views were very different from hers. After being accused of financial scandals in 2017, Temer was replaced in 2019.

PRESIDENTIAL SUCCESSION POSES DILEMMAS AROUND THE WORLD!

BECAUSE OF ITS AMBIGUITIES, EVERY PRESIDENT SINCE REAGAN'S SHOOTING HAS FILED A PLAN FOR WHEN AND HOW THE 25TH AMENDMENT WOULD COME INTO PLAY.

CONGRESS COULD PASS A LAW THAT CLARIFIES THE SITUATION, BUT IT HAS NOT DONE SO YET.

IF THE GAP IN LEADERSHIP AFTER THE SHOOTING HAD LASTED LONGER, THERE COULD HAVE BEEN A BRAWL.

BUSH HAS JUST LANDED— HE'S IN DC!

FORTUNATELY, REAGAN RETURNED TO THE OVAL OFFICE TWO WEEKS LATER.

17

the duck's in charge, january 20

inauguration day

SPRING 1992. SOMALIA.

CIVIL WAR AND ANARCHY HAD CAUSED WIDESPREAD FAMINE. THE UNITED NATIONS TRIED TO DELIVER FOOD, BUT ARMED GANGS HIJACKED THE CARGO AND ASSAULTED AID WORKERS.

IN THE FALL, BOUTROS BOUTROS-GHALI, THE SECRETARY-GENERAL OF THE U.N., APPEALED TO ITS MEMBER NATIONS TO SEND MILITARY FORCES TO THE EAST AFRICAN COUNTRY.

THE TROOPS WON'T FIGHT, I ASSURE YOU.

THEY WOULD JUST STOP THE LOOTING SO FOOD CAN BE DISTRIBUTED.

United Nations

DECEMBER 4, 1992. FOUR WEEKS AFTER PRESIDENT GEORGE H. W. BUSH LOST RE-ELECTION TO BILL CLINTON.

LET'S GET THE MARINES, AIR FORCE, AND ARMY ON THIS.

AMERICAN FORCES WILL ASSIST IN OPERATION RESTORE HOPE.

SHOULD WE CONSULT WITH CONGRESS?

WHAT ABOUT CLINTON?

BUSH WOULD BE OUT OF OFFICE IN SIX WEEKS . . .

BUT AT THIS MOMENT, HE WAS STILL THE COMMANDER IN CHIEF.

EVEN THOUGH HE ASSURED THE COUNTRY THIS WAS A HUMANITARIAN, NOT MILITARY, MISSION, THE ACTION WAS CONTROVERSIAL.

WE WILL NOT TOLERATE ARMED GANGS.

EVEN THOUGH BUSH PROMISED THE TROOPS WOULD BE HOME BY INAUGURATION DAY, WHEN PRESIDENT CLINTON MOVED INTO THE OVAL OFFICE, THE TROOPS WERE STILL THERE.

CLINTON BELIEVED HE HAD NO CHOICE BUT TO CONTINUE BUSH'S POLICY.

AS THE MONTHS STAGGERED ON, ARMED SOMALIS ATTACKED AMERICAN SOLDIERS, MAKING FOOD DISTRIBUTION NEARLY IMPOSSIBLE.

BY FALL 1993, THE MISSION HAD CHANGED FROM HUMANITARIAN AID TO RESTORING A WORKING GOVERNMENT IN SOMALIA

A GOAL NO ONE IN THE CLINTON ADMINISTRATION HAD SIGNED ON FOR.

IN OCTOBER, A FORAY THAT WAS SUPPOSED TO BE A QUICK ARREST OF TWO ENEMY LEADERS TURNED INTO A FIFTEEN-HOUR MILITARY BATTLE.

ONE AMERICAN PILOT WAS CAPTURED, EIGHTEEN SOLDIERS WERE MURDERED, AND ANOTHER EIGHTY-FOUR WERE WOUNDED. HUNDREDS, POSSIBLY THOUSANDS, OF SOMALIS WERE KILLED.

IF CLINTON WITHDREW AMERICAN FORCES, HIS CRITICS WOULD CHARGE HIM AS WEAK.

BUT IF HE SENT MORE TROOPS, THEY WOULD PROBABLY DIE BEFORE GETTING TO DISTRIBUTE FOOD.

HE FACED A DILEMMA NOT OF HIS OWN MAKING.

Meanwhile, back in 1787 (and 1933) . . .

AFTER CONSIDERABLE DEBATE AND UNCERTAINTY . . .

THE EXECUTIVE POWER SHALL BE VESTED IN A PRESIDENT OF THE UNITED STATES OF AMERICA.

HE SHALL HOLD HIS OFFICE DURING THE TERM OF FOUR YEARS.

BUT THE FRAMERS DIDN'T SPECIFY EXACTLY WHEN THE TERM WOULD BEGIN OR END.

MY FIRST INAUGURATION WAS ON APRIL 30, 1789, BUT MY SECOND WAS ON MARCH 4, 1793.

NOT VERY CONSISTENT, ARE WE?

THE FIRST CONGRESS TO MEET UNDER THE NEW CONSTITUTION CONVENED ON MARCH 4, 1789, WHICH WAS ESTABLISHED AS THE STARTING POINT FOR MEASURING ALL TERMS OF OFFICE. THIS LASTED FOR 139 YEARS.

BUT IN 1932, THE WORLD WAS IN THE MIDST OF THE GREAT DEPRESSION; AND HERBERT HOOVER, A TERRIBLY UNPOPULAR PRESIDENT, WAS RUNNING FOR A SECOND TERM.

RE-ELECT HOOVER

IF A NEW PRESIDENT IS TO REPLACE HOOVER, HE'LL HAVE TO WAIT UNTIL MARCH 4 OF NEXT YEAR TO GET TO WORK.

WE CAN'T HAVE USELESS PRESIDENTS HANGING AROUND FOR THAT LONG!

SO, ON MARCH 2, 1932, CONGRESS PROPOSED MOVING INAUGURATION DAY TO JANUARY 20, BEGINNING IN 1937.

IT WILL BE THE 20TH AMENDMENT!

JANUARY 20

IT TOOK ONLY THIRTEEN MONTHS FOR THE MINIMUM THIRTY-SIX STATES TO RATIFY IT.

SO, WHAT'S THE BIG PROBLEM?

THE 20TH AMENDMENT REDUCED THE PERIOD BETWEEN THE PRESIDENT'S ELECTION AND INAUGURATION FROM FOUR MONTHS TO LESS THAN THREE.

BUT THAT STILL LEAVES A LOT OF TIME FOR DEPARTING PRESIDENTS (OFTEN CALLED *"LAME DUCKS"*) TO CAUSE TROUBLE FOR THEIR SUCCESSORS.

This term comes from the 18th century, when English people called businessmen who couldn't pay off their debts "lame ducks" because they waddled away. In the early 20th century, an American magazine referred to losing candidates that way because their wings had been clipped.

A LAME DUCK MIGHT MAKE A MONUMENTAL DECISION THAT SHOULD INSTEAD HAVE BEEN MADE BY THE PERSON WHO WOULD HAVE TO IMPLEMENT IT.

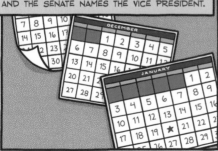

THE GAP BETWEEN ELECTIONS AND INAUGURATION DAY IS LINKED TO THE ELECTORAL COLLEGE.

IF A MAJORITY OF THAT GROUP CAN'T AGREE ON A WINNER, THEN THE HOUSE OF REPRESENTATIVES PICKS THE PRESIDENT FROM THE TOP THREE ELECTORAL VOTE-GETTERS, AND THE SENATE NAMES THE VICE PRESIDENT.

BUT, SINCE SOME REPRESENTATIVES UNDOUBTEDLY LOST THEIR SEATS IN THE ELECTION, IT'S THE INCOMING CONGRESSPEOPLE WHO ARE ASSIGNED THE JOB . . .

AND THEY AREN'T SWORN IN UNTIL THE FIRST MONDAY IN JANUARY!

THERE ARE OTHER WAYS . . .

ALL STATES INAUGURATE GOVERNORS MORE QUICKLY THAN THE NATIONAL GOVERNMENT DOES PRESIDENTS.

ALASKA AND HAWAII HOLD INAUGURATIONS IN EARLY DECEMBER!

NEW YORK INAUGURATES ON NEW YEAR'S DAY!

NO OTHER COUNTRY RELIES ON AN ELECTORAL COLLEGE, SO NO OTHER COUNTRY WAITS MONTHS BETWEEN SELECTING A NEW LEADER AND LETTING THAT PERSON LEAD.

IN FRANCE, THE PRESIDENT TAKES OFFICE WITHIN TEN DAYS OF THE ELECTION.

IN ENGLAND, PRIME MINISTERS TAKE OFFICE THE DAY AFTER THEY'RE ELECTED!

IF INAUGURATION DAY OCCURRED SHORTLY AFTER ELECTION DAY, THE AMERICAN PEOPLE WOULD BE LED BY THE PERSON THEY'VE ELECTED TO OFFICE RATHER THAN BY A LAME DUCK.

BUT BECAUSE THE INAUGURATION DATE IS INSCRIBED IN THE CONSTITUTION, IT WOULD REQUIRE AN AMENDMENT TO CHANGE.

UNTIL THE ELECTORAL COLLEGE IS ELIMINATED (WHICH WOULD ALSO REQUIRE AN AMENDMENT) INAUGURATION DAY HAS TO BE POSTPONED IN CASE THE RESULT ON ELECTION DAY IS NOT DECISIVE.

STUCK BY LAME DUCKS

Seven states seceded from the Union after Abraham Lincoln was elected but before he was inaugurated. The Civil War began a month after Lincoln was sworn in.

The international economy nearly collapsed after Barack Obama was elected but before he was inaugurated.

NEXT!

Probably the most dramatic
example of one leader immediately
replacing another was the defeat of
Prime Minister Winston Churchill
in the British election of July 1945.

He had heroically led World War II efforts,
but a majority of Brits was not confident
he would be a great peacetime leader.

They replaced him with Clement Attlee
of the opposition Labour Party two
months after Germany surrendered in
Europe but before the war ended in Asia.

Churchill was in Potsdam, Germany
at a conference that included U.S.
President Harry S. Truman and Prime
Minister Joseph Stalin of the Soviet
Union. They were discussing the shape
of the postwar world, including how to
end the war against Japan. Attlee flew
to Potsdam and took over the chair in
which Churchill had been sitting.

Churchill returned
to London.

FOLLOWING THE TRAGEDY IN SOMALIA IN OCTOBER 1993, CLINTON SENT MORE MARINES AND ARMORED TANKS TO SOMALIA, NOT TO FIGHT BUT TO SUPPORT THE WITHDRAWAL OF SOLDIERS ALREADY THERE.

THEY NEGOTIATED THE RELEASE OF THE CAPTURED PILOT AND ALMOST ALL AMERICAN TROOPS LEFT THE COUNTRY BY THE END OF MARCH 1994.

OPERATION RESTORE HOPE SAVED THOUSANDS OF SOMALIS FROM STARVATION BUT DID NOT ESTABLISH A WORKING GOVERNMENT.

THE EVENTS REMAINED A BLACK MARK ON BILL CLINTON'S PRESIDENCY.

★ PART VII: ★
emergency! emergency!

The Constitution can trip us up at the worst possible time: when we are involved in **wars** of various sorts.

In these situations, the victims of the Constitution's fault lines aren't members of Congress or the president; they're ordinary citizens, possibly **you**.

Did you know that there are limitations on what you can **say** during wartime?

And the government can restrict your **freedom** of movement during an **epidemic**!

18

at war

emergency powers

BY FEBRUARY 1917, WORLD WAR I HAD BEEN RAGING IN EUROPE AND THE MIDDLE EAST FOR TWO AND A HALF YEARS.

BUT MOST AMERICANS HAD NO INTEREST IN ENTERING THE WAR. THE ISSUES BEING FOUGHT OVER SEEMED CONFINED TO EUROPE, AND IT WAS RUMORED THAT BATTLEFIELD CONDITIONS WERE DREADFUL.

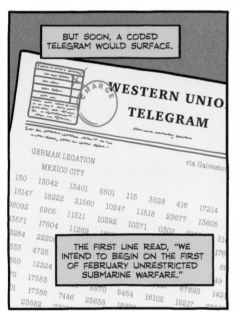

BUT SOON, A CODED TELEGRAM WOULD SURFACE.

WESTERN UNION TELEGRAM

GERMAN LEGATION
MEXICO CITY
via Galveston

THE FIRST LINE READ, "WE INTEND TO BEGIN ON THE FIRST OF FEBRUARY UNRESTRICTED SUBMARINE WARFARE."

DESPITE HAVING RUN A RE-ELECTION CAMPAIGN WITH THE SLOGAN "HE KEPT US OUT OF WAR," PRESIDENT WOODROW WILSON ASKED CONGRESS TO DECLARE WAR ON THE CENTRAL POWERS.

THE WORLD MUST BE MADE SAFE FOR DEMOCRACY.

CONGRESS AGREED.

Members adopted a resolution to go to war and passed several related laws.

The **Selective Service Act** required men in their twenties to register for the draft.

The **Espionage Act of 1917** made it criminal to obstruct the draft and to send unpatriotic materials through the mail.

The **Sedition Act of 1918** declared it a federal offense to use "disloyal, profane, scurrilous, or abusive language" about the Constitution or the American government, flag, or military uniform.

MOST AMERICANS QUICKLY CAUGHT WAR FEVER.

PATRIOTISM WASN'T MERELY IMPORTANT . . .

I WANT **YOU** FOR U.S. ARMY

SUPPORT UR BOYS!

VOLUNTEER TO WORK ON THE HOME FRONT!

IT WAS A POLITICAL AND SOCIAL IMPERATIVE.

HOWEVER, SOME PEOPLE CONTINUED TO OPPOSE AMERICA'S INVOLVEMENT IN THE GREAT WAR. ONE SUCH PERSON WAS EUGENE V. DEBS.

WHEN HE WAS FOURTEEN, DEBS DROPPED OUT OF SCHOOL TO WORK ON THE RAILROADS.

THE OWNERS AMASS FORTUNES, WHILE THE LABORERS REMAIN IMPOVERISHED. THAT'S NOT RIGHT!

HE ORGANIZED STRIKES AGAINST MANAGEMENT TO DEMAND HIGHER PAY.

WE DEMAND FAIR WAGES

New York New Haven and H

OVER TIME, HE JOINED AND THEN LED THE SOCIALIST PARTY OF AMERICA.

SOCIALISTS ARGUED THAT THERE SHOULD BE NO PRIVATE OWNERSHIP OF BUSINESSES OR PROPERTY.

EVERYTHING SHOULD BE SHARED!

IN 1912, DEBS RAN FOR PRESIDENT UNDER THE SOCIALIST BANNER. MORE THAN 900,000 PEOPLE VOTED FOR HIM.

VOTE FOR DEBS

WARS ARE LIKE RAILROADS. THEY ARE UNDERTAKEN TO BENEFIT THE WEALTHY, BUT ARE BUILT AND OPERATED BY THE DOWNTRODDEN!

DEBS FOR PRESIDENT

CANTON, OHIO.

JUNE 1918. DAYS AFTER NEARLY 10,000 AMERICAN SOLDIERS WERE KILLED AT A BATTLE SITE IN FRANCE.

VOTE FOR DEBS

RULERS HAVE ALWAYS TAUGHT AND TRAINED YOU TO BELIEVE IT TO BE YOUR PATRIOTIC DUTY TO GO TO WAR AND TO HAVE YOURSELVES SLAUGHTERED AT THEIR COMMAND.
BUT IN ALL THE HISTORY OF THE WORLD, YOU, THE PEOPLE, HAVE NEVER HAD A VOICE IN DECLARING WAR.

DEBS UNDERSTOOD THAT THE GOVERNMENT MIGHT CONSIDER HIS SPEECH DISLOYAL, AND HE WAS CAREFUL NOT TO URGE THE CROWD DIRECTLY TO REBEL OR RESIST CONSCRIPTION.

HE DID, HOWEVER, PRAISE THREE PEOPLE WHO HAD BEEN JAILED FOR OBSTRUCTING THE DRAFT.

FURTHERMORE, THE SOCIALIST PARTY HAD RECENTLY ADOPTED A RESOLUTION CALLING FOR "CONTINUOUS, ACTIVE, AND PUBLIC OPPOSITION TO THE WAR, THROUGH DEMONSTRATIONS, MASS PETITIONS, AND ALL OTHER MEANS WITHIN OUR POWER."

FEDERAL AGENTS, WHO HAD BEEN SHADOWING DEBS, WROTE DOWN HIS WORDS.

DEBS FOR PRESIDENT

DEBS WAS ARRESTED, TRIED, AND CONVICTED OF VIOLATING THE ESPIONAGE ACT OF 1917.

HE WAS SENTENCED TO TEN YEARS IN PRISON.

DEBS'S LAWYERS APPEALED TO THE SUPREME COURT.

HE HAD A RIGHT TO FREE SPEECH!

IN ANY CASE, HE HADN'T ADVISED ANYONE TO DESERT OR RESIST CONSCRIPTION.

WRITING FOR A UNANIMOUS COURT, JUSTICE OLIVER WENDELL HOLMES, JR. DISAGREED.

EVEN THOUGH DEBS DID NOT EXPLICITLY TELL HIS LISTENERS TO AVOID THE DRAFT, THAT WAS THE BASIC IDEA OF HIS TALK.

HE CREATED A CLEAR AND PRESENT DANGER TO A COUNTRY AT WAR.

WHEN A NATION IS AT WAR, MANY THINGS THAT MIGHT BE SAID IN TIME OF PEACE ARE SUCH A HINDRANCE TO ITS EFFORT THAT THEIR UTTERANCES WILL NOT BE ENDURED SO LONG AS MEN FIGHT.

DEBS REMAINED IMPRISONED.

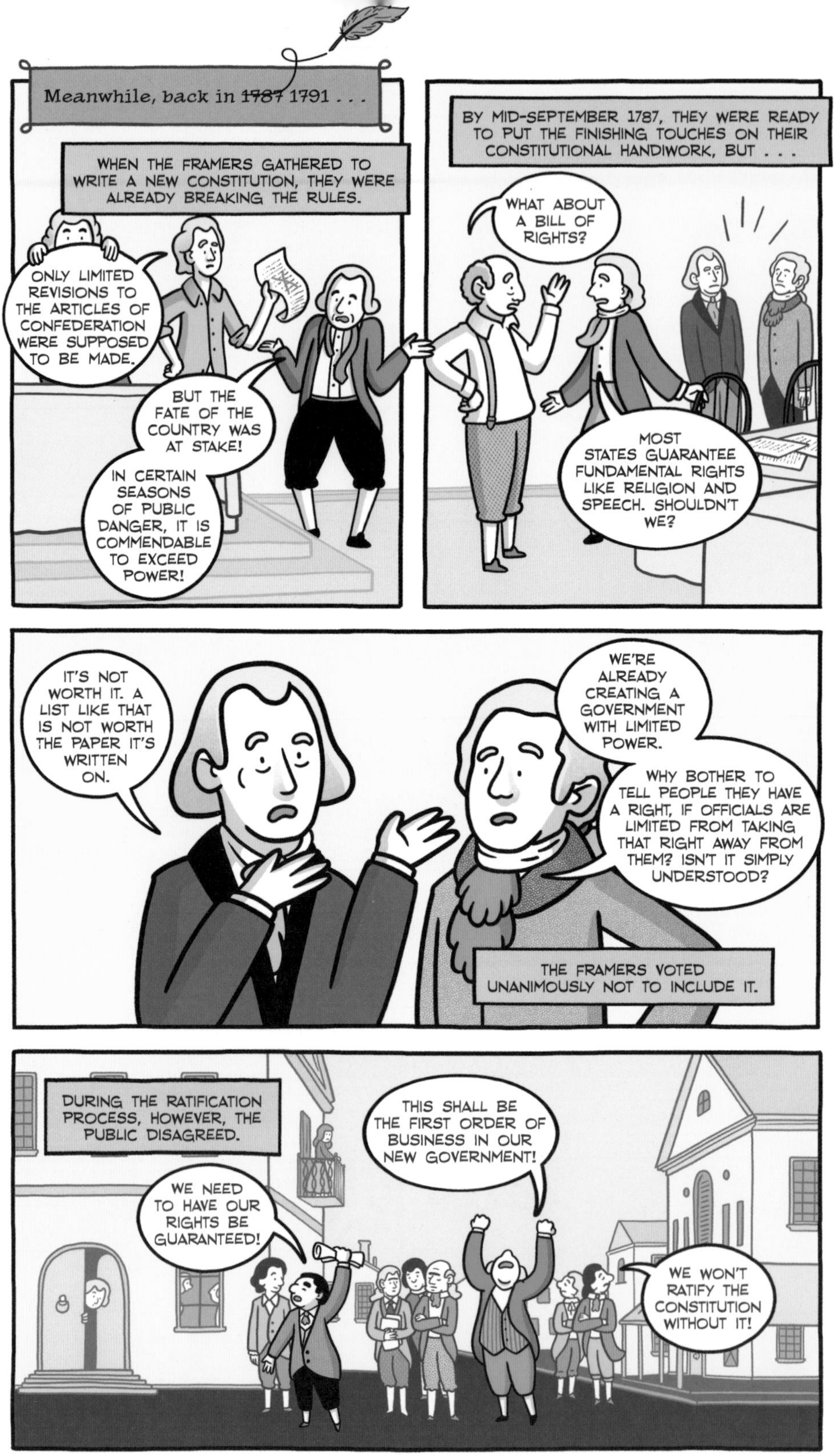
Meanwhile, back in ~~1787~~ 1791 . . .
WHEN THE FRAMERS GATHERED TO WRITE A NEW CONSTITUTION, THEY WERE ALREADY BREAKING THE RULES.
ONLY LIMITED REVISIONS TO THE ARTICLES OF CONFEDERATION WERE SUPPOSED TO BE MADE.
BUT THE FATE OF THE COUNTRY WAS AT STAKE!
IN CERTAIN SEASONS OF PUBLIC DANGER, IT IS COMMENDABLE TO EXCEED POWER!
BY MID-SEPTEMBER 1787, THEY WERE READY TO PUT THE FINISHING TOUCHES ON THEIR CONSTITUTIONAL HANDIWORK, BUT . . .
WHAT ABOUT A BILL OF RIGHTS?
MOST STATES GUARANTEE FUNDAMENTAL RIGHTS LIKE RELIGION AND SPEECH. SHOULDN'T WE?
IT'S NOT WORTH IT. A LIST LIKE THAT IS NOT WORTH THE PAPER IT'S WRITTEN ON.
WE'RE ALREADY CREATING A GOVERNMENT WITH LIMITED POWER.
WHY BOTHER TO TELL PEOPLE THEY HAVE A RIGHT, IF OFFICIALS ARE LIMITED FROM TAKING THAT RIGHT AWAY FROM THEM? ISN'T IT SIMPLY UNDERSTOOD?
THE FRAMERS VOTED UNANIMOUSLY NOT TO INCLUDE IT.
DURING THE RATIFICATION PROCESS, HOWEVER, THE PUBLIC DISAGREED.
WE NEED TO HAVE OUR RIGHTS BE GUARANTEED!
THIS SHALL BE THE FIRST ORDER OF BUSINESS IN OUR NEW GOVERNMENT!
WE WON'T RATIFY THE CONSTITUTION WITHOUT IT!

MADISON WAS CONVINCED. AFTER HE WAS ELECTED A REPRESENTATIVE FROM VIRGINIA IN THE FIRST U.S. CONGRESS, HE BECAME THE CHIEF DRAFTSMAN OF THE BILL OF RIGHTS.

ORIGINALLY, TWELVE AMENDMENTS WERE SUBMITTED TO THE STATES FOR RATIFICATION.

ONLY AMENDMENTS THREE THROUGH TWELVE WERE RATIFIED BY 1791.

WHAT TURNED INTO THE 1ST AMENDMENT (ORIGINALLY IT WAS THE 3RD) OPENS POWERFULLY AND WITHOUT COMPROMISE.

CONGRESS SHALL MAKE NO LAW ABRIDGING THE FREEDOM OF SPEECH.

IF THAT'S THE CASE, HOW COULD CONGRESS PASS THE ESPIONAGE ACT OF 1917?

THE FRAMERS DISOBEYED RULES, AND THE COUNTRY WAS FOUNDED ON A REVOLUTION, AFTER ALL. PERHAPS FUTURE MEMBERS OF CONGRESS BELIEVED THEY COULD DISOBEY THE CONSTITUTION'S RULES, AS WELL?

IN 1798 (JUST SEVEN YEARS AFTER THE BILL OF RIGHTS WAS ADOPTED), CONGRESS PASSED A SEDITION ACT WHILE AMERICA WAS INVOLVED IN A "QUASI-WAR" OF NAVAL INCIDENTS AGAINST FRANCE.

ALL I DID WAS WRITE THAT I WISHED PRESIDENT JOHN ADAMS WOULD GET WALLOPED WITH A CANNONBALL IN THE REAR. SO MUCH FOR FREE SPEECH!

LEADERS AT THE TIME RESPONDED THAT THE CONSTITUTION ALLOWED CONGRESS TO BAR SEDITION, AS IT WAS SEEN AS A THREAT TO THE "DOMESTIC TRANQUILITY" PROMISED IN THE PREAMBLE.

BUT THOMAS JEFFERSON BELIEVED THE ACT WAS UNCONSTITUTIONAL. WHEN HE BECAME PRESIDENT, HE PARDONED THOSE WHO REMAINED IN PRISON.

SO WHAT'S THE BIG DEAL?

Do we lose our rights when the president and Congress agree that our country is threatened?

THE CONSTITUTION BARELY ADDRESSES ITS "EMERGENCY POWERS," THE ADDITIONAL AUTHORITY THAT THE GOVERNMENT MIGHT ASSUME DURING A TIME OF CRISIS.

BUT APPARENTLY, WHAT I THOUGHT WAS FREEDOM OF SPEECH, THE U.S. GOVERNMENT THOUGHT WAS UNLAWFUL.

SIMILAR CONCERNS ABOUT NATIONAL SECURITY AROSE WHEN AMERICA ENTERED WORLD WAR II IN 1941. TWO MONTHS AFTER JAPANESE AIRCRAFT BOMBED PEARL HARBOR, A U.S. MILITARY BASE IN HAWAII, PRESIDENT FRANKLIN D. ROOSEVELT BANNED ALL AMERICANS OF JAPANESE ANCESTRY FROM LIVING IN A LARGE SECTION OF THE WESTERN U.S.

I FEAR THEY WILL BE MORE LOYAL TO THE COUNTRY OF THEIR FOREFATHERS THAN TO THE COUNTRY IN WHICH THEY LIVE.

THE MILITARY ROUNDED UP MORE THAN 110,000 PEOPLE OF JAPANESE ANCESTRY AND CONFINED THEM IN INTERNMENT CAMPS SO MISERABLE THAT JUSTICE OWEN ROBERTS CALLED THEM CONCENTRATION CAMPS.

ONE JAPANESE AMERICAN, *FRED KOREMATSU*, REFUSED TO FOLLOW ORDERS. HE APPEALED TO THE SUPREME COURT, BUT A MAJORITY RULED AGAINST HIM.

APPARENTLY, DURING WARTIME, IT WAS MORE IMPORTANT TO PREVENT POSSIBLE THREATS TO NATIONAL SECURITY THAN TO ALLOW INDIVIDUALS THEIR RIGHT TO FREEDOM.

The Framers defined danger as being under attack.
Today, we understands that peril can take many forms:
technological, medical, biological, even environmental.

How much does the Constitution control the decisions
the government can make when we face a crisis?

And what other ways could such crises be handled?

STATES OFTEN DECLARE A STATE OF EMERGENCY AFTER A NATURAL DISASTER OR DURING SIGNIFICANT CIVIC UNREST. THIS ALLOWS FOR TEMPORARILY SUSPENDING CITIZENS' ORDINARY RIGHTS, LIKE IMPOSING A CURFEW, FOR EXAMPLE.

BUT BY THE MID-20TH CENTURY, COURTS AGREED THAT THERE IS NO SUCH THING AS SEDITION OR TREASON AGAINST A STATE, THE WAY THERE IS AGAINST A COUNTRY.

IN OTHER COUNTRIES, WAR IS THE FUNDAMENTAL STRESS TEST FOR ANY DEMOCRATIC CONSTITUTION.

LEADERS ARE TEMPTED TO TAKE CONTROL AND SHUT THE PEOPLE OUT OF THE PROCESS. CITIZENS CLAMOR TO BE PROTECTED FROM ENEMIES, YET THEY ALSO WANT THEIR FREEDOMS PROTECTED.

THE CONSTITUTIONS OF 178 COUNTRIES ADDRESS EMERGENCY POWERS, WHICH GIVE THE HEAD OF STATE THE ABILITY TO SUSPEND ALL OR SOME OF THE PEOPLE'S RIGHTS.

EUROPEAN COURT OF HUMAN
COUR EUROPEENNE DES DROITS DE I

FORTY-SIX EUROPEAN COUNTRIES HAVE SIGNED ON TO THE EUROPEAN CONVENTION ON HUMAN RIGHTS, WHICH PROTECTS FUNDAMENTAL RIGHTS AND POLITICAL FREEDOMS IN MORE DETAIL THAN THE BILL OF RIGHTS.

IN THE U.S., THE CONSTITUTION NEEDS TO BE AMENDED TO DEFINE MORE CLEARLY WHEN THE COUNTRY FACES A TRUE EMERGENCY AND WHAT THE GOVERNMENT CAN AND CANNOT DO.

FRED KOREMATSU DAY

In 1988, Congress passed a Civil Liberties Act, which President Ronald Reagan signed into law.

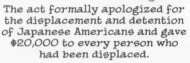

The act formally apologized for the displacement and detention of Japanese Americans and gave $20,000 to every person who had been displaced.

President Bill Clinton bestowed the Presidential Medal of Freedom on Korematsu in 1998.

And in 2011, California established January 30 as the annual Fred Korematsu Day of Civil Liberties and the Constitution.

Hawaii, Virginia, and Florida have since passed legislative bills recognizing Fred Korematsu Day, and multiple other states have submitted resolutions and bills to do the same.

STAND UP FOR WHAT IS RIGHT

It is the first day in U.S. history to be named after an Asian American.

JUSTICE HOLMES ADMITTED THAT HE HAD A HARD TIME DECIDING THE CASE OF EUGENE DEBS.

I COULD NOT SEE THE WISDOM OF PRESSING THE CASES . . .

ESPECIALLY WHEN THE FIGHTING WAS OVER.

THE GREAT WAR ENDED ON NOVEMBER 11, 1918. THE DECISION IN DEBS V. UNITED STATES WAS HANDED DOWN IN 1919.

DEBS APPEALED TO PRESIDENT WILSON.

THIS MAN WAS A *TRAITOR* TO HIS COUNTRY.

HE WILL NEVER BE PARDONED DURING MY ADMINISTRATION.

IN 1920, DEBS RAN FOR THE PRESIDENCY FOR THE FIFTH TIME, ALTHOUGH THIS WAS DURING THE TIME HE WAS IMPRISONED.

DEMOCRATIC	REPUBLICAN	SOCIALIST	FARMER-L
◯	◯	◯	◯
For President JAMES M. COX	For President WARREN G. HARDING	For President PRISONER 9653	For Preside PARLEY CHRISTENS
For Vice President FRANKLIN D. ROOSEVELT	For Vice President CALVIN COOLIDGE	For Vice President SEYMOUR	For Vice President MILLIA AYES
or Electors f President and Vice resident	For Electors of President and Vice President	Electors of President and Vice	For Electors of President

AGAIN, MORE THAN 900,000 PEOPLE VOTED FOR HIM.

THE WINNER OF THAT ELECTION WAS WARREN G. HARDING. ON CHRISTMAS DAY IN 1921, HE FREED DEBS AND INVITED HIM TO THE WHITE HOUSE.

I HAVE HEARD SO DAMNED MUCH ABOUT YOU, MR. DEBS, THAT NOW I AM VERY GLAD TO MEET YOU PERSONALLY.

19

at war with bugs

habeas corpus

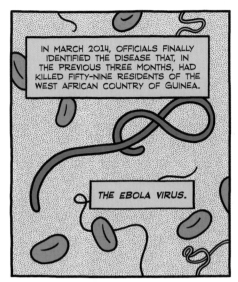

IN MARCH 2014, OFFICIALS FINALLY IDENTIFIED THE DISEASE THAT, IN THE PREVIOUS THREE MONTHS, HAD KILLED FIFTY-NINE RESIDENTS OF THE WEST AFRICAN COUNTRY OF GUINEA.

THE EBOLA VIRUS.

AN ILLNESS THAT CAN LEAP FROM ANIMAL TO HUMAN, EBOLA WAS CROSSING BORDERS AND SPREADING RAPIDLY. MANY WERE CONCERNED THAT IT WOULD GO GLOBAL.

IN OCTOBER 2014, TWO NURSES IN TEXAS WHO HAD CARED FOR AN EBOLA PATIENT BECAME INFECTED.

WE MUST DECLARE EBOLA A NATIONAL SECURITY PRIORITY.

PRESIDENT BARACK OBAMA

THE CENTERS FOR DISEASE CONTROL AND PREVENTION

SOME MEMBERS OF CONGRESS CALLED FOR A TRAVEL BAN BETWEEN THE U.S. AND WEST AFRICA, AND THE GOVERNORS OF NEW YORK, NEW JERSEY, AND ILLINOIS ISSUED A MANDATE:

ALL HEALTHCARE WORKERS WHO HAD CONTACT WITH EBOLA PATIENTS IN WEST AFRICA MUST BE QUARANTINED FOR TWENTY-ONE DAYS UPON ENTERING THE U.S.

THE SAME DAY ON WHICH THE MANDATES WERE ENACTED, KACI HICKOX, A SPECIALIST IN TROPICAL NURSING, WAS RETURNING TO THE U.S. AFTER CARING FOR EBOLA PATIENTS IN SIERRA LEONE.

FOLLOWING A TWO-DAY RETURN TRIP, SHE LANDED IN NEWARK, NEW JERSEY.

YOU'RE TRAVELING FROM WHERE??

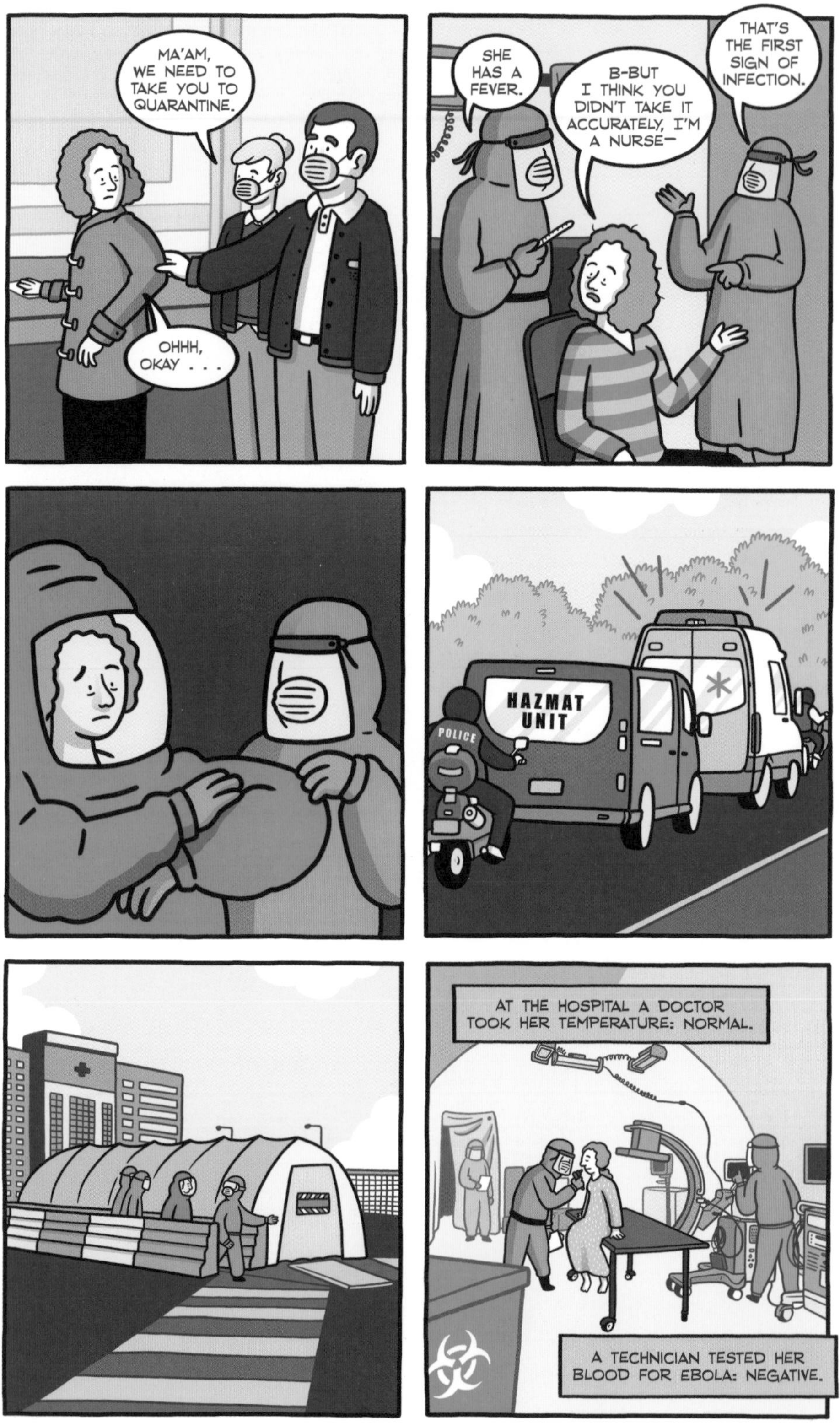
MA'AM, WE NEED TO TAKE YOU TO QUARANTINE.
OHHH, OKAY . . .
SHE HAS A FEVER.
B-BUT I THINK YOU DIDN'T TAKE IT ACCURATELY, I'M A NURSE—
THAT'S THE FIRST SIGN OF INFECTION.
POLICE
HAZMAT UNIT
AT THE HOSPITAL A DOCTOR TOOK HER TEMPERATURE: NORMAL.
A TECHNICIAN TESTED HER BLOOD FOR EBOLA: NEGATIVE.

DR. THOMAS FRIEDEN, DIRECTOR OF THE CENTERS FOR DISEASE CONTROL AND PREVENTION (CDC)

IT'S NOT NECESSARY TO QUARANTINE HICKOX.

SHE SIMPLY NEEDS TO CHECK HER TEMPERATURE TWICE A DAY FOR TWENTY-ONE DAYS.

NEW JERSEY GOVERNOR CHRIS CHRISTIE

HICKOX MUST REMAIN ISOLATED!

AFTER TWO DAYS OF STAYING IN AN UNHEATED TENT, HICKOX HIRED A CIVIL RIGHTS LAWYER TO ARGUE HER CASE AGAINST THE STATE OF NEW JERSEY.

I FEEL LIKE MY BASIC HUMAN RIGHTS HAVE BEEN VIOLATED.

IT'S NOT CONSTITUTIONALLY JUST.

THE NEXT DAY, AFTER AGAIN TESTING NEGATIVE, CHRISTIE ALLOWED FOR HICKOX'S RELEASE—ON THE CONDITION THAT SHE PROCEED DIRECTLY TO HER HOME IN MAINE.

BUT PAUL LEPAGE, MAINE'S GOVERNOR, INSISTED THAT SHE REMAIN THERE FOR THREE MORE DAYS AND THEN FOLLOW THE CDC'S GUIDELINES.

I REMAIN APPALLED BY THESE HOME QUARANTINE POLICIES THAT HAVE BEEN FORCED UPON ME, EVEN THOUGH I AM IN PERFECTLY GOOD HEALTH.

I WILL GO TO COURT TO FIGHT FOR MY FREEDOM.

BUT LEPAGE TOOK HICKOX TO COURT TO ENFORCE THE QUARANTINE. SHE WAS CONFINED TO HER HOME, WITH STATE POLICE POSTED OUTSIDE.

Meanwhile, back in 1787 . . .

IN ADDITION TO FREEDOM OF SPEECH, WHAT OTHER RIGHTS NEED TO BE INCLUDED IN THE CONSTITUTION?

WELL, WITH ENGLAND WE HAD THE RIGHT OF *HABEAS CORPUS.*

PERHAPS THIS SHOULD BE INCLUDED?

LATIN FOR "THAT YOU HAVE THE BODY," HABEAS CORPUS IS A COURT ORDER THAT GUARANTEES AN IMPRISONED PERSON THE RIGHT TO PRODUCE THE *GREAT WRIT,* WHICH DIRECTS THE COURT TO EITHER EXPLAIN WHY THE GOVERNMENT HAS THE POWER TO HOLD THE PERSON IN JAIL, OR IF IT CANNOT, THEN TO RELEASE THEM.

UNJUSTIFIED IMPRISONMENT IS A FATAL EVIL!

SHOULD THERE BE EXCEPTIONS TO THIS?

REBELLION OR INVASION WOULD JUSTIFY SUSPENDING THIS RIGHT!

NEARING THE END OF THEIR WORK, THE FRAMERS AGREED TO INCORPORATE HABEAS CORPUS, WITH THIS EXCEPTION, INTO THE CONSTITUTION.

THE FIRST CONGRESS THEN PASSED A LAW GIVING U.S. COURTS THE POWER TO ISSUE WRITS, OR COURT ORDERS, TO ENFORCE THIS.

THE COURTS CAN DEMAND THAT THE GOVERNMENT JUSTIFY DETENTIONS AND, IF IT CANNOT, THEN DEMAND THE RELEASE OF THE PRISONER.

But how would this right be protected?

The 5th Amendment guarantees individuals the right to protect themselves through a legal process, such as by making their case in a court of law. (This is called due process). The 14th Amendment does the same in relation to state governments.

But in times of rebellion or invasion, the government does not necessarily have to follow these rules!

DURING TIMES OF CRISIS, THE WRIT OF HABEAS CORPUS CAN BE SUSPENDED, AND SUSPECTS CAN BE KEPT IN JAIL INDEFINITELY WITHOUT ANY EXPLANATION WHY.

UNDER A CIRCUMSTANCE LIKE THE CIVIL WAR, THE PUBLIC SAFETY MAY REQUIRE IT!

THAT'S WHY I SUSPENDED HABEAS CORPUS.

SO WHEN JOHN MERRYMAN, A FARMER AND MILITIAMAN FROM MARYLAND, WAS ACCUSED OF DESTROYING INFRASTRUCTURE TO PREVENT UNION SOLDIERS FORM DEFENDING WASHINGTON, DC, HE WAS ARRESTED AND IMPRISONED WITHOUT THE OPTION OF THE GREAT WRIT.

PRESIDENT LINCOLN ORDERED ME TO REJECT ALL WRIT UNTIL THE PRESENT UNHAPPY DIFFICULTIES ARE AT AN END!

MANY, FROM BOTH THE NORTH AND SOUTH, OBJECTED TO THIS SUSPENSION, SAYING THAT ONLY CONGRESS COULD TAKE THIS ACTION.

BUT THE CONSTITUTION ITSELF IS SILENT AS TO WHICH, OR WHO, IS TO EXERCISE THE POWER.

I THINK THE MAN WHOM, FOR THE TIME, THE PEOPLE HAVE, UNDER THE CONSTITUTION, MADE THE COMMANDER-IN-CHIEF OF THEIR ARMY AND NAVY, IS THE MAN WHO HOLDS THE POWER.

MERRYMAN'S CASE WENT TO A FEDERAL CIRCUIT COURT.

SUPREME COURT CHIEF JUSTICE ROGER B. TANEY WEIGHED IN.

I DO BELIEVE LINCOLN IS GRABBING A POWER WHICH HE DOES NOT POSSESS UNDER THE CONSTITUTION.

EVEN THE ENGLISH MONARCH CANNOT SUSPEND HABEAS CORPUS WITHOUT APPROVAL BY PARLIAMENT!

MANY AGREED.

BUT STILL OTHERS PRAISED LINCOLN FOR DOING WHAT WAS NECESSARY TO DEFEND THE UNION . . . AND CONSTITUTIONAL ORDER.

SO WHAT'S THE PROBLEM HERE?

Nowadays, we face many possible emergencies that didn't occur to the Framers.

NATURAL DISASTERS

CYBERTERRORISM

In frightening instances, we might need someone who can make fast, unquestioned decisions; but it's not clear who has the authority to do what.

THE HABEAS CORPUS CLAUSE LIMITS THE FEDERAL GOVERNMENT'S ABILITY TO SUSPEND IT TO CASES OF "REBELLION OR INVASION."

BUT CAN AN INFECTIOUS MICROBE BE CONSIDERED AN "INVASION," AND CAN THE PRESIDENT ORDER EVERYONE IN THE COUNTRY TO STAY HOME?

CONGRESS HAS AUTHORIZED THE PRESIDENT TO ISSUE AN EXECUTIVE ORDER IDENTIFYING PARTICULAR DISEASES AS "QUARANTINABLE."

THE CENTERS FOR DIS AND PREVEN

ATLANTA, GE

WITH THAT, U.S. LAW ALLOWS THE PRESIDENT TO ORDER THE APPREHENSION, DETENTION, OR CONDITIONAL RELEASE OF INDIVIDUALS FOR THE PURPOSE OF PREVENTING THE INTRODUCTION, TRANSMISSION, OR SPREAD OF SUCH COMMUNICABLE DISEASES.

IF THE PRESIDENT ISSUES THIS EXECUTIVE ORDER, THE CDC'S POWERS TO OVERSEE THESE PROCESSES KICK IN.

FURTHERMORE, THE CDC USES *THE COMMERCE CLAUSE* OF THE CONSTITUTION TO JUSTIFY CONGRESS'S ABILITY TO DELEGATE SUCH AUTHORITY.

ARTICLE I, SECTION 8 GIVES CONGRESS THE POWER TO REGULATE COMMERCE WITH FOREIGN NATIONS, AND AMONG THE SEVERAL STATES, AND WITH THE INDIAN TRIBES.

IN THE LATE 18TH CENTURY THIS HAD NOTHING TO DO WITH EMERGENCIES, BUT THE CDC ASSERTS THAT TRANSPORTING SICK PEOPLE IS NO DIFFERENT FROM TRANSPORTING WASHING MARCHINES, OR ANY OTHER PRODUCT THAT CROSSES BORDERS.

THE AUTHORITY TO ENFORCE QUARANTINE IS AMONG THE "POLICE POWERS" (THE PROTECTION OF THE PUBLIC HEALTH, SAFETY, AND WELFARE) THAT STATES COMMONLY CARRY OUT.

ROOM 236

NOTICE OF QUARANTINE

STATES CAN'T VIOLATE THE U.S. CONSTITUTION, BUT THEY ARE GIVEN WIDE LATITUDE IN DEFINING SUCH PROTECTION, ESPECIALLY IN CASES OF PUBLIC HEALTH EMERGENCIES.

LIKE IN 2001, WHEN SEVERAL CONGRESSMEN RECEIVED ENVELOPES IN THE MAIL THAT CONTAINED ANTHRAX, A POISONOUS POWDER.

4TH GRADE
GREENDALE SCHOOL
FRANKLIN PARK NJ 08852

SENATOR LEAHY
433 RUSSELL SENATE OFFICE
BUILDING
WASHINGTON DC 20510-4502

THE CDC ASKED LAWYERS AND HEALTH SPECIALISTS TO DRAFT A SET OF LAWS THAT STATE LEGISLATURES COULD ADOPT BEFORE ANOTHER THREAT LOOMED.

WE CAME UP WITH THE *MODEL STATE EMERGENCY HEALTH POWERS ACT.*

IT GAVE STATES ALLOWANCE TO DO THINGS LIKE COMMANDEER PRIVATE PROPERTY TO COPE WITH AN EMERGENCY AND DEFINE "PUBLIC HEALTH EMERGENCY" HOWEVER THEY LIKE.

AROUND FORTY STATES HAVE INTRODUCED THEIR OWN VERSIONS OF THE ACT.

229

BOTH LIBERALS AND CONSERVATIVES HAVE STRONGLY CRITICIZED THESE BROAD POWERS THAT STATES HAVE GIVEN THEMSELVES.

OFFICIALS COULD QUARANTINE WITH NO JUSTIFICATION, JUST LIKE WITH KACI HICKOX!

SUCH "MODEL" LAWS COULD TURN GOVERNORS INTO DICTATORS IF THEY PANIC!

AND WITH EACH STATE DEVELOPING ITS OWN LAWS, THE COUNTRY COULD BECOME A CRAZY QUILT OF PROCEDURES.

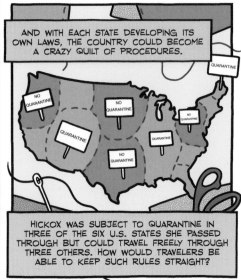

HICKOX WAS SUBJECT TO QUARANTINE IN THREE OF THE SIX U.S. STATES SHE PASSED THROUGH BUT COULD TRAVEL FREELY THROUGH THREE OTHERS. HOW WOULD TRAVELERS BE ABLE TO KEEP SUCH RULES STRAIGHT?

THERE MUST BE OTHER WAYS, RIGHT?

ALTHOUGH THEY CAN MAKE SUCH "MODEL" LAWS, STATES CANNOT SUSPEND DUE PROCESS AND ROUND PEOPLE UP IN TIMES OF EMERGENCY. BUT MOST STATES DO GIVE THEIR GOVERNORS THE POWER TO CALL OUT THE NATIONAL GUARD UNDER MANY MORE CIRCUMSTANCES THAN JUST REBELLION OR INVASION.

IN 2018, THE GOVERNORS OF TEXAS AND ARIZONA DEPLOYED TROOPS ALONG THE U.S.-MEXICO BORDER IN SUPPORT OF PRESIDENT DONALD TRUMP'S IMMIGRATION POLICIES.

IN 2016, FLORIDA'S GOVERNOR RICK SCOTT DECLARED A STATE OF EMERGENCY WHEN A MASS SHOOTING OCCURRED AT AN ORLANDO NIGHTCLUB.

AND IN 2019, WASHINGTON GOVERNOR JAY INSLEE DECLARED AN EMERGENCY BECAUSE OF A MEASLES OUTBREAK.

 Other countries have different approaches, too. The constitution of South Africa offers a modern model of emergency powers.

Only the national legislature, not the president or the courts, can declare a state of emergency.

Parliament can declare a state of emergency only when two conditions are met: the life of the nation is threatened and the declaration is necessary to restore peace and order.

The courts can still determine whether the emergency is valid and overrule Parliament's declaration and any emergency laws it passes.

The Constitution recognizes many kinds of emergencies, including "war, invasion, general insurrection, disorder, natural disaster, or other public emergency."

A declared state of emergency can last no more than twenty-one days. It can be extended by the lower house of Parliament, but only for three months at a time.

THE U.S. CONSTITUTION WOULD SERVE THE COUNTRY BETTER IF IT WERE AMENDED TO SPELL OUT MORE CLEARLY THE ACTIONS PARTICULAR FEDERAL OFFICIALS COULD TAKE IN TIMES OF CRISIS.

IN ADDITION, THE DEFINITION OF CRISIS NEEDS TO INCLUDE MORE THAN INVASION AND REBELLION.

SEVERAL DAYS AFTER LEPAGE TRIED TO CONFINE HICKOX TO HER HOME, THE LEGAL SYSTEM IN MAINE RULED IN HER FAVOR.

THE COURT IS FULLY AWARE OF THE MISCONCEPTIONS, MISINFORMATION, BAD SCIENCE, AND BAD INFORMATION BEING SPREAD FROM SHORE TO SHORE IN OUR COUNTRY WITH RESPECT TO EBOLA.

THE COURT IS FULLY AWARE THAT PEOPLE ARE ACTING OUT OF FEAR AND THAT THIS FEAR IS NOT ENTIRELY RATIONAL.

JUDGE LAVERDIERE

IT WAS A GOOD DAY.

MY THOUGHTS, PRAYERS, AND GRATITUDE ARE WITH MY PATIENTS IN WEST AFRICA.

I DON'T TRUST HER.

GOVERNOR PAUL LEPAGE

In early 2017, the CDC adopted rules that allow the federal government to impose national quarantines and prohibit travel from one state to another. In 2018, the Trump administration disbanded the Global Health Security Team, which was in charge of our country's response in case of a pandemic.

Authorities are likely to get into a free-for-all at the first uncertain sign of an epidemic.

20

we can change it, right?

amending the constitution

> Equality of rights under the law shall not be abridged by the United States or by any State on account of sex.

THIS IS THE **EQUAL RIGHTS AMENDMENT**.

THE **ERA** HAD PASSED IN THE HOUSE OF REPRESENTATIVES IN 1971 AND THEN IN THE SENATE IN 1972. BY 1979, THIRTY-FIVE STATES APPROVED IT.

THIS IS PHYLLIS SCHLAFLY. MOTHER, LAWYER, POLITICAL ACTIVIST.

I AM DEEPLY CONCERNED ABOUT THIS PROPOSED ERA. WITH SUPPORT FROM ONLY THREE MORE STATES, RADICAL FEMINISTS WILL ADD THIS AMENDMENT TO THE U.S. CONSTITUTION!

GIVING WOMEN ALL THE SAME RIGHTS AS MEN IS A DANGEROUS PROPOSITION, SCHLAFLY THOUGHT.

IF EQUALITY IS FORCED ON WOMEN, THEY'LL HAVE TO MARCH INTO BATTLE JUST LIKE MEN, SHARE BATHROOMS WITH MEN, AND ALLOW THEIR EX-HUSBANDS TO GET CUSTODY OF THEIR CHILDREN AND STOP PAYING ALIMONY!

GOVERNMENT-FUNDED CHILDCARE WILL ENCOURAGE WOMEN TO GO TO WORK AND PAY LESS ATTENTION TO THEIR FAMILIES, THE BOY AND GIRL SCOUTS WILL HAVE TO MERGE, AND BOTH ABORTIONS AND GAY RIGHTS WOULD BE LEGALIZED!

A WOMAN SHOULD HAVE THE RIGHT TO BE IN THE HOME AS A WIFE AND MOTHER!

SCHLAFLY'S OPPONENTS, LIKE THE *NATIONAL ORGANIZATION FOR WOMEN*, ARGUED THAT THE ERA WAS NECESSARY.

IT WILL GIVE WOMEN THE SAME PROTECTIONS UNDER THE LAW THAT WERE GRANTED TO FREED SLAVES BY THE 14TH AMENDMENT IN 1868.

ERA NOW

VOTE ERA

SUPPORT THE ERA

THE ERA HAD FIRST BEEN INTRODUCED INTO CONGRESS IN 1923 BUT SUBSEQUENTLY FELL INTO OBLIVION. IN THE 1970S, *NOW* HAD REVIVED IT.

BUT PEOPLE LIKE SCHLAFLY PREDICTED THAT THE ERA WOULD LEAVE WOMEN LESS PROTECTED BY THE MEN IN THEIR LIVES THAN THEY HAD BEEN BEFORE.

IN 1972, SCHLAFLY FORMED AN ORGANIZATION CALLED *STOP ERA*.

STOP ERA

SCHLAFLY HAD REASON TO BELIEVE THAT HER TACTICS WERE WORKING. SUPPORT FOR THE ERA IN THE STATES HAD SLOWED CONSIDERABLY, AND FIVE STATES HAD EVEN RESCINDED THEIR RATIFICATION.

PRESERVE US FROM A CONGRESSIONAL *JAM!*

VOTE AGAINST THE *ERA SHAM!*

BEGINNING IN 1918, CONGRESS HAD OFTEN PLACED SEVEN-YEAR TIME LIMITS ON THE RATIFICATION OF CONSTITUTIONAL AMENDMENTS.

THE LEGISLATION PROPOSING THE ERA WAS FILED IN 1971 AND PASSED IN 1972. PROPONENTS HAD UNTIL MARCH 22, 1979 TO ROUND UP THE THIRTY-EIGHT STATES NEEDED TO RATIFY IT. BUT . . .

WE ASK THAT CONGRESS EXTEND THE DEADLINE BY THREE YEARS TO GIVE US TIME TO PERSUADE THREE MORE STATES TO SIGN ON!

SCHLAFLY WAS INCENSED; HER OPPONENTS WERE RELENTLESS AND MIGHT SUCCEED.

BUT I ALSO KNOW I HAVE THE EASIER JOB AHEAD:

IT'S HARDER TO GET AN AMENDMENT ADOPTED THAN IT IS TO STOP ONE IN ITS TRACKS!

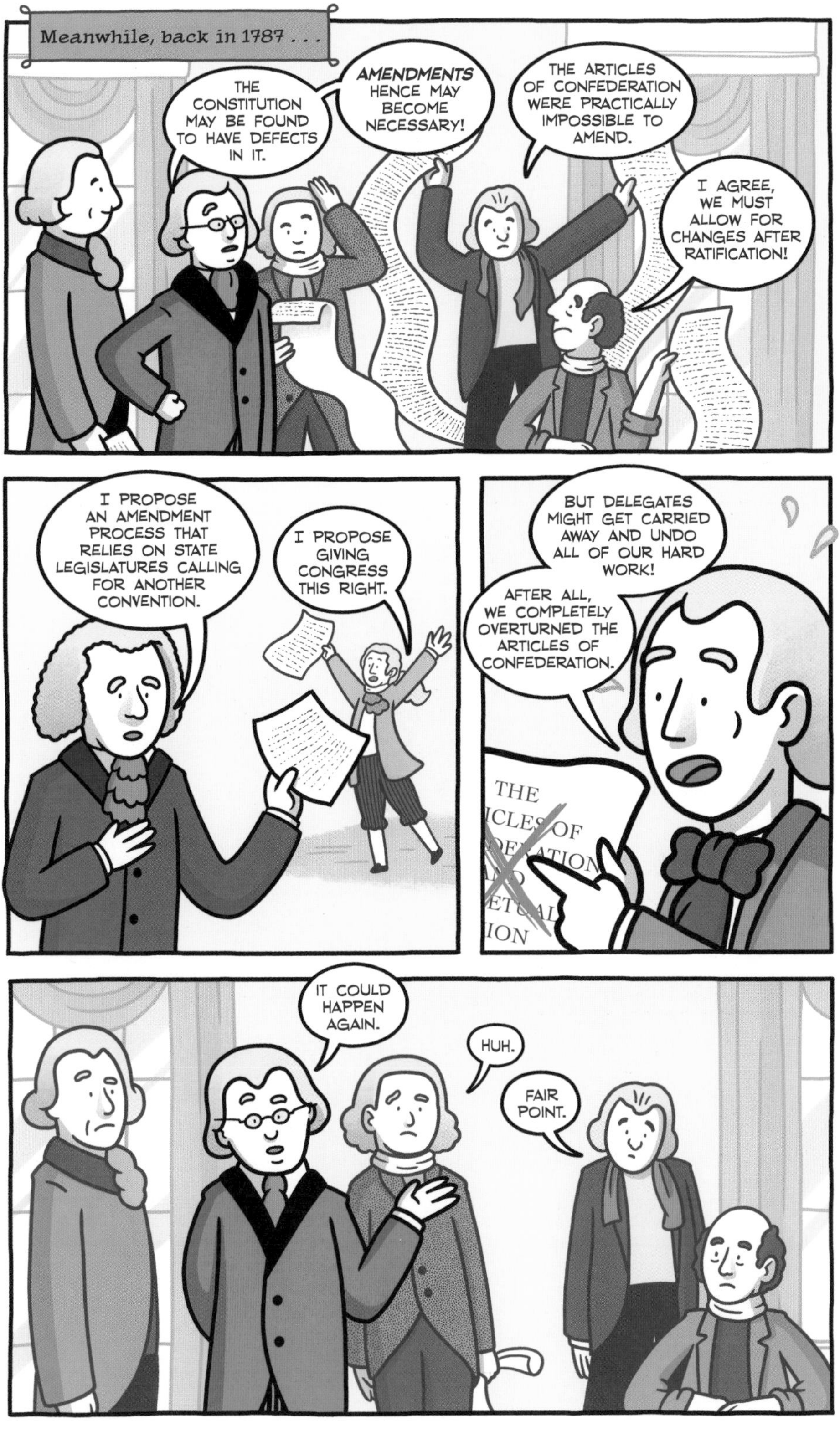
Meanwhile, back in 1787 . . .
THE CONSTITUTION MAY BE FOUND TO HAVE DEFECTS IN IT.
AMENDMENTS HENCE MAY BECOME NECESSARY!
THE ARTICLES OF CONFEDERATION WERE PRACTICALLY IMPOSSIBLE TO AMEND.
I AGREE, WE MUST ALLOW FOR CHANGES AFTER RATIFICATION!
I PROPOSE AN AMENDMENT PROCESS THAT RELIES ON STATE LEGISLATURES CALLING FOR ANOTHER CONVENTION.
I PROPOSE GIVING CONGRESS THIS RIGHT.
BUT DELEGATES MIGHT GET CARRIED AWAY AND UNDO ALL OF OUR HARD WORK!
AFTER ALL, WE COMPLETELY OVERTURNED THE ARTICLES OF CONFEDERATION.
THE
IT COULD HAPPEN AGAIN.
HUH.
FAIR POINT.

AFTER SOME DEBATE, THE FRAMERS MANAGED TO CONCOCT A MORE OR LESS HAPPY MEDIUM.

PROPOSALS FOR AMENDMENTS COULD COME UP IN TWO WAYS:

CONGRESS COULD PROPOSE AN AMENDMENT WHEN TWO-THIRDS OF BOTH HOUSES SEE THE NEED,

OR TWO-THIRDS OF STATES COULD PETITION FOR A SPECIAL CONVENTION.

BUT PROPOSING AMENDMENTS WAS ONLY HALF THE JOB. THE OTHER HALF IS *RATIFYING* THEM.

LET US RAISE THE ANTE WITH REQUIREMENTS FOR RATIFICATION!

AMENDMENTS WILL OFFICIALLY BE ADDED TO THE CONSTITUTION, OR CLAUSES DELETED FROM IT, ONLY AFTER THREE-QUARTERS OF ALL THE STATES APPROVE.

CONGRESS WILL DECIDE WHETHER THE APPROVAL COMES FROM THE STATES' LEGISLATURES OR SPECIAL STATE CONVENTIONS.

THIS COMPROMISE SATISFIED ALMOST ALL THE FRAMERS, BUT A CONTENTIOUS ISSUE REMAINED.

WHAT IF FREE STATES TRY TO ALTER THE CONSTITUTION TO HINDER SLAVERY?!

I PROPOSE THAT NO AMENDMENT ALLOW CONGRESS TO BAN THE INTERNATIONAL SLAVE TRADE BEFORE 1808.

IN ADDITION, THE SENATE WOULD ALWAYS BE COMPOSED OF TWO SENATORS PER STATE UNLESS EVERY STATE IN THE UNION AGREED TO A CHANGE.

I VIEW THIS AS AN EVIL!

BUT, I SUPPOSE, A NECESSARY ONE.

IT'S THE PRICE WE MUST PAY TO JUST GET A DANG CONSTITUTION ALREADY.

WELL, IT'S VERY DIFFICULT TO AMEND THE CONSTITUTION!

SINCE THE BILL OF RIGHTS WAS EASILY RATIFIED IN 1791, ONLY SEVENTEEN AMENDMENTS HAVE BEEN ADDED.

TO CHANGE THE CONSTITUTION, YOU HAVE TO PLAY OFFENSE, AND THE RULES ARE COMPLICATED.

So far, all amendments have been proposed by Congress, which involves getting support from two-thirds of the members of both the House and Senate.

This is no small task! To propose an amendment by this method, you need 67 out of 100 senators plus 288 of the 435 House members (assuming everyone is present and voting).

OR

If that seems too difficult, you could try to get two-thirds of the states to sign petitions and force Congress to call a new Constitutional Convention.

The hitch is that a majority of both houses of thirty-four of the fifty states have to agree. This method never occurred, although what turned into the 17th Amendment came close.

But holding a convention is no guarantee that any particular proposal will even be considered. Once it's called, the convention can do whatever it wants . . . or nothing at all.

Moreover, given that all a convention can do is propose amendments, one-quarter of states plus one more (a total of thirteen) could torpedo efforts at change.

Let's say that, by one route or another, your amendment is officially under consideration.

Now it must be **ratified**.
There are two ways to do that.

Most likely you'll need the approval of both houses of the legislature in three-quarters of the states. That amounts to at least seventy-five chambers in at least thirty-eight states.

(This assumes that one of the states is Nebraska, with its unicameral house. Should Nebraska not approve of an amendment, then you will need a total of seventy-six houses in the same thirty-eight states to win.)

OR

Congress can designate state ratifying conventions as the method by which the amendment is voted on. Again, three-quarters of the states must approve.

This has happened only once, with the 21st Amendment (which repealed the 18th Amendment: the prohibition of liquor).

Blocking an amendment is far easier.

You have two options:

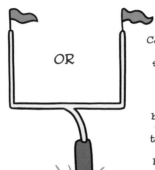

Persuade one-third of the members plus one more in either house of Congress to vote against it.

OR

Convince one legislative house in thirteen states to vote against ratification.

For example, the ERA came up every year between 1972 and 1982. Some years it passed the House; other years, the Senate; but never both in the same year.

More than 11,000 amendments to the Constitution have been proposed.

A few would . . .

prohibit anyone involved in a duel from holding federal office

expel congressmen who miss more than 40% of roll call votes on bills.

choose the president by lot

prevent bankers from serving in Congress

THE TERM PAPER AMENDMENT

The 27th Amendment says that when Congress votes to give its members a raise, they will not receive it until the following term. The point is to discourage congresspeople from raising their own salaries as soon as they're elected.

This was originally the second of twelve proposed amendments, ten of which became the Bill of Rights. James Madison introduced it in 1789, but it was not approved.

IN 1982, GREGORY WATSON, A STUDENT AT THE UNIVERSITY OF TEXAS AT AUSTIN WAS RESEARCHING A TERM PAPER ON THE ERA.

HUH, CONGRESSIONAL SALARIES WERE GOING TO BE AN AMENDMENT?

THIS IS A MUCH BETTER TOPIC!

WATSON DIDN'T STOP AT THE TERM PAPER. FOR THE NEXT TEN YEARS, HE WORKED TO DRUM UP SUPPORT AROUND THE COUNTRY FOR RATIFICATION OF THIS FORGOTTEN AMENDMENT.

27TH AMENDMENT LETTER-WRITING CAMPAIGN!

IN MAY OF 1992, MICHIGAN BECAME THE 38TH STATE TO RATIFY IT. WATSON SUCCEEDED.

IN 1982, WATSON HAD RECEIVED A GRADE OF *C* ON HIS PAPER.

A BIT OF A FANCIFUL SUGGESTION TO THINK AN AMENDMENT COULD BE RATIFIED AFTER 193 YEARS, DON'T YOU THINK?

BUT IN 2017, HIS PROFESSOR CHANGED THAT GRADE TO AN *A+*.

Would YOU like to help pass an amendment to the Constitution?

The **Child Labor Amendment** would protect workers under the age of eighteen. Congress approved it in 1924, and it has no time limit for ratification.

By 1937, twenty-eight states had approved it. You just need to collect ten more states, and it will become a law!

EVEN A SUCCESSFUL AMENDMENT CAN TAKE AN AGONIZINGLY LONG TIME TO BECOME OFFICIAL.

CONSIDER THE *19TH AMENDMENT*.

VOTES FOR WOMEN

THE FIRST MEASURE WAS INTRODUCED IN CONGRESS IN 1878. NINE YEARS PASSED BEFORE THE PROPOSAL EVEN GOT OUT OF COMMITTEE. THEN THE SENATE VOTED IT DOWN.

FORTY-ONE YEARS LATER, IN 1919, CONGRESS FINALLY APPROVED THE AMENDMENT . . .

PRESIDENT WILSON SAYS: "THIS IS THE TIME TO SUPPORT WOMAN SUFFRAGE."

HOW LONG MUST WE WAIT?

. . . ALTHOUGH NOT UNTIL PRESIDENT WOODROW WILSON HAD CALLED A RARE SPECIAL SESSION OF CONGRESS TO NUDGE IT THROUGH THE SENATE.

RATIFICATION FOR THE 19TH AMENDMENT REQUIRED AGREEMENT OF THIRTY-SIX OF THE FORTY-EIGHT STATES THEN IN THE UNION. TENNESSEE BECAME THE LAST STATE TO RATIFY IT. THEIR VOTE AMOUNTED TO FIFTY IN FAVOR AND FORTY-NINE OPPOSED.

HAD ONE REPRESENTATIVE CHANGED HIS VOTE, THE AMENDMENT WOULD HAVE FAILED.

MANY AMERICANS AGREE THAT THE CONSTITUTION SHOULDN'T BE EASY TO CHANGE.

BUT MAKING IT IMPOSSIBLE TO AMEND IS ONLY GOOD IF IT'S NOT FLAWED, RIGHT?

THERE ARE OTHER WAYS!

IN GENERAL, STATE CONSTITUTIONS ARE EASIER TO AMEND THAN THE U.S. CONSTITUTION. FLORIDA HAS MORE WAYS TO AMEND ITS CONSTITUTION THAN ANY OTHER STATE.

EVERY TWENTY YEARS, AN APPOINTED COMMISSION CAN PROPOSE CHANGES. THE LEGISLATURE AND CONSTITUTIONAL CONVENTIONS CAN ALSO DO SO.

ORDINARY CITIZENS CAN USE AN INITIATIVE PROCESS, AND A TAX AND BUDGET COMMISSION CAN RECOMMEND REVISIONS TO TAXES.

EIGHTEEN STATES ALLOW THE PUBLIC TO PROPOSE AND THEN VOTE ON AMENDMENTS AS AN INITIATIVE-AND-REFERENDUM PROCESS, AND FOURTEEN STATES ALLOW THE ELECTORATE TO CALL A CONSTITUTIONAL CONVENTION ON A SCHEDULED BASIS.

NEW YORK, FOR INSTANCE, DOES SO EVERY TWENTY YEARS.

AMENDMENT PROPOSAL TX7

AMENDMENT PROPOSAL NJ11

AMENDMENT PROPOSAL VA13

ALL FIFTY STATES ALLOW THEIR LEGISLATURES TO PROPOSE AMENDMENTS, THOUGH THEY FOLLOW DIFFERENT PROCEDURES.

ALL EXCEPT DELAWARE THEN REQUIRE THAT THE ELECTORATE RATIFY ANY PROPOSED AMENDMENTS.

NO OTHER COUNTRY HAS A CONSTITUTION SO DIFFICULT TO AMEND AS THE U.S.

IN SWEDEN AND AUSTRIA, THE PARLIAMENT CAN AMEND THE CONSTITUTION AS EASILY AS IT PASSES LAWS.

IN ARGENTINA AND NORWAY, THE REQUIREMENTS ARE MORE COMPLEX, BUT THE LEGISLATURES HAVE THE POWER TO ADD AMENDMENTS.

A NUMBER OF COUNTRIES REQUIRE REFERENDA (VOTES BY THE ELECTORATE) TO CHANGE THEIR CONSTITUTIONS.

IN AUSTRALIA, FOR EXAMPLE, THE PROCESS BEGINS IF AN ABSOLUTE MAJORITY OF THE HOUSE AND SENATE AGREE . . .

. . . BUT THE ELECTORATE MAKES THE FINAL DECISION.

THIS MAKES IT A BIT DIFFICULT TO AMEND.

SEVERAL COUNTRIES' CONSTITUTIONS ABSOLUTELY PROHIBIT CHANGING SOME OF THEIR PROVISIONS THROUGH WHAT ARE CALLED "IMMUTABILITY" PROVISIONS OR "ETERNITY CLAUSES."

GERMANY, FOR INSTANCE, FORBIDS CHANGING "HUMAN DIGNITY" AS THE GUIDING PRINCIPLE OF ITS CONSTITUTION.

THE U.S. MIGHT BE BETTER OFF IF IT WAS EASIER TO MAKE AMENDMENTS.

PERHAPS A NUMBER OF THE CONSTITUTION'S FAULT LINES COULD BE CORRECTED IF THAT WAS THE CASE!

REVISING THE PORTION OF THE CONSTITUTION THAT COVERS THE AMENDMENT PROCESS WOULD, OF COURSE, REQUIRE AN AMENDMENT.

MAYBE THIS WOULD BE DESIRABLE IF, LIKE IN GERMANY, CERTAIN PROVISIONS WERE OFF-LIMITS.

LIKE FREEDOM OF SPEECH.

CONGRESS GRANTED AN EXTENSION FOR THE ERA UNTIL JUNE 30, 1982.

BUT NO ADDITIONAL STATES RATIFIED THE AMENDMENT.

SCHLAFLY HAD WON.

HOWEVER, SOME LEGAL STRATEGISTS ARGUE THAT SINCE OTHER AMENDMENTS HAD NO TIME LIMIT FOR RATIFICATION, THE ERA SHOULD NOT HAVE ONE, EITHER.

IN 2017, THE NEVADA ASSEMBLY RATIFIED THE ERA, AND IN 2018, ILLINOIS DID SO, TOO, BECOMING THE 37TH STATE TO RATIFY THE AMENDMENT.

IF ANOTHER STATE STEPS UP TO BECOME THE 38TH—THE MINIMUM NEEDED FOR FINAL APPROVAL—WILL THE ERA BECOME THE 28TH AMENDMENT?

NOBODY KNOWS.

IF I COULD CHOOSE AN AMENDMENT TO ADD TO THE CONSTITUTION, IT WOULD BE THE EQUAL RIGHTS AMENDMENT.

I THINK WE HAVE ACHIEVED THAT THROUGH LEGISLATION, BUT LEGISLATION CAN BE REPEALED, IT CAN BE ALTERED.

I'D LIKE TO SEE THE ERA AS A BASIC PRINCIPLE OF OUR SOCIETY.

Supreme Court Justice Ruth Bader Ginsburg

keeping pace with the times

The Framers' Constitution didn't remain intact for long. Shortly after signing it and sending it out for public discussion, Alexander Hamilton wrote,

ORDINARY AMERICANS HAVE THE OPPORTUNITY TO PARTICIPATE IN "REFLECTION AND CHOICE" ABOUT HOW THEY WISHED TO BE GOVERNED.

The 1st Congress took him up on that offer in 1789 by proposing the series of amendments now called the Bill of Rights.

In order to perfect the union, "reflection and choice" should be an ongoing process.

The next steps ask you to accept Hamilton's invitation and follow the First Congress's example by taking part in

reflection on how well the Constitution meets its goals, as laid out in the Preamble

and

decisions about what to change and how.

It's up to you to offer your own reflections and suggest your own choices about the issues involved!

21

grading the constitution

now what?

IN 2012, SUPREME COURT JUSTICE RUTH BADER GINSBURG VISITED EGYPT.

EGYPT'S LEADERS ARE TRYING TO REFORM ITS GOVERNMENT.

DO YOU THINK THEY SHOULD EXAMINE CONSTITUTIONS FROM AROUND THE WORLD FOR IDEAS?

YES, BUT . . .

I WOULD NOT LOOK TO THE U.S. CONSTITUTION IF I WERE DRAFTING A CONSTITUTION IN THE YEAR 2012.

IT'S TOO OLD AND NOT LIKELY TO BE AS HELPFUL AS, SAY, THE SOUTH AFRICAN CONSTITUTION THAT WAS DRAFTED IN 1994.

WE ARE STILL FORMING THE MORE PERFECT UNION.

SUCH COMMENTS WOULD LAND HER IN HOT WATER WITH POLITICIANS AND NEWSCASTERS BACK HOME.

HOW UNPATRIOTIC!

IF SHE DOESN'T LIKE THE DOCUMENT THAT ESTABLISHED THE SUPREME COURT, SHE SHOULD FIND ANOTHER JOB!

IS IT TOO MUCH FOR A UNITED STATES SUPREME COURT JUSTICE TO HAVE A LITTLE REVERENCE FOR THE CONSTITUTION OF THE UNITED STATES?

HOWEVER, THE FRAMERS DID BELIEVE THAT AMERICANS WOULD FOREVER NEED TO PERFECT THE UNION, CHANGING THE CONSTITUTION ALONG THE WAY.

So which is it:

Should the Constitution be revered or considered outdated? Or both?

To what extent does the Constitution meet the Framers' goals, as laid out in the Preamble?

Looking at the document's successes and problems in each area allows us to give it a **grade**.

The Framers' most basic aim was to transform the people who thought of their state as their country into citizens of the United States.

We certainly have **a more perfect union** than we did in 1787.

Americans, by and large,

obey laws passed by Congress

celebrate Independence Day and put their hands over their hearts while pledging allegiance to the American flag

vote in national elections (though not enough people do so).

pay federal taxes

However, many aspects of the Constitution produce problems as well as pride.

Our bicameral system, the presidential veto, and requirements for overcoming Senate filibusters make it very difficult to pass new and necessary laws.

This gridlock has led many Americans to lose faith in government, especially Congress.

Fracturing into separate realms was a threat in 1787.

Less than seventy-five years later, America went to war against itself to prevent Southern states from seceding. 750,000 people lost their lives in the Civil War. This slaughter has discouraged further efforts at secession.

But can we be confident that will last?

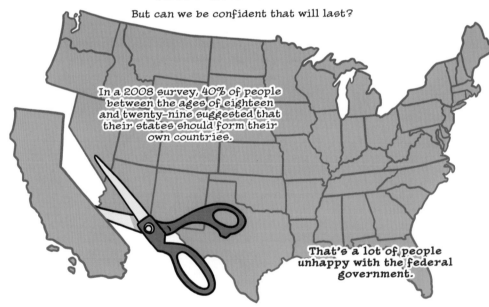

In a 2008 survey, 40% of people between the ages of eighteen and twenty-nine suggested that their states should form their own countries.

That's a lot of people unhappy with the federal government.

GRADE: C-

ESTABLISH JUSTICE

The Constitution created a system of federal courts that has often protected people's rights, as the Framers intended.

There are many examples of ways in which the Constitution has succeeded in establishing, or at least seeking, justice:

Article VI says that elected and appointed officeholders can be any religion.

Federal courts have overruled states' voter ID laws and gerrymandering practices.

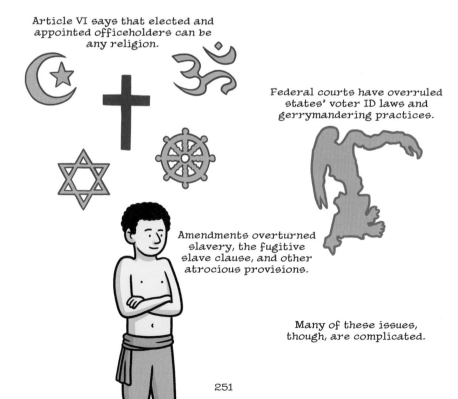

Amendments overturned slavery, the fugitive slave clause, and other atrocious provisions.

Many of these issues, though, are complicated.

After all, a majority of legislators in some states supported voter ID laws and congressional districts with weird shapes. They might think the courts' decisions are unjust.

Americans' definitions of "justice" have broadened since 1787, but we don't agree on the specifics any more than the Framers did.

For example, by not addressing national guidelines for elections, the Framers allowed states to develop inconsistent rules, some of which limit citizens' ability to vote.

And the provision that assigns two senators to every state, regardless of its size, is unfair.

If the Constitution allowed **direct democracy**, Americans might be able to overturn or work around some of these hardwired problems.

But it doesn't.

GRADE: C

INSURE DOMESTIC TRANQUILITY

To the Framers, **domestic tranquility** meant that people could live without being distracted by political bitterness or violent uprisings.

Over time, the Constitution did help resolve the issues they faced.

Farmers no longer raid munitions depots as Daniel Shays's followers did.

Enslaved persons don't rebel because chattel slavery was repealed.

States agree on the locations of their borders.

Americans in general have enjoyed periods of tranquility, but minority groups and poor people have often felt ignored and even oppressed.

In the 19th century, the government forcibly displaced Native Americans.

END SEGREGATED RULES IN PUBLIC SCHOOLS

In the 1950s and '60s, attempts to prevent desegregation triggered mass demonstrations.

Urban riots in poverty-stricken neighborhoods and protests against America's involvement in the Vietnam War also roiled the nation.

The country quieted down for several decades.

Then the deaths of African Americans at the hands of police sparked more demonstrations.

Native Americans opposed a government plan to lay an oil pipeline across an Indian reservation.

About three million people took to the streets to protest the inauguration of President Donald J. Trump in early 2017.

BLACK LIVES MATTER

PRESERVE STANDING ROCK

THE FUTURE IS FEMALE

Many people remain at odds
with one another about

RACE
RELATIONS

GUN CONTROL

IMMIGRATION

AND

TERRORISM

In addition, many Americans express
dissatisfaction with Congress and other
government institutions, and elections
seem increasingly bitter and hostile.

GRADE: C

The Framers wrote into the Constitution that the federal government has the right to raise and support armies and to provide and maintain a navy.

OF COURSE, AN AIR FORCE OR SPACE FORCE DIDN'T OCCUR TO THEM!

POLITICAL LEADERS OFTEN PROCLAIM THAT WE HAVE THE FINEST-TRAINED ARMED FORCES IN THE WORLD.

The government collects taxes from the citizenry to pay for the military protection of the nation as a whole.

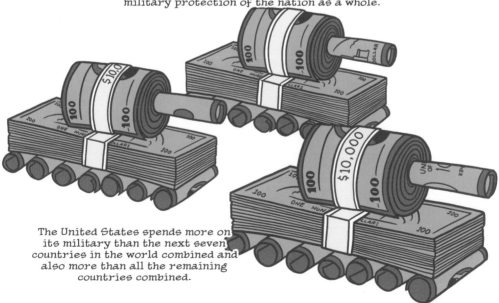

The United States spends more on its military than the next seven countries in the world combined and also more than all the remaining countries combined.

Yet because of the Senate and funding formulas that play favorites with small states, the states that need the most protection might not receive it.

And Congress sometimes funds weapons programs, even ones the Pentagon opposes, because they give jobs to constituents.

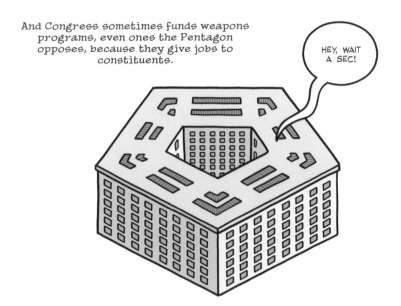

HEY, WAIT A SEC!

Furthermore, some threats might overwhelm our armed services' ability to respond. Biological weapons and telecommunications shutdowns might make a military response almost irrelevant.

CLIMATE CHANGE POSES THREATS TO NATIONAL SECURITY, TOO.

GRADE: B

The Framers eliminated taxes on goods exported from one state to another and gave authority and funds to the government to build roads.

In the 21st century our interstate infrastructure and economic system is fully national, thanks in part to the Interstate Highway System built in the 1950s.

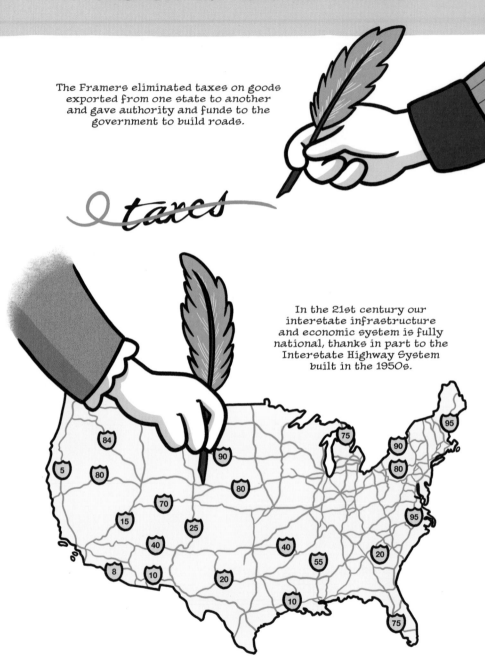

Even in the 18th century, though, leaders hoped for more, including a national rather than local frame of mind.

It's possible that a **federal** government, in which **states** form the basis of representation in Congress, limits our ability to think about the needs of the country as a whole.

Even if we do all care about one another, Congress and the other institutions established in the Constitution are having trouble resolving these issues.

GRADE: C-

The Framers defined "liberty" as citizens being able to govern themselves.

Americans certainly have more liberties today than in 1787. Some of these result from decisions by the Supreme Court, which has interpreted the First Amendment to mean freedom of expression.

So, people can march in the streets, wave signs, even burn the flag—actions that used to be barred. People are also more free to express their gender orientation and sexuality than in the past.

On the other hand, participation in government is restricted in many ways: through gerrymandering, limits on running for national office, the Electoral College, and habeas corpus.

Furthermore, unless the problems of continuity in government are resolved, there might not be much of a government to participate in following a catastrophe.

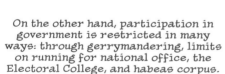

GRADE: B-

THE CONSTITUTION'S REPORT CARD

SUBJECT	GRADE
FORM A MORE PERFECT UNION	C-
ESTABLISH JUSTICE	C
INSURE DOMESTIC TRANQUILITY	C
PROVIDE FOR THE COMMON DEFENSE	B
PROMOTE THE GENERAL WELFARE	C-
SECURE THE BLESSINGS OF LIBERTY TO OURSELVES AND OUR POSTERITY	B-
AVERAGE	**C**

Combining these grades, assuming they're all equally important, the Constitution gets an overall grade of C.

So now, we must ask: how can the Constitution be improved?

The metaphor of fault lines refers
to shifting tectonic plates beneath
the earth's surface that can cause
rumbles ranging from mild vibrations to
catastrophic earthquakes.

Architects safeguard residents in these
zones by constructing buildings that
can withstand shaking.

But what if you lived in a building that
got a C on an earthquake safety test?
Assuming you decided not to move, you'd
want your home shored up.

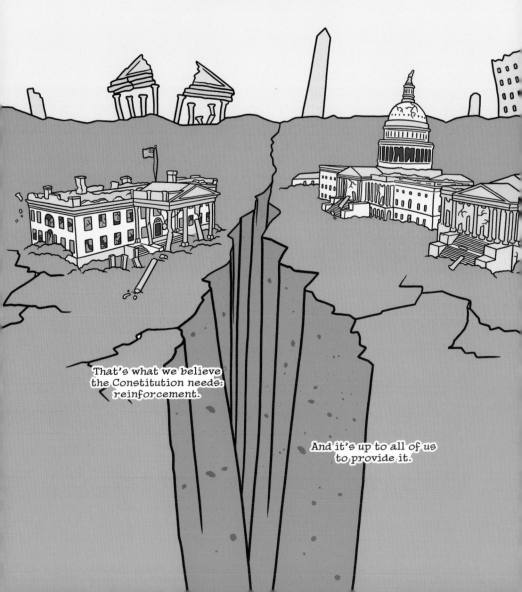

That's what we believe
the Constitution needs:
reinforcement.

And it's up to all of us
to provide it.

Even while praising the Framers for
their work and urging adoption of the
new Constitution, James Madison wrote,

IT IS INCUMBENT ON THEIR SUCCESSORS TO IMPROVE AND PERPETUATE IT.

The year 1787 was a beginning,
not a conclusion. There are still
actions that can be taken.

REDUCE CONGRESSIONAL GRIDLOCK

GIVE CITIZENS WAYS TO DIRECTLY AFFECT LAWS

PASS NEW LAWS

REVISE THE VETO

CHANGE SENATE RULES

HOLD ANOTHER CONSTITUTIONAL CONVENTION

DEFANG THE ELECTORAL COLLEGE

AMEND THE CONSITUTION

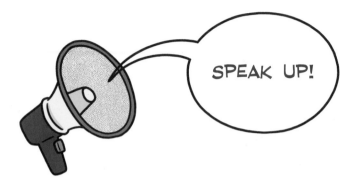

SPEAK UP!

Throughout the Constitutional Convention,
the Framers held straw votes on the issues they
debated. These votes didn't count; they weren't
official. But they gave the delegates a chance to
express their opinions at a given moment and then
change their minds without committing themselves
or the country to a final decision.

In the same way, America could hold straw
conventions—discussions of the Constitution's fault
lines, which ones are the most pressing, and what
to do about them.

You can take part. In fact, you can help get the
conversation started. When you hear people say
that they don't trust the government or that
Congress doesn't seem able to fix big problems like
immigration—tell them it's the Constitution's fault!
Then explain how, banding together, we can repair it.
And when you're old enough, make your vote count.

that would make us a true union.

a constitutional convention?!

At this point, "We the authors" part ways, at least in this book, in our points of view about a convention. Just as the Framers debated the original document, we'll share our debate with you.

SANDY: Most Americans don't connect the dots from what's happening in their lives—including what's in their food—to the Constitution. They have no idea how dangerous the Constitution is.

And what's really bad is that people get angry at politicians they don't like— or place excessive faith in those they do—without realizing that many of the government's failures result from limitations in the Constitution rather than the defects of individual leaders.

CYNTHIA: But why a convention? That's such a drastic suggestion. We could get a lot done simply by changing the rules, putting some work-arounds in place, and passing laws.

SANDY: But it's the Constitution that makes it harder and harder for legislation to succeed. Moreover, as you and I agree, in many cases amendments are necessary. The question is whether we can trust Congress to step up

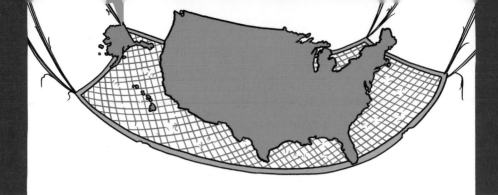

and propose the amendments we need. I have no confidence that they can and will.

Members of Congress protect their own political interests—so that some might oppose eliminating gerrymandering that benefits them personally, for instance. And they're not even willing to face the possibility of a massive attack and state clearly who's going to lead the country in the aftermath.

CYNTHIA: All of that is true. However, once you open the Constitution to wholesale revisions, there's no knowing what might happen. A convention could erase the Bill of Rights. We could end up returning to a president and vice president from different parties or we could have a House of Representatives with five thousand members. Conventioneers might eliminate half of the president's cabinet—and the services those agencies provide, like food programs for Americans in need.

SANDY: If we believe in government by the people, that's the risk we have to take. But I'm more optimistic than you are. Though we discuss a few rights, like habeas corpus and freedom of speech, this book concentrates almost totally on the structures established by the 1787 Constitution. If we ever had the kind of convention I want, almost all of the discussion would focus on those structures.

People are calmer when they're talking about structures—where there aren't obvious winners and losers—than when they are arguing about rights.

CYNTHIA: People are not necessarily calmer when talking about structures. Those who live in the forty-one states with relatively low populations would not graciously relinquish one of their senators to a larger state like California or New York. Anyway, you can't control the agenda at a Constitutional Convention. You couldn't order people to leave the amendments alone. Look what the Framers did to the Articles of Confederation.

SANDY: If people start shouting about their favorite (or least favorite) rights, then a "runaway" convention would break up, as almost happened in 1787 over voting power in the Senate. I'm confident that the country wouldn't stand for repealing the Bill of Rights. I believe that "we the people" are capable of "reflection and choice."

CYNTHIA: I agree with you in principle. But just trying to call for a convention could cause a crisis. How would the delegates be chosen? Who

would make the rules—Congress or the delegates? Would we follow the one-state/one-vote rule, like in 1787? Or would we demand proportional voting? Delaware would never allow that.

SANDY: These are good questions, to which we don't have answers. That provision— Article V—is probably my least favorite part of the Constitution. It provides no clue how to run a convention. I wish the Framers had called for a convention every twenty-five years.

CYNTHIA: But they didn't. And Congress has no incentive to call for a convention, which would change how Congress is selected and operates.

SANDY: If Congress doesn't call a convention, two-thirds of the states can petition to call one. If there's a groundswell of support for the idea, it could happen. As of 2019, there are actually quite a few people who take this option seriously. If a new convention happens, it will be because millions of Americans realize there really are fault lines that need to be fixed before some kind of political earthquake destroys our government's ability to function.

CYNTHIA: If there's that much interest in changing the Constitution, then I believe the people's representatives in Congress would propose the amendments we need. And the states would ratify them. I'm sticking with the amendment route.

SANDY: And I believe we need a Constitutional Convention.

CYNTHIA AND SANDY: But, like the Framers, we can agree on a compromise.

articles and amendments cited in
fault lines in the constitution

Chapter 15
Knock Knock. Is Anybody There? / Continuity in Government

Article I, Section 5
Article I, Section 2
Article I, Section 3
Seventeenth Amendment

Chapter 16
Is There a Leader in the Room? / Presidential Succession

Article II, Section 1
Article I, Section 6
Twenty-fifth Amendment

Chapter 17
The Duck's in Charge, January 20 / Inauguration Day

Article II, Section 1
Twentieth Amendment

Chapter 18
At War / Emergency Powers

First Amendment

Chapter 19
At War with Bugs / Habeas Corpus

Article I, Section 8
Article 1, Section 9
Fifth Amendment
Fourteenth Amendment

Chapter 20
We Can Change It, Right? / Amending the Constitution

Article V
Twenty-seventh Amendment
Seventeenth Amendment
Twenty-first Amendment
Nineteenth Amendment

acknowledgments

Many scholars, colleagues, friends, writers, and family members shared their expertise and opinions as we wrote *Fault Lines in the Constitution: The Framers, Their Fights, and the Flaws That Affect Us Today*, published by Peachtree Publishing Company Inc. in 2017 and updated in 2019. They are thanked with gratitude in those books.

For the development of this graphic novel version, we are especially grateful to Ally Shwed, who with Gerardo Alba Rojas transformed our text-based book with tremendous humor, skill, knowledge, imagination, and patience. Deep thanks also to Ed Sullivan for proposing this project, and to the team at First Second—Mark Siegel for overseeing it, Robyn Chapman, Kirk Benshoff, and Samia Fakih.

This book would not have been possible without the support of Margaret Quinlin, Kathy Landwehr, and Farah Gehy. We are always grateful to Erin Murphy.

And our family members remain as thoroughly splendid as ever.

—CYNTHIA AND SANDY

Foremost, my endless gratitude to Cynthia and Sanford, for sharing the foundation upon which this graphic novel was built; thank you for entrusting your writing to me. A special thank-you to Mark Siegel, for introducing this project to me and believing I was the right woman for the job. To everyone at First Second, including Robyn Chapman, Samia Fakih, Sunny Lee, and Kirk Benshoff, thank you for your editorial skills, design prowess, and unfailing patience, without which this work would not have crossed its finish line so smoothly. To my family and friends, for your endless support of everything I do; and finally, especially, to Gerardo, who deserves more credit than the credit page allows.

—ALLY

bibliography

In researching the Constitutional Convention of 1787 and the Framers' decisions that affect Americans today, we consulted a wide range of online, print, primary, and secondary sources, which are cited in the text edition of *Fault Lines in the Constitution*. The following books were especially helpful.

SELECTED BOOKS

Amar, Akhil Reed. *American's Constitution: A Biography*. New York: Random House, 2005.

Beeman, Richard. *Plain, Honest Men: The Making of the American Constitution*. New York: Random House, 2009.

Bickerstaff, Steve. *Lines in the Sand: Congressional Redistricting in Texas and the Downfall of Tom DeLay*. Austin: University of Texas Press, 2007.

Epps, Garrett. *American Epic: Reading the U.S. Constitution*. Oxford: Oxford University Press, 2013.

Hakim, Joy. *The History of US: From Colonies to Country: 1735–1791*. New York: Oxford University Press, 2007.

————*The History of US: The New Nation: 1789–1850*. New York: Oxford University Press, 2007.

King, Anthony. *The Founding Fathers v. The People: Paradoxes of American Democracy*. Cambridge: Harvard University Press, 2012.

Klarman, Michael. *The Framers' Coup: The Making of the United States Constitution*. New York: Oxford University Press, 2016.

Kurland, Philip B. and Ralph Lerner (eds). *The Founders' Constitution*. press-pubs.uchicago.edu/founders/tocs /toc.html.

Levinson, Sanford. *Framed: America's 51 Constitutions and the Crisis of Governance*. Oxford: Oxford University Press, 2012.

———*Our Undemocratic Constitution: Where the Constitution Goes Wrong (And How We the People Can Correct It)*. Oxford: Oxford University Press, 2006.

McGann, Anthony J., Charles Anthony Smith, Michael Latner, Alex Keena. *Gerrymandering in America: The House of Representatives, the Supreme Court, and the Future of Popular Sovereignty*. Cambridge: Cambridge University Press, 2016.

Paulsen, Michael Stokes and Luke Paulsen. *The Constitution: An Introduction*. New York: Basic Books, 2015.

Rakove, Jack N. *Original Meanings: Politics and Ideas in the Making of the Constitution*. New York: Alfred A. Knopf, 1996.

———*The Annotated U.S. Constitution and Declaration of Independence*. Cambridge: The Belknap Press of Harvard University Press, 2009.

SANFORD LEVINSON is a professor both at the University of Texas Law School and the University of Texas at Austin Department of Government. The author of many books on the U.S. Constitution and other subjects, he is a member of the American Academy of Arts and Sciences and received the lifetime achievement award of the Law and Courts Section of the American Political Science Association in 2010.

CYNTHIA LEVINSON writes award-winning nonfiction books about social justice for young readers, including *The Youngest Marcher* and *We've Got a Job*. She also braids bread with six strands, juggles up to two balls, and takes a constitutional most days. The co-authors have four thoroughly splendid grandchildren and divide their time between Austin, Texas, and Boston, Massachusetts.

ALLY SHWED is a cartoonist, writer, and editor, originally from Linden, New Jersey. She received her Master of Fine Arts degree in Sequential Art from the Savannah College of Art & Design and has worked with *The Boston Globe*, *Topic*, *Jezebel*, and *The Intercept*. She regularly contributes to the comics journalism website The Nib and is the editor-in-chief of Little Red Bird Press, a comics publisher and printmaking studio. She currently lives in Belmar, New Jersey with her partner, cartoonist Gerardo Alba, and their cats, Egon and Schneider.

First Second

First published in the United States under the title *Fault Lines in the Constitution*
by Cynthia Levinson and Sanford Levinson
Text copyright © 2017, 2019, 2020 by Cynthia Levinson and Sanford Levinson
Illustration copyright © 2020 Ally Shwed
Published by arrangement with Peachtree Publishing Company Inc.

This book is a graphic novel adaptation of the nonfiction book *Fault Lines in the Constitution: The Framers,
Their Fights, and the Flaws That Affect Us Today*, which was originally published in 2017 by Peachtree
Publishing Company Inc. and updated in 2019. Please note that the nature of a graphic novel is different
from that of a nonfiction text; the latter uses exact quotations and clear attributions, while a graphic novel
illustrates reenactments of events as seen through the imagination of the artist. Therefore, dialogue and scenes
included here do not necessarily reflect actual or exact statements or actions by the people portrayed. Source
notes and additional informational material are available in the text version of this book.

Published by First Second
First Second is an imprint of Roaring Brook Press,
a division of Holtzbrinck Publishing Holdings Limited Partnership
120 Broadway, New York, NY 10271

Don't miss your next favorite book from First Second! For the latest updates go to firstsecondnewsletter.com
and sign up for our enewsletter.

Library of Congress Control Number: 2019947763
ISBN: 978-1-250-21161-3

Our books may be purchased in bulk for promotional, educational, or business use. Please contact your local
bookseller or the Macmillan Corporate and Premium Sales Department at (800) 221-7945 ext. 5442 or by
email at MacmillanSpecialMarkets@macmillan.com.

First graphic novel edition, 2020

Graphic novel edition edited by Mark Siegel and Samia Fakih
Cover design by Kirk Benshoff
Interior design by Angela Boyle
Color by Gerardo Alba Rojas
Lettering by Angela Boyle
Printed in Hong Kong

Penciled, inked, and colored digitally in Adobe Photoshop.

10 9 8 7 6 5 4 3 2 1